A Cluttered Life

MY SEARCH FOR GOD, SERENITY AND
MY MISSING KEYS

Pesi Dinnerstein

SEAL PRESS

A Cluttered Life
Searching for God, Serenity & My Missing Keys

Published by
Seal Press
A Member of the Perseus Books Group
1700 Fourth Street
Berkeley, California

Library of Congress Cataloging-in-Publication Data

Dinnerstein, Pesi, 1948-
  A cluttered life : searching for God, serenity & my missing keys / by Pesi Dinnerstein.
    p. cm.
  ISBN 978-1-58005-310-5
  1. Self-management (Psychology) 2. Self-evaluation. 3. Behavior modification. 4. Dinnerstein, Pesi, 1948- I. Title.
  BF632.D56 2011
  158.1--dc22

                          2011001397

9 8 7 6 5 4 3 2 1

Cover design by Gopa & Ted2, Inc.
Interior design by Tabitha Lahr
Printed in the United States of America
Distributed by Publishers Group West

In the interest of creating a book that is less cluttered than the life it describes, I have occasionally chosen to merge people and alter events. Even where these changes have occurred, however, the essence of each experience remains truthful and reflects a genuine step on my journey.

Dedication

This book is dedicated to my mother, Sylvia Jacobs-Bernfeld—a true light in our world—who taught me everything I know about clutter, except how to get rid of it.

"In all chaos there is a cosmos; in all disorder a secret order."

—Carl Jung

Contents

Introduction

This is a book about my relationship with clutter—not an instruction manual about how to get rid of it (I wish I knew) nor a practical guide explaining how to better organize it (another big mystery to me), but an exploration of my intensely ambivalent affair with the subject.

As with most conflicted relationships, there is an unresolved tension here. It seems that I am continually drawn to the abundance that creates clutter in my life and then repulsed by the chaos that inevitably grows out of it.

For many years, I gave the matter little thought. I was on a serious quest for spiritual truth and had no time for issues of such minor consequence. In fact, I generally thought of my run-ins with clutter as nothing more than bothersome interruptions on my journey. I certainly wasn't about to stop searching for God so that I could sort through a stack of neglected papers or mend a torn hem. But, eventually, it occurred to me that the piles of unfinished business disturbing my concentration in *this* world were probably blocking my way in the higher worlds as well.

 9

I have to admit that my natural tendency to accumulate and lose myself in the overflow very likely qualifies as an addiction and certainly makes for an unmanageable life. I instinctively fill time and space with far more than they can reasonably hold and then find myself overwhelmed and unable to cope with it all.

A large part of the problem, I believe, is that I have little respect for boundaries, particularly those of my own making. Somehow, I don't see them as protective fences that keep me from exceeding my limits, but, rather, as hurdles to be jumped and overcome. And, so, with a shoehorn in my pocket, I travel through life—always trying to slide in one more object, one more experience, one extra moment. . . .

In writing this book, however, I've come to realize that the cause of my behavior is not simply a character defect in need of remediation. My desire for abundance has many dimensions—some of them, no doubt, dysfunctional and better lived without; but others, deeply complex in nature and not so easy to write off.

What I am faced with, it seems, is a rather odd paradox. My chronic struggle with clutter keeps me too preoccupied with the physical world to focus on anything that transcends it. Yet, the clutter I attract is often a source of creative stimulation to me, as well as a natural outgrowth of my desire to embrace life spontaneously and without restraint. It is free borders and poor boundaries; infinite possibilities and overloaded circuits. When all is said and done, the whole thing is quite a tangled maze . . . a very strange and complicated relationship, indeed.

The following pages are my attempt to sort it all out and return to my spiritual path—hopefully, a bit wiser and less cluttered. However, my story is not being told from a quiet shore on the other side. Armed with new insights and fresh resolve, I may have finally begun the march toward simplicity and order, but I remain far from my destination; and, on most days, my life continues to feel overcrowded, off schedule, and likely to spin out of control at any moment.

Nevertheless, there is joy for me in the unfinished journey. And if, in the end, it takes a lifetime of zigzagging and circling and retracing my steps to gradually inch my way closer to freedom, I consider it a trip well worth the effort.

CHAPTER ONE

The Journey of a Thousand Miles

"Things fall apart; the center cannot hold."
—William Butler Yeats

*I*t all began quite unexpectedly on the eve of my fiftieth birthday—December 23—which almost always turned out to be the last day of the fall semester. After turning in my final grades, I decided to stop at the All-Night Bagel Hole for one last decadent snack. It was here that I ran into Barbie Bomzer and made the decision to finally change my life.

I hadn't seen Barbie in over twenty years, which actually suited me just fine, since I never liked her very much anyway. For a brief time in the 1970s, we taught remedial English together at a wild-west high school in the South Bronx. However, other than sharing an office and an occasional joke about the alliteration we each married into—she had recently become Mrs. Barbara Bomzer, and I had been newly renamed Paulette Plonchak—we had almost nothing in common. I certainly never expected to see her again after I left the Bronx.

But there she was, sprawled across a table-for-four at the Bagel Hole. Never one to tolerate mess—although, God knows, I gave her plenty of opportunity for practice—she now seemed fixated on trying to contain the cream cheese and chives oozing out of her pumpernickel bagel. Preoccupied as she appeared to be, I was hoping to slip out before she had a chance to notice. Unfortunately, I never made it past the checkout counter.

"Paulette Plonchak, is that you?" she called across the aisle in a voice that rang an octave higher and a decibel louder than necessary.

Since I had remarried and changed my last name, and most of my friends now called me by a different version of my first name, I was tempted to say—with some degree of justification—"No, I'm sorry, it's not," but I couldn't quite bring myself to do it.

"Yes, it is," I finally responded. "And is that you, Barbie Bomzer?"

"Yes, P. P.," she answered, immediately slipping into our old nicknames. "And still known around town as B. B."

After a few moments of strained conversation, we quickly exhausted our small reservoir of overlapping interests and mutual acquaintances and were reduced to commiserating about the difficulties of finding a decent bagel in New York these days. I couldn't wait to finish my coffee and escape.

However, just as I was about to gracefully make my exit, I noticed all the shopping bags filled with holiday-wrapped gifts that

Barbie had piled on the adjacent chairs. I suddenly remembered the many times she had offered to drop me at the D Train when my car wasn't working and I was hauling around a knapsack full of papers to be graded.

"Barbie," I heard myself ask—over the loud protest of my better judgment—"can I give you and your packages a ride somewhere?"

Since I was heading to Brooklyn and she was on her way to Bayside, we settled on a lift to the Long Island Railroad. The station was only a short distance away; but, in the end, the trip proved just long enough to unearth a host of awful memories and send me into my fifty-first year with a substantial dose of humiliation and a firm resolve to change my life once and for all.

The trouble began as soon as we approached my car.

"Look, P. P.," Barbie announced cheerfully, managing to point her finger toward the front windshield despite all of the packages she was balancing. "I think the City of New York has left you season's greetings."

Apparently, it had—in the form of a $55 parking ticket.

"I bet that was the most expensive cup of coffee you ever bought. Even a Starbuck's special double mocha latte with whipped cream and freshly ground cinnamon doesn't cost that much—at least not yet."

"Well, I'm glad to see that your sense of humor hasn't been dampened by my financial loss," I said, trying to keep the tone light, although I could feel myself beginning to bristle with irritation. In truth, it wasn't her lack of compassion that was disturbing me as much as my own inability—or unwillingness—to pay attention to the basic realities of urban life, one of which was clearly the presence of roving ticket writers on the streets of Manhattan at all hours of the day and night.

This was only the most recent in a long string of outrageously priced parking violations that I had received over the past year simply because I'd neglected to look at my watch or read a sign carefully. Barbie was quick to remind me of a few others that had come my way on the streets of the Bronx.

"Remember that time when you left school and found a ticket on your windshield for no apparent reason? You were outraged at the injustice, until I pointed out that your car was, in fact, parked in a 'No Parking Tuesday and Thursday' zone on what was indisputably a Tuesday. And, here, you had gone through the entire day believing, with unshakable faith, that it was actually Wednesday. Even the cop on the corner couldn't stop laughing. . . ."

She then went on—with great enthusiasm—to relate tale after embarrassing tale of my dysfunctional days in the South Bronx, as if she had been planted there for the sole purpose of documenting my inadequacies. Now, more than twenty years later, she seemed overjoyed to have finally found an opportunity to share her recollections with a captive audience.

This was definitely not how I had anticipated spending the last few hours of my fiftieth year, and I couldn't wait to say goodbye to Barbie and resume the quietly reflective evening I had been looking forward to all day. But as soon as I began to feel around for my car keys, I knew—with a familiar surge of panic—that it was going to be a long and difficult night ahead.

In a fitting conclusion to five decades of unmindful living, I suddenly realized that I had no idea where I had put my keys. Not wishing to unloose an avalanche of Barbie's memories about my absentminded past, I quietly began to run my fingers through the zippered pockets and webbed pouches of my down jacket and around the folds and crevices and secret compartments of my handbag, praying to find the missing key ring before its disappearance became apparent. However, I came up with nothing but crumpled tissues, cough drop wrappers, and the extra quarters I should have put into the meter in the first place. In the end, I had no choice but to confess.

Twenty minutes later—after I had turned all my pockets inside out, retraced my steps to the Bagel Hole, and emptied the entire contents of my handbag into one of the new salad bowls Barbie had conveniently purchased that evening—we found the keys tangled in the torn lining of my jacket. My fingers and toes were nearly numb by now, but Barbie—apparently energized by the whole experience—continued to churn out one disturbing reminiscence after another.

"I'll never forget the day you had the entire security staff and a squad of students combing the building for hours in search of your office keys—only to find them, at three o'clock, sitting on the roof of your car beside your mittens. . . . And do you remember that department meeting when you rushed in late because you couldn't find your reading glasses—until our chairperson politely suggested that you try looking on the bridge of your nose? . . . And I really loved the time when all of your students' exams blew away in the Bronx Botanical Garden because you left them lying on a bench when you knelt down to smell a flower. . . ."

I wasn't sure how much more of this I could take, but as soon as I opened the door to my car, I realized that the worst was yet to come. Barbie's eyes opened wide at the sight of my old

Volvo, overflowing, as it typically was, with piles of portable clutter en route to their next destination—the dirty laundry that hadn't yet made it to the laundromat; the old books in search of a new home; the two-by-fours my carpenter had left behind the previous summer, finally being returned to Home Depot; the goods in need of repair on their way to the shoemaker, the tailor, the eyeglass shop . . . and, on the front seat, the stack of magazines and mail-order catalogues I hoped to catch up on at red lights.

"How clever," Barbie remarked, apparently overjoyed at the source of new material. "A basement on wheels. Everything you need and don't need right at your fingertips. And, to tell you the truth, except for the spare tire and booster cables, it's a near-perfect replica of your half of our old office."

With that, she began once again to re-create—in excruciating detail—the moments of my life I had tried so hard to forget. At some point, I simply stopped listening; but, hardly taking notice, she continued pommeling me with one mortifying anecdote after another. It wasn't until our ride was nearly at its end that she finally began to wind down her monologue and turn her attention toward me.

"So, P. P.," she asked, as if we were just about to begin our conversation, "what have you been doing with yourself all these years—I mean, when you weren't busy looking for your keys or trying to get your life organized?"

I was so exhausted by this point that I didn't even attempt to censor my response. Besides, Penn Station was mercifully just around the corner, and the entire ordeal would be over in a matter of minutes. So, I simply gave her a direct and honest answer.

"Well, Barbie, to tell you the truth, I've spent most of the past twenty years searching for God."

This was obviously not the reply she had expected, nor one for which she had a quick and witty retort at her fingertips. It took a moment for her to regain her composure and think of an appropriately sarcastic comeback, but she soon rose to the occasion.

"Hmm . . . searching for God . . . ," she mused. "Rumor has it that He's quite a slippery character. Have you ever thought of looking under all those piles in the back seat of your car? It seems the perfect hiding place for an elusive Deity—or, for that matter, anyone else who prefers not to be easily found."

As soon as Barbara Bomzer and all of her packages were out of my car, I sat back and closed my eyes. My hands were shaking, and my chest felt tight, but I knew I had just been given an amazing birthday present, even if I were not fully able to receive it just yet. Barbie—obviously unaware of what she was doing—had handed me a gift that was certain to change the course of my life. Thanks to her unintentional generosity, I was now in possession of that rarest of commodities—a pure kernel of truth.

God, Barbie had said, was probably hiding in my piles of clutter. It was one of her typically irreverent attempts at humor—a poke in the ribs to the universe, with a little sideways jab to me as well. But embedded within the sarcasm was a truly profound insight.

I had spent a lifetime searching for God, while the details of my daily existence went largely ignored. In the end, not only had I never found Him—at least not in the deeply personal way I had hoped—but, on most days, I couldn't find my checkbook or a matching pair of socks either.

Now, for the first time, I was beginning to understand why. All those piles of unfinished business were not just casualties of the journey, but actual barriers to its completion. The many things I had pushed to the side were now blocking my path and obscuring my view. As Barbie had been only too happy to point out, it was not simply my reading glasses and my car keys that had gone into hiding in the back seat of my car and in the recesses of my closet and at the bottom of my oversized pocketbook—it was the spiritual light for which I had been searching in the first place. Wherever I had created a little mess or a big pile, I had also apparently created a spiritual block that kept the light hidden from me.

Which is not to say that clutter operates this way in everyone's life. Many people seem perfectly capable of functioning normally and even growing spiritually while the world around them is in chaos. But not everyone is as internally cluttered as I am, nor as incapable of filtering out the distractions that surround them.

For me, too much of the physical world has meant not enough of myself nor of anything that transcends myself. And with more years now likely behind me than ahead, I knew that I could no longer afford to remain in a holding pattern.

But December 23 clearly marked the beginning of a fresh opportunity. It was a new year in my life—and a new decade and a new half-century. Soon, it would be a New Year for the rest of the world as well. If ever there were a time to transform my life, the moment had surely arrived; and I was determined not to let it pass me by.

"Thank you, B. B.," I said aloud, as I pulled away from the curb. "I hope I can return the favor someday—but, please, may it be from afar."

*W*as Barbie right, after all? I asked myself over and over again, as I inched my way down Seventh Avenue toward the Brooklyn Bridge. Had my spiritual path become as oppressively cluttered as my physical one? I could easily imagine the inner chambers of my soul beginning to resemble the walk-in closet in my bedroom that no one could any longer walk into.

It was clearly time for an uncompromising look at my life. No sugarcoating; no prettying up the ugly details; no hiding the unpleasant truth beneath layers of deeper meaning. Tonight, I simply wanted to observe what was there—just move the lens from scene to scene and let the images speak for themselves. And what better opportunity to do so than a bumper-to-bumper traffic jam of holiday shoppers and late-evening commuters that was sure to keep me stuck in my car and disconnected from the world for the next hour and a half?

I decided to begin by taking a closer look at my immediate surroundings. Barbie had already declared my car the latest exhibit in the history of my hopelessly cluttered life. And, really, who could argue with her? In fact, the longer I reflected upon the mess, the more I was inclined to agree.

Now, to make matters worse, the piles were beginning to attract the attention of the drivers alongside me—most of whom were, no doubt, simply looking for a little diversion from the tedium of their slow crawl home. I soon found myself being stared at by rubbernecking drivers on my left and on my right, eyeing me with growing curiosity, as if they were trying to decide whether I was a homeless person living out of the back seat of her car or a woman on the run with all of her worldly possessions in tow or just another eccentric New Yorker wearing her life on her sleeve.

But it was a precocious little preschooler in a nearby minivan who came closest to the truth when he rolled down his window, pointed a sticky finger in my direction, and announced loudly to his mother: "Look, Mommy—there's a funny-looking lady hiding in a mess."

The little professor was clearly on to something there. Hiding in a mess—definitely an interesting choice of words. No one could accuse *him* of sugarcoating the truth. It certainly appeared that my journey was off to a brutally honest start.

Not wanting to lose my momentum, I immediately turned my lens toward another long-term source of embarrassment—my distinctly unprofessional office at the College.

During my sabbatical several years ago, a part-time colleague in need of office space had asked to borrow mine for the year. When I returned the following September, I found all of her possessions still in my file cabinets, with my own items piled in boxes on the floor. I'm sure she fully intended to restore everything to its original location; but at the end of the semester, she suddenly became ill and never returned to the College, leaving no forwarding address or phone number.

Now, a normally functioning person in my position would probably have waited a few weeks, packed up the unclaimed items, and asked the secretary to store them somewhere out of the way. I, however—not being a normally functioning person who could easily orchestrate such a complicated rearrangement of things—chose a more passive approach. I simply left the woman's papers in my file cabinets and her personal belongings in my desk drawers and began to conduct my professional life out of the cardboard boxes on the floor—which, not surprisingly, soon gave rise to more cardboard boxes and mounting stacks of paper.

Before long, the little piles had spread from one end of my tiny room to the other and were beginning to grow into towering beanstalks. My office was now well on its way to becoming the laughing stock of the Department. You would think the humiliation alone would have provided sufficient motivation for a massive cleanup effort; but my time was as cluttered as my space, and the two-hour project had now turned into an all-day affair.

I kept hoping for the return of the missing teacher, which would have solved a good part of the problem, but she never came back. So, in the end, I simply hung a thick sheet of oak tag over the hallway window, began turning off the lights and locking the door at all times, and spent my office hours seeing students in an empty classroom—in other words, dealing with the situation by not dealing with it at all.

The mere thought of it now filled me with overwhelming shame. I guess I had forgotten just how discomforting clarity could be.

Yet, on I went—slogging through visions of everything in my life that was unfinished, disorganized, out of place, overdue, swirling in chaos. The list was endless; it covered my entire existence. Nothing, it seemed, was in order or being attended to in a timely fashion. I had no idea how I'd ever managed to maintain a home, a marriage, a full-time job, and a good number of meaningful relationships all these years, but I was sure I was living on borrowed time.

Driving down Ocean Parkway, almost home at last, I was finally struck with the disquieting but undeniable conclusion I had been trying all evening to avoid: Barbie was absolutely right. Somewhere along the way, my life had slipped off track; and amid the clutter and confusion of it all, I had lost my direction. Now, just about every aspect of my existence was in some form of disarray, and I was so busy trying to contain the scattered pieces that I no longer had any sense of how they all fit together.

Tonight, however, as I was about to officially turn the corner into middle age, I realized that I could not go on like this any longer. I needed to make an unequivocal commitment to order and simplicity. It was time, once and for all, to gain control over this unwieldy life of mine so that I could focus my attention on its meaning rather than the management of its infinite details. I wanted to spend my remaining years in pursuit of spiritual wisdom—not trying to remember where I had last seen my W-2 form.

As I parked the car and walked toward my house, I made myself a promise that tomorrow—no matter what—I would take the first step toward changing the course of my life. But, tonight . . . well, tonight, I was still forty-nine, and I had some celebrating to do.

"*I*'m home!" I shouted, as I burst through the door, dropping my bags where I stood and creating an instant mess in the narrow foyer.

"Happy almost-birthday to you!" my husband sang out from his armchair, while he attempted unsuccessfully to stifle a yawn. Not a late-night person by nature, Yankel (pronounced 'Yahn-kəl) tried to flow with my evening schedule, but usually faded out just as my second wind was coming in.

"I'm sorry it took me so long to get home," I said, "but after I called you from that phone booth in the Village, the traffic just kept getting worse and worse. And, of course, I had no way of letting you know."

"Maybe—sometime before the new millennium arrives—we should begin to think about beginning to think about getting cell phones," he suggested.

"You know what will happen," I reminded him. "I'll lose mine in the first two hours, and yours will end up in that shoebox beneath your desk with all the T.V. remotes, electronic battery chargers, and atomic watches that we can't figure out how to operate."

"You're a wise woman," he observed proudly.

"Thank you—and soon to be an older one."

"Well, that's as good an excuse as any for opening a bottle of champagne," he said, leading me to the dining room, where I was shocked to find the table set for a candlelight dinner.

"It all got a bit overcooked," he explained, tactfully not making reference to the obvious reason. "But the wine is perfectly chilled."

Between mouthfuls of wilted salad and burnt lasagna, I shared with him the events and revelations of my evening. Then, I blew out the many candles on my triple layer chocolate fudge birthday cake, and we drank a toast to the beginning of my new journey:

"Here's to order and simplicity . . ."

"To an uncluttered life . . ."

"To empty time and open space . . ."

"To freedom . . ."

"And, finally," Yankel concluded with a satisfied yawn, "to sweet dreams. . . ."

But there were no sweet dreams for me that night. Hours after he had gone to bed, I found myself still sitting at the dining room table, wide awake and too agitated to even contemplate sleep. I couldn't stop thinking about the fifty years of disorganized living

I was now determined to leave behind. But how was I ever going to make such a radical change when my every waking moment was consumed with looking for something I had forgotten somewhere or running frantically to make a meeting that had begun ten minutes before I arrived or trying to remember what I was about to do just as I got distracted from doing it?

It was a life of total anarchy, and I had no idea how to infuse it with order and structure and everyday normalcy. And, so, I feared that all my efforts would once again be scattered to the winds, and my life would remain in perpetual chaos.

I was clearly in need of some guidance here, but at three o'clock in the morning, I couldn't think of too many places to find it—until I reminded myself that it wasn't 3:00 AM everywhere in the world. I could still call my friend Laya in Portland, Oregon. It was only midnight on the West Coast—and she did say that she wanted to wish me a happy birthday the moment I hit the Big One. (Of course, when I thought about it afterwards, it was obvious that she meant the moment I hit it in *my* time zone.)

"Am I calling too late?" I began apologetically.

"No, no," she assured me. "It's fine." But I'm certain I heard a muffled yawn on the other end.

I seemed to be having that effect on everyone tonight. Perhaps my timing was more out of synch than I had realized. Another potential dysfunction to consider . . .

But Laya quickly pulled herself together, sang "Happy Big Birthday" to me in perfect German—she'd spent ten years studying opera in Vienna—and then listened attentively to my story.

At the end, she said, "I think you should call an emergency meeting of the Holy Sisters to discuss the issue."

"But do you think this is really an emergency?" I asked.

"Absolutely," Laya responded with certainty. "You've got to make a decision and take action immediately. This is the perfect time to change your life—and it only comes once every half a century. You can't let the moment slip through your fingers."

Then, being the good friend and Holy Sister that she was, she added, "And if anyone there has a speaker phone, I'll be at the meeting myself—no matter what time it is in Portland."

The Holy Sisters were not due to meet for another few weeks— and who knew if my fragile resolve could sustain itself that long? Rather than take a chance, I decided to follow Laya's advice and try to pull together an impromptu meeting of anyone who could attend on such short notice. I began making phone calls first thing the next morning, which—my mornings being what they were—turned out to be somewhere around 11:00. Nevertheless, despite everyone's extremely busy schedule, by noon, I had gotten four definite yeses and three strong maybes for a meeting at Etta's house the following day.

I couldn't imagine a life in New York City without my Holy Sisters. What the environment here lacked in terms of civility and access to nature was more than compensated for by the friendship of these uncommonly wise and caring women. Over time, we had evolved into a seriously committed—if somewhat unconventional—group of spiritual seekers, trying to help each other find our way to the higher worlds while struggling to keep things together down below.

I'm not sure just how we found each other in the first place, but we seem to have naturally gravitated toward one another, as if we instinctively sensed that we had arrived simultaneously at the same bend in the road. From here, many of us went on to develop deeper connections with each other, while others just touched lightly and continued on; but we all recognized that, in one way or another, we had become part of a circle that extended far beyond our individual friendships.

Once a month, we would meet in someone's living room. Each meeting was slightly different, depending on whose home we were in and who was leading the group. Usually, we meditated together, shared our writing, and discussed whatever was on our mind that day. We also sang and danced and ate, and, in general, tried to support one another's attempts at living a spiritual life. The rest of the time, we got together individually and in small groups, always grateful to be part of an extended family in which we were all fluent in the language of personal growth, and no one had to explain why she cried at the end of the movie.

Yet, we knew that our Holy Sister Jill was right when she encouraged us to always keep the entrance to the tent open.

"We need to move beyond ourselves," Jill would often say. "There are all these amazing women out there waiting to be discovered. We don't know who they are, and many of them are so hidden that even *they* don't know who they are—but we have to keep trying to find each other because we're all holy sisters traveling on this journey together."

And, so, we began to call ourselves—and all of our unfound travel companions—the Holy Sisters. At first, the name seemed a bit pious for a group as offbeat as ours. And, as Yankel pointed out, it made us sound more like an ancient order of medieval nuns than a contemporary group of spiritual seekers. But, in the end, we decided to adopt it anyway because in addition to reinforcing our bond with spiritually conscious women everywhere, it also reflected the ways of a very special teacher who had personally touched the lives of many of us.

Rabbi Shlomo Carlebach used to greet everyone he met by saying, "Hey, my holy brother!" or "How are you doing, holy sister?" One of his many gifts was a rare ability to see the holiness in every single person who crossed his path. As he walked up and down Broadway at all hours of the day and night, Reb Shlomo would greet the hidden saints of the Upper West Side—the unwashed street people, the nickel-and-dime hustlers, the wild-eyed prophets reminding us that the end was near. They were all his holy brothers and sisters, and he made it his practice to stop and tell them so.

One Saturday afternoon, as he left his synagogue on 79th Street in Manhattan, he met up with a would-be mugger in Riverside Park. The thief demanded his wallet and all of his money. Reb Shlomo patiently explained to him that Orthodox Jews do not carry money on the Sabbath, so, unfortunately, he could not comply with the request. However, he invited his accoster to stop by the synagogue after the Sabbath, when he would have the money available to give him. Sure enough, that evening the mugger showed up to collect the debt; and, true to his word, Reb Shlomo pressed a wad of bills into his palm. As the astonished thief was about to depart, Reb Shlomo took his hand and said, "Stay in touch, holy brother." And, as the thief no doubt realized, Reb Shlomo truly meant it.

We, too, wanted to be able to recognize the goodness and spiritual potential in each person—and in ourselves as well. And, therefore, we decided to continue calling ourselves the Holy Sisters, not because any of us thought we were particularly holy, but only because we yearned to see the world—as Reb Shlomo did—through holy eyes; and, by seeing, hopefully come a bit closer to making it so.

As much as I always welcomed the opportunity to spend time with the Holy Sisters, this morning I didn't feel any of my usual enthusiasm. Even when I turned onto the walkway leading to Etta's house and was met with the scent of freshly brewed coffee with a hint of vanilla, my footsteps did not quicken in anticipation. It was only when Etta came out to greet me with my special mug in her outstretched hand that I began to soften a bit.

"For you," she said, handing it to me. "Two heaping teaspoons of maple syrup, twice as much half and half as anyone our age should ever consider having, and water hot enough to scald . . . everything in excess, just the way you love it."

"Etta . . ." I began, but immediately my voice caught, and I could feel myself fighting back tears.

"You're going to ruin a perfectly good cup of coffee if you go and add salt to it," she said, reaching in her pocket for a tissue. "Okay, before everyone gets here, why don't you come inside and tell me what happened."

"Well," I said, slipping off my jacket and reaching for the coffee mug, "what happened, I think, is that my life snuck up on me when I wasn't looking; and all those little details I've been ignoring for so many years finally ganged up on me and jumped me from behind. Now, suddenly, wherever I turn, I see a mess. My house is a mess; my car is a mess; my office is a mess—my entire life has become one huge, unmanageable mess. Everything seems to be falling apart—or maybe it always was, but I just never noticed—and I have no idea how to put the pieces back together again."

Besides being one of my closest friends, Etta was also an exceptionally warm and loving therapist. She wanted so much to help me, but before she had a chance to say a word, the doorbell rang, and the Holy Sisters began to arrive.

Everyone gratefully took a cup of something hot to drink—coffee for Yitta and Etta and me; herbal tea for Yidis, Ruchama, Atara, and Judy—and carried it into the living room, where we each headed for our favorite armchair, loveseat, or pillow on the floor. Since it was an informal meeting, we skipped our usual opening rituals; and as soon as everyone said hello to Laya on the speakerphone, they immediately turned their eyes toward me.

Now, being the center of attention in a group of my peers—any group, even the Holy Sisters—is a bit more than I can comfortably handle. And having my life scrutinized by everyone present—even at my own request—creates anxiety. Add to this the distress I was already experiencing, and I found myself barely able to compose a coherent sentence.

Feeling as fragile and unsure of myself as I did, I wanted to tread lightly and choose my words with care. However, as soon as I opened my mouth, my thoughts began to fly in all directions at once, so that my explanation turned out to be every bit as fragmented and unfocused as the life it was describing.

Yet, the Holy Sisters sat quietly, sipped their hot drinks, and listened attentively to every word—shaking their heads in commiseration and nodding supportively as I rambled on. I finally concluded with the events of the past two days—my awful encounter with Barbie and the unsettling realization I had on my drive home.

"I think," Etta suggested, "that we should all close our eyes for two minutes and visualize Pesi's life free of all clutter. Then, we can discuss how to help her get from here to there. But, first, refills anyone?"

Settling back in our seats with fresh mugs of coffee, tea, and hot chocolate, we all silently envisioned what my transformed life would look like. Going around the room, each of the Holy Sisters shared her image of a world unfolding before me filled with order and tranquility. And I believed—if only for this one inspired moment—that it could really be just as they described.

"You know," I said, after everyone had finished speaking, "among my many collections, I have a shoe box filled with old buttons from the 'sixties, and one of my all-time favorites says—in bright day-glo orange—'I'll see it when I believe it.' Well, now that you've gone and made a believer of me, I think I'm finally ready to see it—whatever *it* turns out to be."

"And we're here, ready to help," Etta offered, having apparently become the group leader by default today, since it was her living room in which we were sitting, and no one else seemed to be volunteering for the position. "So tell us what we can do to support you."

"Okay," I said. "I feel like I'm lost in a maze, and I can't find my way out. What I need from everyone is advice on what my next step should be—but it's got to be simple and specific, or I'll become too overwhelmed to follow it."

Since I was obviously looking for practical guidance, we agreed that everyone should take an index card and anonymously write down the first concrete step she thought I needed to take, with Laya dictating her suggestion over the phone. Then, Etta would read aloud the cards without anyone knowing who said what, so that we could discuss all the possibilities objectively.

A few minutes later, Judy supplied the drum roll, and Etta began to read:

"Number One: Find a therapist who understands the psychology of clutter. You need to know *why* you clutter in order to permanently break out of the cycle.

"Number Two: Hire a clutter coach. Professional help is available—Why not use it?

"Number Three: Time can be more difficult to control than space. Maybe you should look for a time management specialist. (Maybe we all should—See if you can get a group rate.)

"Four: Before you begin, take some time to meditate. You've got to be spiritually centered to do this job properly.

"Five: Join a clutterers' support group—if there is such a thing. If not, maybe you could start one yourself.

"Six: Buy a large supply of super-size garbage bags, and recite twice a day: 'When in doubt, throw it out' (And you can begin by tossing that shoe box of old buttons.)

"Seven: Take notes. Try to process your experience on paper."

"Great suggestions," Etta said, placing the index cards on her lap. "Before we discuss them, Pesi, is there anything you want to add?"

"Well, they're all so good, I think I'd like to use every one of them as part of my first step."

"Of course you would," Yidis said, beginning to laugh. "Given seven choices, why not choose all seven? It's a clutterer's dream."

I started to laugh, too, and soon everyone joined in as well. Of course, she was absolutely right. My thinking process was every bit as cluttered as my closet. Why choose one when you could have them all? Complicated was so much more fun than simple.

"Okay," Etta said, trying to do her thankless job and keep us all on track. "Back to those suggestions . . ."

It wasn't too difficult to figure out who had made which recommendation, but we went on to discuss each one without mentioning its author. In essence, the debate was a philosophical one, a latter-day version of faith vs. good works or nature vs. nurture or the chicken vs. the egg. What it basically boiled down to was whether change was more likely to come from the outside in or from the inside out.

Everyone agreed that both were important, but the question was which was more essential to my process. Should I act now and reflect later, or study my inner world before I turned my attention outward? Pick up my clothes and put them where they belong, or try to figure out why I dropped them on the floor in the first place?

Now, the Holy Sisters—being composed mainly of psychologically oriented women who were, for the most part, therapists, teachers, social workers, writers, and artists—naturally leaned toward the introspective. However, struggling with the material world—as most of us did on a daily basis—we also recognized the limitations imposed upon us by our tendency to turn inward. And, so, we came up with what we considered a reasonable compromise: Begin with more active work on clutter and less personal reflection, and then gradually move on to more personal reflection and basic clutter maintenance. In the end, it would all even out and hopefully lead—someday—to a balanced life.

"It sounds like a plan," I said with guarded enthusiasm, as the enormity of the task began to dawn upon me. "But I'm afraid it might take an entire village to make it happen. Where am I going to find all these people, and how am I going to afford to pay them?"

"Well, that's where the Holy Sisters come in," Etta explained. "What do you say—can we create a team to help Pesi get started? I'll begin by volunteering to be her clutter therapist. Of course, we're too close for me to really be her therapist, but since we're only going to deal with issues related to clutter, I think it might work.

"All right. Next, we need a volunteer to be her clutter coach. You don't have to be perfectly organized yourself. You just have to remain a few steps ahead of her."

"I think I can handle that," Yidis said.

Yitta volunteered to be the literary gadfly and keep me writing about my experiences as I was living them.

And since the four of us saw each other regularly outside the group and all dealt—to one degree or another—with issues of clutter, Yidis and Yitta and Etta agreed to function as my inner circle of advisors.

Ruchama and Judy agreed to be on call for crisis intervention and general back-up support. Atara offered to bring me food when I was too immersed in my clean-up efforts to eat properly. And from the speaker phone, Laya signed up for the graveyard shift, promising to keep the hotline open every night from midnight our time until whenever she fell asleep in Portland.

Unfortunately, nobody felt capable of overseeing the nuts and bolts of the operation or dealing with issues of time management, so those positions remained unfilled.

"Our next meeting is in less than three weeks," Etta reminded us, as we were carrying our empty cups into the kitchen. "Is that too soon for a progress report?"

"Not if I actually make some progress," I responded. "But that remains to be seen."

"No, it doesn't," Yidis whispered, slipping her arm in mine as we walked out the door. "We're definitely going to make progress. And quite a bit of it."

"I like the *we*," I said, beginning to feel hopeful again.

"Well, of course," Yidis assured me. "You know we're in this together. So, here's my plan: Since you and I already speak at least once a day, why don't we just add a ten-minute check-in to our conversation. You can report on your experience—your success, your lack of success, your insights, your resistance—whatever comes up for you that day. You'll share, I'll listen; and, then, I'll give you my feedback."

"Yidis," I asked, as I opened the door to my car and climbed in, "do you really believe there's hope for me? I mean, do you honestly think that my life will ever be in a normal place?

"Pesita," she said slowly, "I believe that your journey to the other side of clutter will bring you to truth and serenity and un-imaginable joy. I'm not sure if that's what you'd call a normal place, but why would you want to go anywhere else?"

Chapter Two

The First Step

"Simplify, simplify . . . We are happy in proportion to
the things we can do without."
— Henry David Thoreau

*I*n the weeks that followed, my life became less and less recognizable to me. Not because it changed in any appreciable way—in fact, I was in such a state of paralysis most of the time that it barely changed at all—but simply because the lens through which I viewed the world had suddenly developed a new and unfamiliar focus. The foreground had faded into an obscure corner, and what used to be the backdrop had now moved to center stage.

For most of my life, I pretty much ignored my clutter. It was simply there—a chronic irritation that I lived with, the way most people live with a mosquito in their bedroom. You wish it would go way—you even swat at it from time to time—but you don't take out a shotgun and start blasting holes in your ceiling. In fact, until it starts to buzz in your ear and disturb your sleep, you barely notice it.

However, now that I *had* noticed, I could see nothing but clutter everywhere. It seemed to be rapidly consuming my life. It woke me in the morning and chased me through the night. It multiplied before my eyes and mocked my inability to restrain it. Yet, although I complained incessantly, in truth, I did little to free myself.

"I can't seem to move forward," I confessed to Yitta one evening. "No matter how much my clutter torments me, I just sit here and stare at it, as if I'm waiting for it to get up and walk out the door on its own."

"Don't be discouraged," she reassured me. "You're simply pupating. You know, like a caterpillar. And when the time is right, you'll emerge and be ready for action."

Pupating. I liked that. It transformed my inertia into a respectable stage of development. Leave it to Yitta.

In the meantime, while I was busy pupating, the Holy Sisters were hard at work encouraging me, coaching me, trying to push the project forward. I was on the phone with Yidis and Yitta and Etta nearly every day, and Laya and I usually had a late-night cup of tea by telephone as well. In between, I consulted with Ruchama and Judy; and Atara saved the day on several occasions with emergency deliveries of macrobiotic care packages. Yet, despite all the support, I seemed to be making absolutely no progress.

Nevertheless, as Yidis said, "Once you start to chip away, you're on the road to a Shawshank Redemption—and before you know it, you'll be tunneling your way to freedom." I wasn't sure if I had that much chipping in me, but I hoped she was right.

$\mathcal{T}$oday's gathering was being held at Laurie's house. When we first began our get-togethers, Laurie was single and shared this small apartment with two roommates and a parrot. Now, seven years later, she was married with two children and another on the way—and still living comfortably, parrot and all, in the same quarters. Meanwhile, Yankel and I—with no children and no pets—had moved several times and outgrown each apartment or house we rented before we ever finished unpacking.

At Etta's house, we were transported into the living room on a wave of freshly brewed coffee. Now, as we stood on Laurie's front porch, the aroma of cinnamon cookies warming in the oven came out to greet us. Everyone, it seemed, had her signature scent. Mine, unfortunately, had become the smell of forgotten food left burning on the stove as I ran off in pursuit of whatever it was that distracted me.

But, someday, I fantasized, I, too, would have a pleasing scent floating out the window of my well-organized kitchen. And when guests knocked at the front door, I would run to welcome them, as Etta and Laurie graciously did, instead of looking to dive behind the couch because I was running an hour late and my house was still a mess.

I shared some of these thoughts as we went around the circle, but I saved most of what I was feeling for later. Whoever needed to talk about her issues in greater depth or with more group feedback was given an opportunity to do so at the end of the meeting, when we had a more informal discussion with everyone who could stay. I had never before requested this extra time, and I felt uncomfortable doing it now—but I was too desperate to pass up the opportunity for help.

Etta suggested that I briefly describe my clutter crisis—gentle emphasis on the word *briefly*—so that those who had not been at our last meeting would understand what was going on. This time, I was able to sum it all up in just a few relatively focused statements—no doubt, a sign of progress itself. When I finished, Etta invited the Holy Sisters who had not yet become part of our support team to participate in what we were now calling The Project.

Everyone present stepped forward and offered to help in one creative way or another; and even those who were already helping volunteered to expand their roles. Laurie—an inspiring teacher and also a great dessert maker—promised to keep baking my favorite blueberry muffins for me, as well as providing unlimited telephone support between baby feedings. Myriam—who always had words of wisdom at her fingertips—said she would call once a week with a spiritual teaching on the topic of order and simplicity. And Atara—a gifted artist and art therapist—suggested painting her vision of an uncluttered universe so that I could hang it on my wall for inspiration.

After refueling with another round of Laurie's cookies, more Holy Sisters came forward. Ruchama—everyone's favorite teacher of creative writing, as well as a successful author herself—volunteered to put together a reading list of practical and inspirational books. Julie—one of the better organized among us—said she would work with me on prioritizing and list-making. Golda—always eager to lend a helping hand—signed on to be the designated driver in charge of clutter removal and recycling. And Judy—a natural social worker and clutter sympathizer—agreed to round out the team by coordinating all the unassigned Sisters to run interference with my life—return a library book, mail a letter, pick up an emergency pint of half and half—so that nothing would get in the way.

"With such an army behind me, how could I possibly lose this war?" I asked with rising confidence.

"Very easily," Yidis responded. "Without a timetable and some sort of battle plan, your soldiers won't even know where the front line is."

"That's why you're my coach," I said with a little bow.

After many suggestions and countersuggestions, we finally came up with a strategy and a target date. Between now and the end of May, I would do the best I could; but given the demands of my job and my life, it probably wouldn't be all that much. However, as soon as the semester was over, I would spend my entire summer vacation tackling my clutter. From the beginning of June until the end of August, my quest for order would take center stage. And whenever I ran into a psychological roadblock, Etta would be there with an emergency therapy session.

By the time I went back to school in September, my house and my car would be thoroughly organized and free of all clutter. That would enable me to spend the entire fall semester working on my office.

When my birthday came around again at the end of December, I would be ready to face, not only the next year of my life, but also a new century and a new millennium (The timing would have been amazingly synchronistic had it not been for the fact that it was all based upon one huge chronological error. The New Century and the New Millennium were not actually arriving until the year 2001. But since the entire world was planning a wild celebration of this miscalculated event on January 1, 2000, I decided to jump on the bandwagon and join them. After all, I wasn't about to go up to my roof the following year and shoot off firecrackers by myself at the dawning of the real Millennium.)

And so, I left the meeting filled with renewed hope, the support of good friends, and a concrete plan of action—as well as a large bag of warm cookies to get me through the challenges that lay ahead.

*B*efore stepping into this new and promising future of mine, I decided to take a moment to reflect upon my less successful past. I wanted to understand just where I had gone wrong in all of my previous attempts to create order. What was there about the simple, uncluttered life that I could not seem to fully embrace? Or, at least, not for very long.

Several years ago, I was granted a twelve-month sabbatical in which I was supposed to produce a book of essays. Eager to begin before I could find a good excuse not to, I immediately sat down in my rocking chair, with a pen in my hand and a notebook propped on my lap . . . and waited.

I rocked and waited and rocked and waited, but nothing came through. So, I decided to try sitting at my desk. Change your location; change your luck, they say. But I soon realized that my options for changing my location were severely limited. Every potential writing surface in my home was already occupied by the unfinished projects that had landed there first.

Mail waiting to be opened and bills in need of payment had staked their claim to one side of my desk, while the other side had been appropriated by an avalanche of receipts and coupons and scraps of paper with unidentified phone numbers that had recently been emptied in a heap from a drawer during a frantic search for a missing paycheck. Items waiting to be filed or recycled or shredded had migrated to the rear of the desk, and the center had been taken over by chapters of an old manuscript in various stages of revision.

The dining room table (half of which had recently been ceded to my husband in a battle for territorial rights) did not look promising either. His side was covered with unread newspapers and sailing magazines; my side, with unread newspapers and literary journals. And both sides were being elbowed out from the middle by the breakfast dishes that were awaiting their turn in the sink, which was currently occupied by last night's unwashed dinnerware.

So, I never changed my location, and my luck remained unchanged as well. Every morning, I showed up faithfully at the rocking chair; and every afternoon, I left with the same empty notebook. After a week of this, I was forced to accept the obvious diagnosis: I was suffering from a severe case of writer's block. It would simply have to run its course, which would hopefully not take the entire span of my sabbatical.

But what to do until the muses arrived? I knew from previous experience that there was no rushing these gals. In fact, the more I kept my nose pressed to the glass, the longer it generally took for them to come around.

It finally occurred to me that what I needed was an all-consuming project to take my mind off the one I should have been engaged in. Something real and meaningful that would keep me occupied for a few days or weeks or even months, until my writer's brain unfroze, and I could resume the task at hand.

I gave the matter a great deal of thought, but nothing came to me. So, I did what I usually do when I feel stuck. I sat down with a freshly brewed cup of coffee and stared out my kitchen window. As is often the case, the answer wasn't long in coming. In fact, when

I looked up from my coffee cup, it was sitting right there staring me in the face.

Directly below the window sill, just beyond view of the rest of the house, sat a lonely patch of garden—undernourished, poorly groomed, and generally forgotten by all. A botanic stepchild left out in the noonday sun. It was obviously a victim of shameful neglect, but not one for whom all hope had completely vanished. There still seemed a spark of life among the dry grass and withered leaves.

My new project, it seemed, had arrived at last.

With a pair of pruning shears in one hand and a first aid kit in the other, I pushed past the dying hedges and stepped over the fallen buds. I cut back the tangled weeds that were choking the daylilies and black-eyed Susans and removed the layers of dead foliage crushing the unborn sprouts. As soon as the last twisted vine loosened its grip, I reached for the wounded plants and began CPR. I watered them and fed them, straightened their bent limbs, and provided them with splints and supports. I sang songs of triumphant acorns and crocuses peeking through the snow. Soon, they unfolded their petals and arched their stems toward the sun; and the cycle of nature began to renew itself.

And so, I realized, it could be with everything else in my life as well.

I looked around my house. It was a mirror image of my garden. Untended, overgrown, out of control. Another victim of neglect bordering on abuse.

But the garden was now beginning to heal. Why not apply the same treatment to my many other areas of dysfunction? My home, my office, the back seat of my car . . . they were all gasping for breath beneath a thick layer of clutter.

Armed with a case of industrial-strength garbage bags and a stack of plastic milk crates, I spent the next six months combing my house in search of excess. Determined to smoke out every last item that was not genuinely wanted or needed, I searched from basement to storage shed, from bay window to gabled roof. I looked on every shelf and in every drawer, beneath the bed and behind the refrigerator and above the acoustic tiles in the dropped ceiling. I went through cabinets and closets, suitcases and backpacks. I poked into every bin and basket and cubby hole.

In truth, I didn't really have to try so hard. Most of the time, the clutter was sitting right out there in the open—a humiliating display for all to see. But I was clearly a woman obsessed.

And, in the end, my obsession paid off. Before long, I was hauling bags and boxes to the curb for sanitation pickup and recycling—scores of them, overflowing with broken umbrellas and cans of dried paint, typewriter ribbons and snarled telephone cords, lamps without shades and shades without lamps, old calendars and faded needlepoints reminding me to have a nice day and not forget to smell the flowers. They lined the driveway and sat six deep and three high across the porch. A sad commentary on my relationship with the material world.

Many more piles sat indoors, awaiting delivery to the Salvation Army, the Second Chance for All Thrift Shop, and the We Buy Junk and Sell Antiques Dealer. These items, I must say, were quite impressive—at least from a decluttering point of view. Of course, I had the usual stock of musty books, used clothing, and outdated electronic equipment; but I also had personal treasures here that I never thought I would allow myself to part with.

My mending kit, for example. It had taken me decades to assemble this extensive assortment of buttons and ribbons and spools of thread, squares of fabric and skeins of braided yarn. It was a tribute, at least in part, to my Aunt Minnie, who promoted the view that an ugly patch is more pleasing than a beautiful hole. However, despite the basket of creative options at my disposal, there were many holes and few patches in my wardrobe. Rather than climb all the way up to the top shelf of my closet to reach the kit and then have to decide which of the rainbow assortment of colors best matched the garment in need of repair, I generally opted for a safety pin, with a few staples as back-up. And once I discovered iron-on tape, it was really all over. I never opened the mending kit again. Still, the thought of giving it away . . . it was, after all, the collection of a lifetime . . . and Aunt Minnie would have been so proud. . . .

But I was ruthless. I had to be. And, in the end, it was well worth it. For the first time in my life, I knew just what I had and where I could find it. And if someone happened to approach the door to my closet, I was no longer seized with an uncontrollable urge to throw my body across the entrance and bar their way.

Now, it was obviously time to return to my writing project.

I took a few days off to luxuriate in the spaciousness of my newly uncluttered home; but, in truth, I could hardly wait to get back to work on the project, thrilled to once again have something in my life to create besides order.

Finally, I entered my light and airy study, sat down at my well-organized desk, and spread my writing materials across the empty surface. And, just as I had hoped, the process immediately began to unfold. Once I touched my pen to paper, a half year's worth of ideas scrambled for release.

From the beginning, however, I decided to guide the process along by applying the same principles of clutter management to my writing that I had to my possessions. Delete the excess from sentences the way I had from dresser drawers and closet shelves. Make those paragraphs lean and spare, with fewer adjectives and less exuberant imagery. Become a minimalist in word as well as deed.

I started by tightening the reins on those unruly metaphors of mine, keeping an especially watchful eye on the quick-moving mavericks that had a way of galloping off on their own and sending my essays stampeding down unintended paths. Before my thoughts even hit the page, I tried to clip here and crop there and prevent the energy from dashing in all directions at once.

In general, I thought I was doing a pretty good job; and, therefore, I anticipated the same rush of exhilaration I felt when I discarded the last yellowed newspaper and hung my final Pendaflex folder. Instead, I found myself staring in numb silence at a world gone flat and gray. My writing slowed to a depressing trickle, the words dropping—one by one—in tightly metered sentences that clearly reflected the strain of effort and the absence of inspiration. It wasn't exactly writer's block, but there was definitely something clogging the channel.

After several gridlocked days, it became obvious that by restricting the flow of my imagination, I had cut myself off from my own source of creative energy. Tightening the controls may have staved off verbal clutter, but it apparently sapped the life from my writing as well. The overgrowth, I realized, could always be pruned later—that's where gardeners and editors come in—but, first, the spirit needs to be unleashed and allowed to run free.

Before I knew it, I was joyfully heaping piles of images upon themselves once more, stringing form and color across the page like fresh laundry on a tree-held clothesline. The writing started to spin out of control, as my mind darted off in hot pursuit of each new idea and fresh image. In this highly charged zone, I found my-self once again riding the wave of a writer's high and loving every minute of it.

Yet, despite the joy that unrestrained abundance brings me, I have to admit that my day-to-day existence would be far more manageable if I felt stimulated by the empty rather than the full, by a blank canvas instead of a palette of many colors. But my inspiration seems to come from viewing an array of options spread before me. From there, I can proceed to make my tentative selections, change my mind several times if need be, then mix and match and separate until the samples of paint or colored scarves or jars of fragrance yield the special one I'm searching for or the perfect combination. In this way, I'm able to wander back and forth from the many to the few, from the full spectrum of choices to the ones that beckon to me most enticingly.

This is the method by which I decorate a room, get dressed in the morning, compose a thought, and generally live my life. It's how I make major decisions and prepare a simple meal. It is ineffi-cient and impractical and consumes an inordinate amount of time, space, and energy. Yet, I've been doing it all my life, and it's the only way I know that seems to work for me.

I look with amazement at any woman whose delight in jewelry can be aroused by a string of pearls or a few simple chains that fit neatly into a box—while I require the visual stimulation of a three-foot cork board displaying hand-painted ceramic beads; necklaces of shell, gemstone, and colored glass; macrame chokers; long strands of silver and gold filigree; and crystal pendants dangling from velvet ribbons.

In theory, I admire the smooth lines and refined elegance of a solitary white orchid in a slender glass vase; but, in reality, it can never stir my heart in quite the same way as an uncontrolled explosion of red and purple wildflowers in a watering can. There is, for me, a vitality in the untamed profusion of a thing that is simply not present in its more constrained counterpart.

I am reminded of this fact every time I visit my local vegetable market.

Many of my neighbors simply call in their weekly produce order and never set foot in the store. I, on the other hand, cannot begin to make my decisions without standing at the counter with all the contenders in plain view. I need the full range of possibilities laid out before me so that I can follow my eyes, my nose, my fingertips, and my sense of a good buy to the perfect head of lettuce and cluster of grapes.

One day, I might choose red-veined Swiss chard because I am fascinated by the exquisitely detailed designs etched in crimson on each deep green leaf. Another time, I may go for the nubby little purple potatoes, usually quite a bargain in season, with fresh clumps of farm dirt still clinging to them—simply too endearing to pass up. Or I could find myself irresistibly drawn to a bouquet of spunky magenta beets with the stems and leaves intact that instantly transports me back to my childhood stoop in the Bronx, where I used to sit on late summer afternoons sipping homemade borscht streaked with sour cream from an oversized mug.

The way I walk through that vegetable market is the way I walk through the marketplace of life—wanting to experience it all. Look at each item. Taste it, smell it, feel its texture, relive its memories; then, take some home to keep. The last part, of course, is where the problem comes in.

There is so much to take in and so little space to store it. The joy of creative clutter has stretched my system way beyond its limits. Nevertheless, I continue to seek more because abundance is my way of appreciating life and connecting to its beauty.

And maybe, in the end, that's not so bad. After all, the universe itself seems to mirror my tendency toward excess. Why else would we see such a multiplicity of forms in nature's bounty? Wouldn't a few sweet-smelling flowers and brightly colored butterflies have sufficed? Do we really need over fifteen hundred varieties of subtly differentiated begonias and four thousand species of songbirds, most of whose variations in chirping are indistinguishable to the human ear? Over a million species of insects? Twenty thousand varieties of ferns and 14,000 types of mushrooms?

It would appear that the Master Creator Himself may well be somewhat of an advocate for clutter. After all, He has generously chosen to fill His world with far more variety than seems necessary—which might explain why we seek to do the same.

Nevertheless, when all is said and done, it is clear that the abundance that stimulates my imagination also clutters my path; and when my path becomes cluttered, my imagination begins to shut down. Yet, without that overflow of abundance, my imagination would rarely be activated to begin with. And it is, no doubt, because of this strange irony that as much as I yearn for order and simplicity, I am, at the same time, put off by the prospect of a contained and clutter-free life.

*O*ver cappuccino at Cafe K a few days later, I shared the story of my sabbatical with Yidis and Yitta and Etta.

"It's such an interesting twist on the subject," Yitta said. "I never thought of the connection between clutter and creativity. You should definitely write about it."

"But there won't be any time or space for writing," Yidis said, "if we don't get this project off the ground. I can't wait for the day when we can sit around and talk about the deeper meaning of it all; but, right now, there's no time for that. We've got to start taking action immediately. And we've got to find a way to make Step One really simple, or we'll never get to Step Two."

"Pesi," Etta said, "I think you should keep a log of every psychological and emotional issue that comes up for you, and we'll deal with all of them later. I promise. But, first, we need to get some forward motion going here. You've got to find something to get rid of."

"I have an idea," Yidis suggested. "How about choosing one large item—like a piece of furniture. If you can get rid of something that takes up a lot of space, I think you'll have such a feeling of success that you'll be able to move on to the smaller and more subtle forms of clutter with a lot less difficulty."

"Okay," I agreed. "I have six large tables stored in my landlord's garage. I certainly don't need all of them. Why don't I begin there?"

"Great," Yidis said. "Next week, when we meet for coffee, you can tell us about all the tables you found new homes for. And, by the way, why *do* you have six tables in the garage?"

A good question, I had to admit.

As I walked down Avenue K, I thought about it. How, in fact, did I come to have six tables? Then, slowly, I began to remember.

The very first piece of serious wooden furniture I ever purchased from a real furniture store was a solid oak table that, the salesman assured me, could—with the simple flick of a wrist—be converted into a bench whose seat concealed a hidden storage compartment. Even before I had any awareness of my attraction to clutter, something in me was sparked by the prospect of a secret space in which to store future acquisitions.

The simple flick of a wrist, however, turned out to be more of a project for a skilled carpenter; and the high-backed, hard-seated bench into which it transformed itself never succeeded in attracting anyone but my long-haired cat—and that by default, since he was banned from every upholstered piece of furniture in the house that might require vacuuming.

The salesman described, in fascinating detail, how the table got its name. It was called a monk's bench, he explained, because in medieval times, when bands of marauding barbarians would attack defenseless villages and monasteries, the monks would hide themselves in the secret compartment beneath the seat of the bench, over which the back could then be turned to its table-top position, providing additional concealment.

I was always sorry I hadn't inquired further about the size of medieval monks, since the storage space was only about three feet long and one foot wide. Perhaps fasting and other forms of abstinence retard normal growth; but it would have been nice to know for sure, since every time I've repeated the story over the many decades I've had the table, someone has invariably raised the question.

As to the purchase itself, I was never quite certain if what I bought was a practical piece of furniture or an interesting anecdote, but, in any case, it was the beginning of a lifelong affection for tables. Although I rarely ventured into a retail furniture store after that, I have filled home after home with tables of every size, shape, and suggested function, acquired at flea markets, garage sales, and secondhand shops up and down the East Coast.

There is scarcely a vacation in memory from those early years that did not conclude with a table being strapped to the top of an already sagging vehicle, followed by a late-night phone call to my building handyman, asking him to please remove the front door from its frame so that the table could be carried into my apartment.

"You'd think," Willie would inevitably grumble as he unhinged the door, several screws resting between his teeth, "that folks who been to college would have enough good sense to measure a thing before they went and dragged it home." However, at some point in the operation, he would usually begin to soften and begrudgingly acknowledge the obvious charm of the piece.

Tables are like that. In their own understated way, they quietly strike a responsive chord in even the most unlikely of appreciators.

To this day, my house—and, of course, my garage—remained filled with tables. They were mostly handmade wooden ones with plain, unvarnished tops—blank canvases upon which I could freely splash the beauty of the world. And if not its beauty, then surely its overflow—functioning, as they often did, as the official landing strip for transient objects on their way from one location to another.

Then, there was the unseen world below. With the simple addition of a tablecloth—and, here, almost anything would do, from fine Irish linen to an old madras bedspread—the table could be converted into a horizontal closet. Beneath its newly draped legs, a world of unassimilated possessions could safely be stashed, providing instant refuge from judgment for any objects of questionable value.

Yet, for all their virtues, tables have created an ongoing challenge in my life. My dining room table, in particular, presented a daily temptation not to be lightly dismissed. Every day, that long, sleek expanse of emptiness would spread itself irresistibly before me—and, like Mother Nature herself, I was seized with an uncontrollable urge to fill the vacuum.

"Come a little closer," it beckoned. "Unburden yourself. You can leave that package here for a while. There's plenty of room for those newspapers and magazines, too. Relax. Put your coffee mug down. And that stack of mail you're carrying—why not place it on this empty corner for just a few minutes. . . ."

Dangerously seductive though they may be, tables were still my favorite piece of furniture. And although, at this moment, six of them sat unused in my garage, I remained confident that they would one day find their way back into my home—if not this home, then perhaps the next or the one after that.

"So, how's it going with your tables?" Yidis asked me the next evening at check-in time.

"Well, from a literary point of view, it's going beautifully. I was so inspired by the topic that I came home and wrote a long essay about my relationship with tables."

"I'm sure Yitta will be thrilled. And from a decluttering point of view?"

"That's a bit of a problem. Now that I've gotten more deeply in touch with how much I love my tables, I don't think I want to part with any of them just yet."

"Not even one of the six?"

"I don't think I'm ready. Couldn't we start with something easier?"

"Well, maybe just a little easier," she said. "But, remember, we want you to feel empowered; so, you need something that's going to make a real dent and boost your confidence. After that, you can do whatever you want."

"How about a bag of clothing to Goodwill?"

"No, that's not dramatic enough. We need something with real physical and emotional heft to it."

"How about a really big bag of clothing to Goodwill?"

"It still lacks substance. Let's think for a minute. . . . Wait, didn't I see one of those old metal typewriters sitting on your desk next to your computer? That's perfect. You certainly don't need both of them."

"No, of course not. As a matter of fact, I've been thinking about getting rid of the computer for some time now."

I could hear Yidis taking a deep, exasperated breath.

"Have you ever actually tried to use it?" she finally asked.

"I took a few lessons, but I wouldn't exactly say we're friends yet."

"Well, maybe you could work on the relationship. You don't have to decide this minute. All I'm asking you to do is consider the possibility of giving the typewriter away. You could donate it to a good cause, like an artifacts museum or some third world nation that would probably consider it cutting-edge technology."

"All right," I promised. "I'll think about it. But I've had that typewriter for a really long time. We've been through a lot together; and it works just fine, except for the *q* and the *x*—and how often do you use them anyway?"

"I tried; I really tried," I told Yidis and Yitta and Etta at Café K later that week. "But I love my tables. And my old typewriter, too—I wrote my first term paper on it. I just couldn't bear to part with any of them."

"You know, maybe we're setting the bar a bit too high," Etta said. "Tables and typewriters—those are big items to let go of. Why can't we begin with a few old newspapers?"

"Because, at that rate, the process could go on for decades," Yidis responded. "As it already has. Sometimes, halfway measures only get us halfway there. And Pesi is desperate for a sweeping change right now. Not in twenty years—one faded newspaper at a time."

"I think Yidis is right," Yitta added. "If we start big, we can always narrow it down later. But if we start small, we may never build up the momentum we need."

"I don't know," Etta hesitated. "It doesn't seem to be working."

"I think I just need a little more time," I finally said. "I like the idea of beginning at the top; but if I don't make at least one successful deposit in the giveaway pile soon—say, by our next meeting of the Holy Sisters this month—I'm open to going small."

We all agreed that this seemed reasonable, so we put the subject to rest and, over another round of coffee, went on to discuss Yidis' upcoming conference, Etta's new chiropractor, and Yitta's latest book proposal.

"All right," Yidis said, as we left the café and began to walk home together. "We have two weeks until our February meeting. Any new ideas?"

"Well, since we're aiming high, I've been trying to decide which corner of my basement has the distinction of being the most out of control. It didn't take much thinking. The obvious winner is the corner where we store our exercise equipment and sporting goods. When we first moved in, we piled all of it there in a heap and tacked a sign to the wall that read GREAT EXPECTATIONS. Not too long ago, I amended the sign to read SIGNIFICANTLY REDUCED EXPECTATIONS. I think that pretty well sums it up."

"So," Yidis asked eagerly, "do you think you might be willing to pass some of that equipment on to a needy fitness seeker?"

"I don't see why not. We're obviously never going to use it ourselves."

*F*or several hours that afternoon, I experienced the deep satisfaction of creating empty space. Since exercise equipment and sporting goods are two of the rare categories of items for which I feel absolutely no affection, the process of release was one of unequivocal joy. The objects themselves evoked no sense of longing; no nostalgia; no association with pleasures past, present, or future. In fact, quite the opposite. They induced feelings of guilt and inadequacy, reminding me of how irresponsibly I treat my body and how athletically challenged I've always been. They recalled early childhood memories of being chosen last—if at all—for the team and later recollections of an ungraceful adolescence— memories I was only too happy to pass on to the recycle bin.

Other than a few twinges of remorse at the money wasted, I completed the entire project with virtually no conflicting emotions. And when I was finally done, I felt so energized by my success that I dragged everything to the front door myself. Not wanting to eliminate all sense of hope, however, I left behind the treadmill, the exercise bicycle, and a set of freestanding weights—all of which were too heavy to carry upstairs anyway.

By the time Yankel came home, our narrow foyer was spilling its contents onto the front porch: an old Red Flyer sled from the winter we spent in Buffalo; cross-country skis from our years in the Hudson Valley; several crates of camping equipment that dated back to his summers as an Eagle Scout; the trampoline that was guaranteed to make exercise fun; and half a dozen boxes representing our good intentions and weak follow-through.

"What's all this?" Yankel called from the porch, as he tried to make his way across to the front door. "Is it coming in or going out?"

"Out," I announced proudly. "It's all going out."

"Oh, that's great," he said. "Looks like a lot of junk we'll be better off without. . . . But what's in those unopened boxes?"

"Just more stuff that we'll never use."

"Hmm, let's take a peek," he said, kneeling down for a better look and grunting from the effort.

At this point, I could feel myself beginning to get nervous. His curiosity about my castoffs was never a good thing. As it was, I usually found myself only a step away from reclaiming whatever I was about to discard; and his sudden interest in an object was all it took to cast doubt upon my decision and send me running to the curb to retrieve the item.

It was getting a bit chilly on the porch, so I left him there opening and closing all the boxes, while I stepped inside, hoping for the best. A few minutes later, he burst into the kitchen, obviously overjoyed about whatever he had found.

"It's a good thing I looked through those boxes. You almost threw out something really valuable by mistake."

"What's that?" I asked, hoping the answer wasn't going to bring anything too big back into our lives.

"My roller skates," he said, raising the dusty boots high into the air.

I was too shocked to respond.

It was true, of course, that Yankel had once been a great skater. But over the past decade, he had developed all sorts of middle-aged maladies—high blood pressure, diabetes, bursitis, loss of balance, sciatica, and arthritic knees, to mention just a few. And, on most days, he was grateful to walk a straight line from his car to the front door of the house, and from the front door to his favorite easy chair. Now, the thought of him barreling down Ocean Parkway on roller skates . . .

"I know I've gotten a bit rusty," he conceded in response to my silence, "but I feel really motivated to get back in shape again."

An hour later, I could hear him humming one of his favorite melodies as he oiled and polished the skates and carried them back down to the basement along with every other box and piece of equipment I had brought up. To his credit, he did stack them more neatly than I had originally found them, but it didn't really make much of a difference since, in the end, they took up the same amount of space.

"We really got a lot accomplished here today," he said, breathing heavily but beaming with satisfaction. "Doesn't it feel great to finally make order?"

"*I* couldn't believe it," I told Yidis later that evening. "In one fell swoop, Yankel managed to undo everything I had accomplished the entire day; but, at the same time, his actions made a beautiful statement about his faith in the possibility of change. And, when you think about it, is holding on to his roller skates any more out of touch with reality than keeping dresses in our closet that we haven't fit into for years? I mean, getting rid of them makes perfect sense, but it would be the ultimate admission of defeat. Isn't it better to have a cluttered closet—or a cluttered pile of exercise equipment—than to surrender all hope?"

"Of course," Yidis said, "but it's all a matter of degree. Most of us have one or two of those fantasy dresses—you probably have a dozen."

"At least," I had to admit.

"Okay," she continued, "I rest my case. But, still, this has definitely been your most successful failure yet. So, I guess you could say we're beginning to make progress."

"And," I reported with great enthusiasm, "I have the perfect location for our next offensive. . . ."

For years, I've called this place The Last Room because I believed it was my final obstacle to an orderly life. In one form or another, some version of this room has existed in every home I've ever lived in, and entering it has inevitably filled me with a profound sense of shame. Which is why it's always been my most avoided place to clean, organize, pack, or unpack.

Another potentially beautiful room transformed into a humiliating eyesore, this once-pleasant area had, like its many predecessors, become the repository for everything I owned that defied classification. Whatever did not fit neatly into one category or another landed here, where it was condemned to spend its days in a purgatory of indecision.

Every morning, the rising sun would attempt to stream through the big bay windows that looked out hopefully from its eastern wall. And every morning, the sun would be met with resistance at all points.

A thick coat of dust clinging to the panes presented the first barrier to any sunlight attempting to enter. Then, there were the piles of my unsettled belongings that reached so high off the ground that the light could only, at best, circle around them and occasionally peek through a little chink in the stack. Finally, there were the yellowed papers rising from every surface—thousands of them; maybe hundreds of thousands—each waiting their turn to be read, reread, filed, cried over, laughed at, fed to the shredder, or, in some way, responded to and finally released. My own personal Tower of Babel, climaxing—like the original one—in a maze of confused words.

Just thinking about this chamber of unmade decisions filled me with anxiety. I couldn't bear its tentativeness and lack of clarity, its stubborn refusal to accept boundaries and submit to the simple order of things that somehow managed to permeate the rest of the universe. Today, however, I was determined to finally take a deep and honest look at the contents of the room.

Whenever I walked through that door—which was as infrequently as possible—I would generally edge my way along the walls until I reached my destination and then immediately depart. I tried to avoid making eye contact with anything there, not wishing to interact more than necessary with a scene that so vividly reflected my own inner chaos.

But, this evening—ready, at last, to confront the truth and act upon it—I took my first step forward by venturing beyond the periphery of the room, climbing over a few of the softer piles, and inching my way toward the center. There, I found myself surrounded on all sides by an assembly of homeless objects, all glaring accusingly at me, their eternal tormentor.

Slowly and awkwardly, I looked around and began to reconnect with these forgotten pieces of my life. They greeted me, one by one, my prodigal children come home: Hippilah, my psychedelic hippopotamus with fringed eyelashes and a pink tulip embroidered on her ear that I bought for a dollar at a garage sale in Woodstock several decades ago; my mildly deformed wicker baskets, all a size or shape too odd to actually fit anywhere or hold anything, but too endearing in their imperfection to be discarded; the dried flowers and discolored wall hangings that added a touch of color and a softening of lines to former homes, but never quite made the transition to this one.

Off to the side, I saw my favorite pieces of old lace draped across a rocking chair, fragments of faded beauty in search of a definition—each too small to be a tablecloth, too large to be a doily, too wide to be a ribbon, too narrow to be a scarf—but all symbols of a time when loveliness was its own reason for being. On the hassock nearby sat my woolly heap of half-knit scarves, shawls, and baby blankets—labors of love suspended indefinitely in a process of becoming, much like the friendships for which they were created. And in the corner closest to the window, the never-used bassinet lifted my flowering cactus to meet the few persistent rays of sunlight that managed to fight their way through.

As I reunited with these lost parts of myself, the hostility melted for the first time into a stream of compassion for the prisoners of this way station, who could find no dwelling place of their own because they would not be reduced to an identity that gave them permanent residence in this drawer or folder or on that shelf. They were the lonely holdouts in a world that clearly believed there was a place for everything, and sooner or later, the slot would be discovered or created, and we would each be assigned to our proper niche.

Suddenly overcome by a wave of love and gratitude, I wanted to thank the inhabitants of this no man's land for simply being what they were. They would never be contained by a label or confined to a pigeonhole because their very essence was a celebration of freedom. Misfits and mess-makers, they were also the sweetness and spirit of life, the wildflowers and shooting stars that wandered from the pack to create their own special magic in an otherwise dull and orderly world.

Now, if I could only figure out what to do with all of them . . .

"Yidis, it was one of the most healing experiences I've ever had—me and all the fragmented parts of myself together in one room, reuniting and finally making peace."

"It sounds like an amazing experience. As your friend and Holy Sister, I wish I could have been there with you. And if I were your therapist, I'd declare it a cathartic breakthrough. But as your clutter coach . . . I mean, I hate to be insensitive, but, in the end, did you actually throw anything out?"

"No, not a single thing. I just couldn't."

"I understand," she said quietly.

We were both silent for a moment.

"You know," she continued, "you should definitely write about this experience—the whole idea of our things and the memories they hold and the parts of ourselves they reflect—it's such a fascinating subject to explore.

"But, maybe, for just a little while, we could put it aside and focus on The Project. Otherwise, I'm afraid you'll go through the rest of your life too overwhelmed to ever write about anything.

"And I still believe that if you were able to let go of even one substantial item—especially something you've been carrying around for a long time—it would give your decluttering efforts a huge lift-off and really propel the process forward."

"I think you're right," I agreed. "But I seem to be much more attached to my things than I ever realized. Not so much as things, but as connections—to myself, to others, to my experiences—I don't know, to everything."

"I really hear what you're saying," Yidis said. "And I'm not suggesting that you part with Hippilah or that you spend hours agonizing over which piece of lace to give away, but maybe you could find just one box in that room that it would actually feel good to get rid of."

"Well," I considered, "there are certainly lots of possibilities in there. The room is piled high with bags and boxes I haven't looked at in many years and many moves. And each one is filled with things I once considered too special to part with, but could never figure out just where to put or how to use. Maybe, now, I'm finally ready to let go of some of them—or at least of *one* of them."

Newly inspired, I promised Yidis that I would go back into the room and stay there until I found at least one significant item to remove. Or until I needed a coffee break—whichever came first.

Given the fact that it was already close to 10:00 PM, I was obviously setting myself up for a long night ahead. But I didn't care. There was now only one week left until the Holy Sisters held their February meeting, and I was determined to have some progress to report. Fortified with a mug of coffee and a handful of chocolate kisses, I reentered the room and began my search.

I quickly bypassed the objects that seemed too heavily laden with memories or romantic overtones—photographs, old cards and perfumed letters, pressed roses, handwritten poems . . . all too big a challenge. I also decided to ignore the piles of paper because I didn't have the patience to deal with such a tedious task. In addition, any memorabilia from my childhood or anything that belonged to someone who had passed away were off limits. So were old books and record albums. The possibilities were definitely narrowing.

Finally, after opening and closing dozens of boxes, I found a potential candidate. It was an old wooden crate filled with pieces of pottery that had all been chipped or broken in ways that made them impossible to use or display. And I don't say that lightly. There are very few pieces of pottery for which I can't find a purpose or a potential home.

At first, I couldn't understand why I had saved them in the first place. Had they begun their journey in good condition and simply gotten damaged along the way? That seemed unlikely, since the pieces that had chipped off were not in the box. And judging from the dates on the newspapers in which they were wrapped, they had been traveling with me unopened for many years.

After working my way through reams of crumpled paper and bubble wrap, I discovered the clue lying inside a cracked demitasse cup with a missing handle. Right in the center was a tiny emerald leaf—the unmistakable symbol of my favorite Greenwich Village pottery store.

The Green Tree Pottery Shop was tucked away in a little cul-de-sac in the West Village on one of those winding cobblestone streets with shuttered cottages and Victorian names. Beside it was an old wooden bench, where I often sat in the early '70s, trying to make sense of my life as I waited for my friend Joanna to arrive from the Bronx.

The store was far too small for the volume of its contents and, therefore, required a certain level of agility just to navigate the cramped quarters. Visitors were routinely required to walk sideways with stomach muscles contracted, stand on tiptoes, twist, climb, crouch, and gracefully duck.

Even the building itself—in an apparent gesture of support—seemed to have curled itself around the bulges, adding a few critical millimeters here and there, and producing a curiously rounded effect. The ceiling arched upward at an unnatural angle, granting a hair's breadth of clearance to an oversized shelving unit; the walls curved slightly outward toward the street, as if to accommodate those whose girth did not permit easy passage; and even the floorboards seemed to sag and dip cooperatively at just the right points. One had to wonder whether this oddly misshapen structure ever actually passed inspection or was simply too charming to condemn.

The owner of the shop was Jeremy Greentree, a gentle artist of advanced but indiscernible age, slight of build, with refined features and incongruously thick eyebrows that sloped over his face like thatched eaves above a cottage window. We considered him—although he, no doubt, would have cringed at the term—a true philosopher of pottery. And throughout the narrow aisles, he had tacked dozens of hand-painted signs expressing his thoughts on the nature of clay and the human condition:

"Please touch. Pottery was meant to be handled."

"Beauty is fragile—but reach for it anyway."

"Stretch to the top shelf, and stoop to the bottom. The best things in life can't always be found at eye level."

"If you break it, don't worry—we'll make another one. Only people are irreplaceable."

A visit to the shop generally began with a freshly brewed cup of sweet and spicy tea, graciously poured by Mr. Greentree from his antique Russian samovar. But no matter when we arrived, we rarely left before he began to play his favorite recording of "Goodnight, Irene," which he did every evening at 6:00 PM to remind his customers that closing time was near. It was also a signal for us to spread our final selections on the tea table for his approval. He would carefully study each piece to make certain that it was not too defective for safe use, since most of our choices came from the low-ceilinged basement where the less-than-perfect specimens were stored.

Beneath a narrow sign that read "BIG BARGAINS for Little People and Those Willing to Bend," we would wander—sometimes for hours—hunched over or crawling on our hands and knees, as we looked through the chipped mugs, wobbly bowls, and mismatched candlesticks. Most of the time, we were able to find a few dusty treasures among what Mr. Greentree affectionately called his "underachieving pieces."

As he carefully wrapped each item in yesterday's *Times* and secured it with a bright green sticker in the shape of a willow leaf, he would thank us for seeing beauty where others saw only damaged goods or bargain-basement prices.

"I can't understand," Mr. Greentree once said as he walked us to the street, "why people don't find beauty in a broken piece of pottery. Sooner or later, we're all broken in one way or another, but no less beautiful—and usually a lot more interesting—than when we were whole."

Later that night, when we arrived home and began unpacking, Joanna and I were each likely to find at the bottom of our bag a little piece of unexpected pottery—slightly damaged, in most cases, with a shiny green leaf inside. And every time it happened, we were as surprised as if it had never happened before and fell in love with Mr. Greentree all over again.

Then, one afternoon, just before the holiday season began, we showed up at the store with large canvas bags and lots of extra newspaper, only to discover that everything was about to come to a sudden and very sad end.

Over the banging of moving crate lids and the tearing of tape, Mr. Greentree explained how he had lost his lease. It was a classic tale of urban bureaucracy, clerical incompetence, and basic human greed.

"There's nothing real about real estate in Manhattan," he concluded with tears in his eyes. "It's all money and no heart."

However, he immediately began searching for a new home; and, before long, he found an empty store in a more gentrified location—for a substantially higher rent, of course. Unfortunately, the new place never quite captured the magic of the old one. It was definitely cleaner and more spacious, with straight walls and proper lighting. It even had a respectable basement where those over 5'2" could actually stand to their full height. But it lacked soul.

The customers were noticeably different as well—more affluent and fashion-conscious, with an affinity for fine lines and smooth edges. In response, the quality and consistency of the merchandise was significantly upgraded, and the prices rose accordingly, until all that Joanna and I could possibly afford was the occasional item too deformed to stand on its own clay feet and certainly too riddled with imperfection to appeal to patrons who saw flawlessness as an artistic virtue rather than an impediment to the creative spirit.

Saddest of all, however, was the fact that these new shoppers were too busy seeking objects of beauty to find time for an eccentric artist's homemade tea and heart-spun wisdom. So, gradually, Mr. Greentree's presence receded farther and farther into the background until, one day, even his samovar vanished from the countertop.

By commercial standards, I suppose the new store was a success; but Joanna and I always went home with a heavy heart, as if we had just witnessed the defeat of David at the hand of Goliath.

Since Mr. Greentree was rarely around anymore, our visits grew less and less frequent as well. I knew, of course, that I would never forget him, but the memories—like the pottery—began to wear with time.

Years passed, with many moves along the way and much broken pottery to show for it. Yet, no matter how badly damaged an item became, I could never quite bring myself to part with it. And, now, looking into this box, which I probably hadn't opened in fifteen years, I found that those forgotten pieces still had the power to connect me to Mr. Greentree, to my old friend Joanna, and to that very special chapter of my life that we all shared.

"Hi, Lay-Lay, it's me. Are you still awake?"

"More or less. What time is it?"

"2:30 AM here—which I guess makes it 11:30 in Portland."

"Okay . . . just give me a second . . . Let me get myself some tea."

"Good idea. I'm about ready for a cup of coffee myself."

"At 2:30 in the morning?"

"Well, it's been a busy night. And it's not over yet."

"I can't wait to hear all about it. . . . Is this a friend call or a hot line call?"

"A little bit of both, I think. I could definitely use a hug—and probably some crisis intervention as well."

Armed with a strong cup of kukicha, Laya could wake up faster than anyone I've ever known and find her way back to sleep just as fast—a great asset to our friendship, given the tendency of my crises to strike in the middle of the night.

We chatted for a few minutes while she pulled herself together, and then I got right to the point.

"Do you remember The Last Room?" I asked her.

"Of course. The Little Shop of Horrors. Who could forget such a sight?"

"Well, I'm standing in the middle of it right now, on the verge of a defining moment—and I need you to help me define it."

"I think it's time for some more kukicha," she said, wisely bracing herself for the task.

When she returned, I gave her the unabridged version of my experience that evening and the evening before.

"Wow," she said at the end. "It's been only two days since we last spoke, and you sound like you've just completed a grand tour of your life."

"Not quite," I said, "but if I stay in this room long enough, I probably will. Apparently, it's all here—in one form or another. The question is, can I get some of it to leave?"

"Well," Laya reflected, "I think the larger issue is not whether you can find an object or two to let go of, but whether you can find a way, in general, to consolidate your memories into fewer objects. Maybe, at this point, you *do* need a piece of broken pottery to connect you to your Green Tree days—but are you really in need of a whole box? Couldn't you choose just one or two items that capture the experience for you and get rid of everything else? And—who knows—maybe someday you won't need anything more than your own imagination to transport you back in time."

That was definitely good advice, and I hoped to put it into practice before the night was over. Reinspired and well-caffeinated, I now felt ready to face the box.

I examined each piece of pottery, one by one, and sat waiting for the memories to emerge. Usually, I'm pretty patient with this slow-moving process—the waiting and circling and free-associating that take place before the trapped memory finally breaks through, sometimes in gentle waves, sometimes in intense spasms, occasionally in one glorious Proustian epiphany.

Tonight, however, I had no time for the drawn-out ritual. I felt pressured to part with something; but in order to choose the right piece, I had to go through a whole retrieval process with every single one—an incredibly tedious exercise, especially for an overtired brain.

Each piece—defective though it was—had its obvious charm and, no doubt, its own special connection to something. How could I decide what to keep and what to pass on? Suppose I made a mistake and discarded something with a precious memory attached to it?

The caffeine was wearing off, and my head was beginning to hurt. I was just on the verge of putting everything back in the box and letting the whole thing go until the morning—which, at the rate I was going, would be the afternoon—when I noticed the bowl. It was more well padded than anything else. Tucked into a corner of the box and swathed in extra paper and bubble wrap, it had almost eluded me entirely.

Slowly, I unwrapped it and held it up to the light. Unlike all the other pieces, it had no redeeming qualities whatsoever. The lid was cracked, but that was the least of its problems. The glaze was a medley of unappetizing shades of green, and the size and structure were not amenable to either serving or storage—and certainly not to countertop display. Even in its pre-damaged days, it had apparently possessed neither practical nor aesthetic value.

So why had I taken such care to make certain that it was more protected than anything else?

There was clearly an important memory here to be mined. For what reason—other than a connection to my past—would I ever have kept this marginal piece of pottery safely preserved for so many years and through so many moves? If only I could unravel the mystery of that association, perhaps I would finally be able to let go of the bowl and give my decluttering project its much-needed boost.

What I sought from this piece of pottery was a simple act of release; a liberating insight rather than an emotionally charged remembrance. I needed only to understand the experience that had created the bond, not necessarily relive it. Right now, I had no time or energy for a complicated interaction with my past. I wanted nothing more than to attain closure and move on.

But memories are strange phenomena. They slip unbidden into our consciousness when we least expect or desire them, yet resist all efforts to appear when summoned. Those that we try most vigorously to uproot often appear immovable, while the ones to which we desperately cling for comfort seem to vanish at our touch.

The memory I was now trying to coax forth was apparently in need of an extra measure of prodding, and I was growing too tired to sustain the effort. All I could manage to do at this point was drum my fingers impatiently on the broken lid, as if to rouse an oversleeping genie who had no business still being in bed at this hour. The genie, however, did not seem about to awaken anytime soon; and, the way the night was going, I expected to be in the same condition when the alarm went off the following morning.

However, just as I was on the verge of admitting defeat, a few tentative ripples of recognition began to make their way to the surface. Fuzzy images at first, only vaguely familiar and with no apparent connection to one another, they slowly began to organize themselves into a coherent stream of memory, eventually carrying me back to a hospital bed at the Beth Israel Medical Center in lower Manhattan.

It was May 1983, and I had just undergone a complicated hysterectomy at the age of thirty four. After years of trying, there had been no children; and, now, there would obviously be none to come. My marriage was in the process of dissolving (not for that reason, but it certainly didn't help); my body felt as if it were no longer my own; and God seemed many miles beyond my reach.

Suddenly, I was seized with an urge to scream. After so many months of positive thinking, New Age affirmations, and enlightened acceptance, I was more than ready to have a well-earned temper tantrum and let all of my negative and distinctly unspiritual feelings have their moment in the sun. I wanted to shout "Unfair! Unfair!" over and over again until my words reverberated so loudly throughout this world and into the next that everyone would know just how shabbily the universe had treated me. And why me anyway? What had I ever done to anyone?

Just as I was working myself up into a frenzy of anger and self-pity, the door swung open, and in burst my old friend Joanna, carrying a big purple box with iridescent blue and violet ribbons streaming in all directions.

"A blast from your past," she announced in a strong, cheerful voice. "How long has it been since I've seen you in pajamas? Or, for that matter, in street clothes? Well, you still look great . . . I mean, considering. . . .

"And here is a special gift for my always and forever special friend. I hope you bond easily with it."

Touched by her awkwardness and overstated good spirits, I tried to force myself to meet her halfway. I couldn't bear to see my usually poised and unflappable friend squirming in discomfort at the sight of me.

"I'm bonding with the box already," I assured her, curling the ribbons around my fingers. "It's so Joanna. Kind of reminds me of that lavender and turquoise shag rug of yours that we dragged back and forth from one end of the Bronx to the other during your wandering gypsy days."

"Oh, yes, that hairy beast. . . ."

It was a pleasant space in which to linger, a safe memory for two old friends to share—warm and familiar, with little risk of turning more intimate than either of us could handle. We stayed as long as we could, savoring the details of simpler days, reluctant to return to the complexities of the present. But the sight of the purple box growing heavy in Joanna's arms brought us back to the reality of the moment.

"It's only half from me," Joanna began to explain, as she brushed aside the IV and placed the package on the bed beside my monitor.

"The better half, I'm sure. And who," I asked "is the mysterious stranger to be thanked for the other 50 percent?"

Fully expecting a detailed account of the new man in Joanna's life, I eagerly awaited a tale of romantic intrigue in which to lose myself.

Instead, Joanna paused, sat down next to me, and said quietly, "Mr. Greentree." She waited a moment for the announcement to register.

"I went there yesterday to buy you a gift, and just as I was about to pay, Mr. Greentree himself appeared. These days, that probably qualifies as a little miracle. When I told him that it was for you and what the nature of the occasion was, he began to cry. I don't mean he got teary-eyed. I mean he really began to cry—right there in front of all those well-dressed customers of his.

"Of course, he refused to take any money, so I told him that the gift would officially be from both of us. He seemed very pleased at that and immediately reached for his fountain pen and wrote you this little note."

She handed me a small parchment envelope that smelled like sweet pipe tobacco and spicy tea. Inside, Mr. Greentree had written:

Choose life every day . . .
Choose love every minute . . .
Don't be afraid to cry. . . .
Your friend always,
Jeremy Greentree

As I read the card, it suddenly occurred to me that I had not shed one tear throughout the entire ordeal—the discussions of divorce, the anticipation of the hysterectomy, the surgery itself, the loss, the grief . . . the whole nightmare.

But now that Mr. Greentree had cried for me and encouraged me to cry for myself, the ice quickly melted, and I found myself shaking with big heaving sobs. I cried for babies unborn and dreams not lived, for sweet marriages gone sour and little pottery shops that were no more. I cried for what was and what wasn't, what might have been and what never again could be. I cried so loud and so hard that two nurses and an aide came running to see if I was hemorrhaging. Joanna told them that I was, but not to worry because I was only hemorrhaging tears.

I found her remark so funny that I began to laugh uncontrollably. I laughed with such intensity that I triggered another full-blown crying jag.

To which Joanna commented in her most exaggerated professorial voice, "What we have here is a fine example of the linguistic relationship between *hysterectomy* and *hysteria,* both derived from the Greek root for uterus."

This time we both began to laugh out loud, although I could feel another wave of tears about to overtake me.

"Please," Joanna finally implored, "open your present before it drowns."

Grateful to focus my attention on something other than the unraveling of my own mental state, I immediately began to work my way through the tangle of ribbons. With accelerating curiosity, I untied the turquoise bow, tore open the purple paper, and slid the top off the box. Then I sat up and stared in silence.

The object I was holding was one of the most uninspired and irredeemably boring pieces of pottery I had ever seen in my life. A perfectly circular bowl, round-bottomed and high-sided with no slope or curve to add character or visual appeal, topped with a dull, flat lid that contributed nothing to the overall design. It looked like a mummified doughnut without the hole that had molded over in sickly shades of gray and green. What could Joanna possibly have been thinking when she chose it?

As if in response to my silent indictment of her taste, Joanna explained, "It was the only piece I could find that was not offensively modern. I know it's not exactly your style or your favorite color, but at least it's simple and earthy and doesn't make an obnoxious fashion statement."

She was probably right. Given the trendy merchandise in the new shop, this may well have been the closest thing to my taste that could be found there anymore. Besides, I told myself, the kindness of my friend was the thing to focus upon here, not the appeal of her gift. However, before I had a chance to express my gratitude, a strange thing happened.

As I was removing the pottery from the box, the lid shifted its position ever so slightly, revealing a hairline fracture running across the center. It was a crack so smooth and delicately etched that it was virtually invisible to the naked eye. Yet, the moment I raised the lid, it split in half. As soon as I placed the two pieces back on top of the rim, they appeared once again to form a seamless whole.

"You know, I think I could really come to love this bowl," I suddenly blurted out, startled by my own dramatic turnabout. "In fact, it's starting to feel like a part of me already."

"But it's broken," Joanna protested, obviously noticing the crack for the first time. "It must have happened at 14th Street when the conductor jammed on his brakes and the train lurched forward. I'll bring it back and get you something else. Mr. Greentree wouldn't want you to have a damaged gift."

"Yes, he would!" I said, with far more emotion than I was aware I was feeling. "He loves his damaged pieces more than the others. And, besides, I like this bowl just the way it is—this broken one that looks whole but really isn't. I can relate to it perfectly well—and, in my eyes, it's beautiful."

"Oh," Joanna said softly. "I see."

I'm sure she did, and I'm sure that when she told Mr. Greentree my reaction, he also understood. It took me, however, quite a bit longer to get there.

Now, some sixteen years later, I was finally beginning to grasp the deeper meaning of my own words as well.

A visual metaphor for my wounded psyche, the bowl's brokenness clearly represented my own; its hidden fissure, a secret gash within myself. But it was not until tonight, with the rediscovered bowl pressed between my palms, that I had been able to enter the world of that lost memory and, once again, relive its sweetness and its pain.

However, now that the bowl had yielded its secret, I began to question whether it was still necessary to maintain my relationship with it. Did I really want to carry this ceramic albatross with me wherever I went for the rest of my life? Once the genie was out of the lamp, did the lamp itself matter anymore—or did it simply become another piece of clutter?

Although the memory hidden in the damaged bowl had been restored to me, I wondered whether the bowl itself would continue to retain the essence of that memory—forever serving as the secret passageway to the heart of the experience, a point of contact not accessible through any other means.

Would it always take the sight of the cracked lid and the smooth touch of the rounded clay to bring me into the presence of my own past? I wanted to reclaim the memory for myself, establish permanent residence for it in some inner chamber where I could reach it directly, not through the assistance of an external mediator. Yet, without an anchor in the physical world, most of my memories seemed to come and go as they pleased, eventually floating off to join all the brightly colored balloons and high-flying kites that have slid from beneath my grip.

Clearly, this was no academic issue I was grappling with here. The consequences were immediate and far-reaching. I was, after all, in the midst of a potentially transformative process, from which I hoped to emerge more deeply connected to what was real and meaningful in my life and less attached to what was not. But what if they turned out to be one and the same? What if my most valuable memories were trapped within objects that, in and of themselves, lacked value? Could I rescue these hostages, or had they become inextricably bound up with their captors?

I looked around the room. Would less of this clutter mean less of *me*—less of the parts of myself that were intertwined with my things? Did fewer objects translate into fewer memories or more breathing space for the memories I chose to keep and the ones yet to come?

In my desire to discard, I had almost thrown out the pottery bowl—and, along with it, the piece of myself it contained. However, if my life had not been so cluttered to begin with, perhaps the memory would have surfaced a lot sooner or never gone underground in the first place.

In the end, what was I to do with all the objects in my Last Room—and everywhere else in my house as well? Were they valuable links to my past or stumbling blocks on the way to my future? I sat down beside them and closed my eyes, trying to determine whether I was in the presence of friends or adversaries or some odd combination of the two.

When I finally looked up, I saw Yankel slouched across the door frame, staring down incredulously at me.

"What are you doing crawling around on the floor at this hour?" he asked. "Are you still trying to find something to get rid of? There must be an easier way."

"I'm sure there is," I agreed. "But until I figure it out, I'm going to sit here and keep trying."

"I understand," he nodded sympathetically, as he headed back to the bedroom. "Trying to simplify life can be really complicated. And all the more so at four in the morning."

*A*t the February meeting of the Holy Sisters, I gave the following Progress Report: "I am sorry to report that there has been absolutely no progress. End of report."

Everyone looked stunned.

"You've all been incredible, and I can't begin to tell you how grateful I am. You've made me gourmet meals and homemade muffins; you've helped me run errands and do paperwork; you've nurtured me and nudged me and supported me in every way possible. But I'm sorry to say that even with all your help, nothing has changed—I'm still every bit as cluttered as I ever was. And I feel terribly guilty that I'm taking so much of our meeting time to discuss this issue—especially when the whole thing is such a hopeless case.

"Yidis and Etta and Yitta don't see it that way. They think I've taken a major step forward—even if it is an internal one. Yidis says I'm finally beginning to understand my relationship with the world of things, and that's an important part of separating from them. Etta tells me I'm doing just fine because the real work is psychological anyway. And Yitta believes that, for a writer, the process can be more valuable than the result.

"Nevertheless, in the six weeks since I've begun, not one single item has left my possession. Not one. Does that sound like progress to anyone?"

Of course, I was hoping everyone would disagree with me; and I was greatly relieved when they did. But, naturally, they all wanted to hear more about this inner process of mine.

"Well," I began to explain, "I've now come to see how deeply my memories are embedded in my belongings. The things I have don't simply recall thoughts of people I've known and places I've been—they actually re-create those moments for me. The other night, when I stumbled upon Hippilah—my tie-dyed hippopotamus—I wasn't just reminded of the summer I found her in Woodstock. I was actually *there* once again, smelling the marijuana and patchouli, drinking carrot juice at the Joyous Lake, watching the bare feet and the Birkenstocks go by.

"Yet, many of the things I hold on to have no memories attached to them at all. They're not connected to anyone or anything in my life, and they're not objects of outstanding craftsmanship or beauty. They're simply things that bring me pleasure—a handmade bamboo flute that I don't know how to play; a basket of old embroidered handkerchiefs that I once picked up at a flea market; an interesting piece of driftwood that I found near the ocean when we lived in Seagate. But looking at them or touching them or simply knowing that they're in a box somewhere makes me happy. I can't really understand the connection, but I also can't seem to easily break free of it.

"And, then, there are the objects that I never use and probably never will. But they're the promise of hope that I give to myself. Someday, I'll pick up that rake and finally plant a vegetable garden; and, on my next summer vacation, I'll read all the books I bought at the library sale on my last summer vacation; and when I'm not busy reading or gardening, I'll string the beads in my mason jars and make beautiful necklaces for my friends. . . ."

"Tell everyone the story of your sabbatical," Yitta reminded me, "and what happened when the things that inspired you to be creative got swept away with all of the clutter you were getting rid of."

I shared that experience with the group, along with my insight that less is not always more, and an environment that lacks abundance can be sterile and deadening as well as easy to maintain.

So far, I seemed to be making an excellent case for the other side; and it was becoming increasingly unclear whether I was, in fact, advocating *for* clutter or *against* it.

"Probably the most illuminating insight of all," I finally concluded, "was seeing just how deeply my things connect me to myself—not simply to where I've been or where I want to go, but to who I really am. They're like little mirrors that reflect the forgotten parts of my psyche back to me—parts I wasn't even aware were missing."

"You know," Yidis said as soon as I finished speaking, "I was really listening to what Pesi was saying just now, and I suddenly realized that I've been wrong about this."

Yidis made that statement more easily and more often than anyone I have ever known. Not because she was wrong more of the time, but simply because she didn't care who was right and who was wrong. She was searching for the truth at any cost; and if being right got in the way, she was perfectly willing to be wrong. Of course, the rest of us also wanted truth, but we wanted sympathy and support as well; and, in a given moment, truth didn't always win out.

"The problem," she continued, "is that I've been encouraging Pesi to start at the top because I wanted to energize her project with a spectacular beginning. But I'm afraid it's had the opposite effect. Instead of propelling her forward, I think the magnitude of the first step has immobilized her. My feeling now is that we should move in the opposite direction and begin with as little drama as possible."

Etta was too gracious to mention that she had been saying that all along, but she did point out another flaw in the group's approach.

"We've been encouraging Pesi to get rid of things that appear *to us* to be clutter—but I'm not so sure that, for her, those objects are really the problem. I bet she could live a perfectly happy life with all of her tables and typewriters and wicker baskets and broken pieces of pottery. I think we need to hear what *she* thinks really makes her life feel oppressive and unwieldy. Then, we can begin with the smallest of the small in those areas and gradually work our way up."

"You're absolutely right," Yidis agreed; and everyone nodded and turned toward me.

"It's true." I said, "The more substantial items that I've tried to get rid of in the Last Room or in the basement or the garage really don't bother me half as much as the little piles of nothing that seem to be taking over my living space and my life. I rarely think about the objects I don't have contact with, but I have nightmares about my closet, my dirty laundry, my paperwork, the back seat of my car, the vegetables rotting at the bottom of my refrigerator—all the pockets of mess that I have to contend with every single day."

"So," Myriam asked, "if you could wave a magic wand and get rid of all those pockets, what do you think your life would look like?"

I was silent for a moment; but, really, I knew the answer before she asked the question. I had spent years trying to imagine what was waiting for me on the other side of my piles. And although the fantasies varied from time to time, the underlying theme always remained the same.

Oddly enough, my vision had little to do with an orderly home or a well-organized workspace or a manageable schedule—although, at the moment, I would have been only too happy to experience any one of the three. Yet, on some level, I had always known that my issues with clutter were there simply as the backdrop to my journey—either to help move it along or to hinder its progress—but never to be its ultimate destination.

"Well," I responded slowly, "I know I'm far from this point, but I believe that if I were truly free of all clutter—I mean, inside and out—I would see a totally different world. I think the physical universe would be transformed into an unobstructed reflection of the spiritual. Instead of blocking the way, every object and situation in my life would somehow connect me more deeply to myself and to God; and, in the end, I would hopefully find my way to a clear and balanced life."

"Pesi, you must write that down," Yitta said, immediately handing me her notebook and a pen. "I think you've just created the perfect mission statement for The Project—and possibly for your entire life."

Chapter Three

A Leap Forward

"Everything should be made as simple as possible,
but not simpler."
—Albert Einstein

"Okay," Yidis announced during our next check-in. "It's time to refocus our lens. What we want to do now is try to find some *little* mess in your life to unclutter—something small and insignificant, but personally irritating. Like maybe a shoe box full of odds and ends that you don't know what to do with or how to organize."

"Oh, I have lots of those," I assured her. "As a matter of fact, I collect shoe boxes for just that purpose."

"I thought you might," Yidis said. "So, tell me, what kind of things do you keep in these boxes?"

"Well, I have a box full of buttons that need to be sewn back on my clothes—but, mostly, I can't remember which button goes with which hole; and, then, there's a box of unsorted nails and screws that were left behind by various handymen; and a box of old recipes that I cut out of newspapers and magazines and plan to copy onto index cards when I have a free moment; and a box of string—little pieces in all different sizes—you never know when you might need one; and a box with all my keys, most of which I can no longer identify; and . . ."

"Wait," Yidis stopped me. "I think we've found it. The box of keys. Just think of all the stories you've shared with me over the years about being locked in here and locked out there and searching high and low for your missing keys—it's one of the most consistently recurring themes in your battle with clutter. And, here, the whole issue is contained in one simple shoe box, probably without too much emotion attached to it. Little resistance and large rewards. It's the perfect place to start."

"It definitely has potential," I agreed. "What exactly do you want me to do?"

"Get rid of every single key that you can't identify or don't absolutely need."

"But just because I can't match each key to its lock at this moment doesn't mean that I never will. What happens if I throw out a key today and then discover that I really need it tomorrow?"

"Has that ever happened in all the years you've been carrying these keys around?"

"Not that I can remember."

"Okay. And it if ever does, you can always call Lenny the Locksmith on Coney Island Avenue. He can open anything."

"I think I'm going to need some help with this," I said, beginning to feel my confidence slipping. "I don't know if I can really tell one key from another, and I'm not sure that I'm ready to throw any of them away."

"Let's call Atara," Yidis suggested. "She's a good friend with an artist's eye, and she dislikes clutter of any sort. You'll make a great team."

The next afternoon, Atara and I took all the keys in my shoe box and laid them out on the dining room table. There were probably well over a hundred. Keys for houses and cars; bicycles and boats; classrooms, offices, and restrooms at school; mailboxes and jewelry boxes and antique wooden trunks; desk drawers and file cabinets and old leather briefcases; keys that looked like they could open medieval dungeons or lost treasure chests; keys to bleed radiators and tighten roller skate clamps and keep diaries safe from probing eyes. Keys to everything I've ever owned or borrowed or thought I might need. Extra sets of keys for my mother, my neighbors, my friends across town. Such an extraordinary collection of keys—but almost none of them could I identify or match up with a lock.

Atara stared at the contents in disbelief, and even I was somewhat taken aback at the extent of my accumulation. I had probably never thrown out a key in my entire life. It was, no doubt, a blessing that I've lost as many keys as I have, or the box would easily have been twice the size by now.

Atara patiently matched up the few keys that were duplicates of what was currently on my keychain. I picked out a few more that I recognized or had actually labeled, and we put those aside as well. All together, we were able to identify about a dozen keys that seemed relevant to my life. The rest, with my reluctant consent, Atara deposited in the recycle bin.

"Don't you feel lighter and less cluttered?" she asked.

"Not really," I said. "In fact, I'm beginning to feel like I made a terrible mistake. What happens if I suddenly remember what one of those keys is for? Some of them looked like one-of-a-kind antiques that we might never be able to duplicate."

"Don't worry," Atara said, having obviously been well prepped by Yidis. "You'll just call Lenny the Locksmith."

"I know," I said. "On Coney Island Avenue. He can open anything."

"So how did it go?" Yidis asked that evening.

"I got rid of most of the keys, so I guess it went well."

"That's great. But you don't sound too happy."

"Well, to tell you the truth, it was a very stressful experience. Atara was wonderful, but even with her support, I felt really uncomfortable about letting go of all those keys. And, in the end, what did I actually accomplish? I got rid of one little shoe box, and now I have all this anxiety to contend with."

"But without that anxiety," Yidis countered, "there would be no challenge—and, ultimately, no triumph. Besides, just think about all the space you've freed up. You have one less shoe box in your closet, one less corner of your brain occupied with cataloguing your clutter, and one less failure in your quest for order."

"Does one less failure mean—finally—one success?"

"Absolutely," Yidis said without hesitation. "And what would you like to do to celebrate—Cappuccino? Champagne? Lunch at Café K?"

I considered the options. Then, I thought about the mess closing in on me from all sides.

"You know," I said after a moment's reflection, "I think I would just like to find another shoe box to organize."

*R*eleasing the contents of my shoe box turned out to be one of the major turning points in my relationship with clutter. At that moment of letting go, all the forces invested in my tendency to hold on suddenly sprang to life. No matter that the prize was only a shoe box full of old keys. The implications of a first victory were not lost upon those elements of my psyche determined to maintain the status quo.

The inner voices opposing change were well-reasoned and relentless:

"You'll regret it if you get rid of those keys. Your most valuable possessions will be locked away beyond your reach forever."

"Someday, when you need to get to something immediately, you'll have to wait until Lenny the Locksmith can fit you into his schedule."

"Why waste all that metal? You could use the keys in an art project—make a wind chime out of them or a mobile or a piece of hanging jewelry."

"Those keys hold many priceless memories. They opened all the doors in your life. How can you just give them away?"

"And why are you in such a big rush all of a sudden? Slow down and really think about what you're doing."

"What's the big deal here anyway? How much room do these keys actually take up? We're only talking about one little shoe box."

"You know, tomorrow would be a better day to start. Get a good night's sleep, and begin fresh in the morning."

But this time I didn't listen. Not to the voices of fear or insecurity or nostalgia or even logic. The only voice I heard—and the only voice I wanted to hear—was the one that loudly proclaimed my right to an uncluttered life of simplicity and freedom.

"Aren't you glad we started with your keys?" Yidis asked the next evening. "Imagine if we had chosen the box housing your rubber band collection or your broken earrings? What kind of symbols would they have made?"

"I don't know," I said. "But I'm sure we would have come up with something."

"Probably," Yidis agreed. "But with this box, we didn't even have to try. The metaphors pretty much created themselves. There you were—searching for the key to an orderly life; trying to unlock the grip of your clutter; preparing yourself to open new doors. . . ."

We both groaned, but the clichés were a perfect fit.

"So, what's next?" I was eager to know. Momentum is a fragile force, and I didn't want to lose the little bit that had finally been set in motion.

"I think that for the next few months, you should choose one small pocket of clutter at a time and stay focused on it until your work there is done. The smaller the pocket, the better. This way, it can slip beneath your radar and not attract the attention of hostile forces. The way I'm looking at it now, big changes—big battle; little changes—well, hopefully, your inner gremlins won't even notice."

"But don't you think, at that rate, the project will take me the rest of my life to complete?"

"Not at all," Yidis said. "But you'll have to make a serious commitment to keep working at it every day—piece by piece, box by box, room by room—until, eventually, you'll get rid of all the clutter you can pry loose; and whatever is left, you'll neatly organize and pack away. If you really stick with it, I bet you'll be done with everything by the time you go back to school in September."

"That would be amazing," I said, not believing for one moment that it was possible. "To start the fall semester with my life in order—it hasn't happened since I began kindergarten. And, even then, my toy chest was a mess."

"But don't become overzealous," Yidis cautioned, "or you'll wind up creating another fiasco like you did on your sabbatical when you made everything so lean and spare that your spirit became anorexic."

"Point well taken," I assured her. "And I know just what I want to work on next. . . ."

And, so, the journey began. It was only March, and I was still quite busy at school; but whenever I could find a moment, I tried to tackle the project of the day. Slowly, I found myself moving forward. I didn't attempt anything too large or challenging—I figured I would leave that for my summer vacation—but the little accomplishments were really starting to mount up. Neater drawers, lighter shelves, smaller piles, and—every now and then—even a patch of empty space.

The Holy Sisters supported me every step of the way. And when I got up at the March meeting to give my Progress Report, I began by proudly announcing that, at last, I had some genuine progress to report.

As I began to see movement, I felt that familiar rush of excitement—the clutterer's equivalent of a runner's high. And I thought back to the first time I had ever experienced it.

I was somewhere in my midtwenties and had undertaken a massive campaign to thin out my life. I can't remember why—perhaps I had just read Thoreau or Kerouac or Ram Dass, or maybe I had misplaced my keys one time too many, or I might have just looked around and decided enough was enough—but, in any case, I went at it with a vengeance. And I was amazed at how sweetly seductive that initial whiff of fresh air and freedom turned out to be.

Suddenly repulsed by my crowded existence, I wanted only to downsize and simplify. Overnight, *empty* became my new *full*; and the sight of unfilled space sent my endorphins into a wild frenzy. Barely stopping to eat or sleep, I worked feverishly around the clock, determined to re-create my cramped studio apartment in the image of a spacious zen monastery.

At some point, it became obvious to me that my cleanup binge was taking on a life of its own and providing an all-consuming drama in which I was only too happy to lose myself. Yet, unlike most other forms of escapist behavior, the compulsion to make order was generally regarded as socially acceptable—in some circles, even virtuous. If one had to experience a touch of madness every now and then, this seemed quite the ideal affliction.

However, my passion for simplicity soon lost its fire. And this, unfortunately, came to be the pattern for most of my attempts at creating order, as enthusiastic beginnings and promising middles quickly gave way to endings that were more likely than not to evaporate into thin air.

Now, here I was—many evaporated endings later—still uncertain of just how to successfully navigate the material world. I was as far from developing a healthy relationship with the physical universe as I had ever been. And, at fifty, I was beginning to hear the clock ticking noticeably louder.

It was apparently time for a change in strategy. Over the past few months, I had replaced the somewhat unrealistic goal of transforming my life in one grand sweep with the considerably less ambitious plan of repairing it one little mess at a time. But that had been more by necessity than design, and only with the ongoing support of the Holy Sisters. Left to my own devices, I predictably lapsed into an all-or-nothing approach: completely ignoring my clutter because I had more important things to deal with or ignoring what I should have been dealing with because my clutter suddenly seemed more important than anything else.

As a result, my belongings tended to be either so well organized and beautifully displayed that they elicited applause from impressed visitors or in a state of such chaos and confusion that even my closest friends could barely suppress their horror and concern for my sanity. Rarely was there the normal blend of order and disorder one would find in the homes of those given to lesser extremes. My friend Edith, who, many years ago, courageously attempted to share an apartment with me, probably summed it up best when she commented in utter frustration one day: "You know, I'll never be as neat as you are—but I'll also never be as sloppy."

Ignoring the larger issue of why I could not seem to maintain more of a balanced rhythm to begin with, what concerned me at the moment was why I experienced these unprovoked outbursts of organizing mania. I could think of no rational explanation for the surge of anxiety and pressure that seemed to come upon me from out of the blue. The piles of clutter that had been sitting around unnoticed for weeks or months or years would suddenly rise up and begin to demand my attention so insistently that I had no choice but to respond with immediate action.

Since I didn't seem able to maintain a consistent approach, why couldn't I simply relax and accept the fact that it might well take me the rest of my life to reform my disorderly ways and finally get the job done? The frightening reality, of course, was that, at the rate I was going, the rest of my life just might not be time enough—and if living in a state of uncontrolled clutter filled me with shame, dying under such conditions surely seemed the ultimate humiliation.

I was haunted by visions of ending up like the Collyer Brothers, buried alive in an avalanche of my own possessions. And even if I were spared such a grisly end, I certainly did not want to leave behind an obituary that commented on the irony of my untimely departure from this world at the very moment that I was finally about to make peace with it: "She died, tragically, with her lifelong quest for order and simplicity only a few piles away. . ."

This was definitely an issue to explore with Etta when we had our first session of clutter therapy at the end of the semester— by which point I would hopefully have made substantial progress with my cleanup. In the meantime, I spent March and April and the better part of May living a relatively productive life, with most of my spare time devoted to getting organized. I tried not to think about the decades of disorder behind me and not to look at the mess to my left or to my right. Instead—for the first time that I could remember—I focused only on the task directly before me. I carefully examined each bit of clutter that came my way and tried to ease it out the door before I could come up with a convincing rationale for keeping it, reminding myself over and over again that every inch of space I cleared would bring me an inch closer to a sane and manageable life.

However, June was rapidly approaching, and I was not at all certain of how to proceed from here. Now that I would be free for the next few months, should I push everything aside and mount an all-out frontal attack on my piles? Or would it be better to try to maintain some sort of balance in my life—bicycle along the boardwalk with Yankel, go on a few day trips here and there, schedule my long-overdue visit to the dentist and the annual checkup I hadn't had in three years—and continue chipping away at the mess slowly but steadily whenever I reasonably could? The question definitely called for some sage advice from the Holy Sisters—and just in time because this month's meeting would be our last before the summer break.

It was a particularly beautiful spring that year; and with all the mimosas and dogwoods and magnolias in full bloom, no one wanted to sit inside and watch the world turn pink and white through a window. The Brooklyn Botanic Garden was everyone's first choice for an outdoor gathering, and it turned out to be even more delightful than we had expected. After a silent walk through the Fragrance Garden, followed by a stroll across Daffodil Hill, we spread our blankets in a grove of wildly colored azalea bushes and prepared for our final meeting of the season.

Soon, everyone would be heading for their summer destination—the mountains, the ocean, a secluded cabin by the lake, or—in my case—a windowless basement and walk-in closet. It was not exactly picture postcard material, but I tried to think of it as a spiritual sweat lodge of sorts—uncomfortable to live through but cathartic in the end.

We had all been looking forward to seeing the magnificent cherry trees in bloom, but by the time we arrived, they had already dropped their last petals. This, of course, should have come as no surprise to me, since I showed up too late to see the cherry blossoms every spring—if I managed to show up at all. Over the course of the ten years I'd lived in Brooklyn, my need for nature had never once overcome my tendency toward procrastination and actually succeeded in getting me to the Garden during the trees' much-heralded month of flowering. And as I was sadly reminded each spring, cherry blossoms, like time and tide, wait for no man—and, it seemed, for no well-intentioned woman either.

For some reason, this unfulfilled opportunity disturbed me out of all proportion to its apparent significance. While missing the breathtaking beauty of cherry trees in bloom was, of course, no small loss, it was hardly a case of high tragedy either. Nevertheless, I found myself reacting as if someone I loved had suddenly passed away. I've certainly missed many moments of far greater consequence in my life and responded with considerably less emotion. As we sat meditating, I tried to understand what this overreaction was all about, but I was too distracted by the colors and fragrances of the garden to really focus on what was going on inside of me.

When it came my turn to speak, instead of raising the issues I had planned to discuss, all I could manage to say was, "The cherry blossoms are gone."

To which Yitta responded, "But the azaleas are now in bloom."

"Yes," I acknowledged, "but the cherry blossoms are gone forever." And, with that, I stopped speaking and started to cry.

Quite some time passed before I was able to compose myself and go on, but no one seemed bothered by the delay. If anything, the Holy Sisters appeared grateful for the chance to sit quietly in the warm sun and inhale the rich scents of the garden.

"Cherry blossoms don't wait," I said, finally breaking the long silence. "That could be the title of my autobiography or the epitaph on my tombstone. What did John Lennon say on his last album? . . . 'Life is what happens while you're busy making other plans?' . . . Well, I feel like life is happening around me all the time, but I'm too busy and too cluttered and too overwhelmed to ever experience it fully.

"Once a year, an opportunity arises to witness a spectacular display of nature. Yet, for one reason or another, I can never manage to step forward and receive the gift. It may be the least important of all the events that I miss; but, somehow, it disturbs me the most deeply. Maybe that's because there's no compelling reason for me to make the effort other than my own desire for a moment of beauty; and that, apparently, does not provide the motivation of a deadline at work or a friend in need.

"Now that I'm beginning to simplify my life, I can envision a day when I will finally be able to do all the things I need to do in a timely fashion. I can even picture myself relaxing more often with family and friends. But, in my wildest imagination, I cannot conceive of ever feeling so totally free of life's obligations that I would choose to do something simply for the joy that it could bring to me and me alone."

An uneasy quiet settled over the group. Everyone looked off in a different direction, and no one said a word. Finally, Yidis stood up and broke the silence.

"And why not?" she demanded loudly. "Don't you deserve a moment that belongs to you and no one else? Aren't you just as important as the people you love?

"Pesita," she continued, her voice softening, "I—and I'm sure all of the Holy Sisters—really want you to value yourself as much as you value everyone and everything around you. And, someday, when you finally get to the other side of your clutter, I hope that one of the things you'll discover there is a quiet space just for you. You'll see—once you get organized, you'll have plenty of time to pay your bills, grade your papers, and return all your phone calls *after* you've given yourself the gift of watching the cherry blossoms in bloom."

"Amen," Etta said. "And thank you, Yidis. I think we now have the topic for our first therapy session."

The following Tuesday, I rang Etta's doorbell at 9:00 AM sharp—a significant accomplishment for me, *sharp* not being a term generally applied to my arrival or departure times. But today's session marked a new beginning in my war on clutter, and I wanted to demonstrate—to myself as well as to Etta—just how seriously I was taking the whole thing.

Etta, obviously making a similar statement, did not appear at the door in her usual T-shirt, denim skirt, and high-top sneakers. Instead, she showed up fashionably dressed in shades of burgundy and mauve, wearing high-heeled boots and a long silk scarf. She greeted me with a warm but professional hug and politely offered me a hot drink.

"This all feels a bit strange," I commented on the familiar walk up the stairs to her office.

"Yes, it does," she agreed, "but I'm sure we'll adjust. Besides, it's only for one hour. Then we can go back to being friends and Holy Sisters."

"Okay," I said, trying to get comfortable with my new role. "For the next sixty minutes, you're the doctor, and I'm the trusting and compliant patient. Do with me as you will."

As we entered her office, Etta sat down on the couch and motioned me toward the recliner. I stretched out my legs, took a sip of hot coffee, and looked around.

"You know," I commented. "I never realized what a great shade of peach this room is. And did you always have these curtains and that wall hanging?"

"Ever since we redid the place three years ago."

"I've been here so many times since then. I wonder why I never noticed before."

"Perhaps," Etta suggested—slipping smoothly into therapist mode—"creating clarity in your own life has helped you to see the rest of the world more clearly."

"An interesting theory," I reflected. "Removing the mess in my house somehow enhanced the color in yours. . . ."

"Something like that," she said, now shifting to the time-to-get-down-to-business tone that therapists frequently employ with unfocused clients such as myself.

We began the session officially with a deep-breathing exercise, a few yoga stretches, and a guided visualization. By then, I was pretty much ready to go anywhere Etta wanted to take me.

"All right," she cleared her throat. "Let's begin with a little review.

"You've been working on your clutter for—what?—about five months now?"

"More or less," I responded. "On the one hand, it seems like forever; and, on the other hand, it feels like I've just begun."

"I know what you mean," she said. "It feels that way just watching you go through the process. So, what I'd like you to do now is to list some of the things you've learned during these past five months—positive and negative—about your relationship with your physical possessions. I'm not talking about the mess they create, just about the things themselves."

She set her timer for five minutes, handed me a notebook and a pen, and asked me to list five of the positive observations I had made.

When the bell rang, I was still busy writing. It was actually a very enjoyable exercise, reminding me once again that my clutter was not simply a distraction and an obstacle to my peace of mind, but a comfort and a joy as well.

I read aloud what I had written, and Etta listened attentively, giving me an encouraging nod every now and then:

"Number One: Many of the seemingly unnecessary things that I possess bring me great pleasure. I could definitely do with less, but much of what I have, I really love.

"Number Two: Abundance stimulates my creativity and energizes my spirit.

"Number Three: Objects help me to access feelings and memories. Much of my past seems to be stored in my belongings.

"Number Four: I identify positively with many of my possessions, especially the ones that defy categories and simple labels.

"Number Five: A lot of the things I hold on to represent my hope for a healthier, better organized, more enlightened version of myself in time to come.

"I stopped here," I explained, "only because the timer went off. I could easily have kept on going."

"You're doing great," Etta said. "Now, let's try the other side. List five of your negative observations."

This, surprisingly, turned out to be more of a challenge. And when the bell sounded, I was still struggling to complete the list:

"Number One: The objects I possess seem to take up space in my brain as well as in my closet and on my shelves. When I get rid of things, not only does my house feel more spacious, but my mind seems lighter as well.

"Number Two: So many old treasures don't leave much room for new ones. I often feel like my home reflects more of who I used to be than who I currently am.

"Number Three: Too much of a good thing is not such a good thing. The items that I really need and love have to vie for space with things of lesser value.

"Number Four: Having so many objects to contend with keeps me too busy to do the things I really want to do in life.

"That's as far as I got. I couldn't think of anything else."

"Interesting," Etta concluded.

"What is?" I asked.

"That you found positives more easily than negatives."

"What do you think it means?"

"Just what I've been feeling all along—that your definition of clutter is very much your own. Six unused tables sitting in a garage may appear excessive to others, but they don't seem to constitute clutter in your mind. Which is not to say that your life wouldn't be simpler without them and all the rest of the overload you carry around with you. However, what the world generally considers clutter doesn't seem to be the issue for you."

"So, what do you think the issue is?"

"Give me a moment," Etta said, leaning back and closing her eyes. Before long, she removed one of her earrings and began to slowly twirl it around her forefinger—a habit she often lapsed into when lost in thought. To my pleasant surprise, the spinning crystal caught the rays of the sun streaming through the window and scattered them in all directions. I sat perfectly still, delighting in the warmth of the sun on my shoulders and the circles of color dancing across the peach walls.

When Etta finally opened her eyes, I pointed to the little rainbows being projected by her earring. We watched them together in silence, until Etta suddenly turned to me and said, "That's it—I think I've found the answer."

"What was the question?" I asked, startled out of my reverie.

"Sorry," she said, trying to suppress a laugh. "My transitions could use a little work. But what just came to me now is that your response to beauty may well be the key to understanding how to deal with your clutter.

"I'm almost certain that it's not what you have that makes you feel cluttered, but what you see. I don't think you really mind living with a box of unlabeled keys and a stack of half-knit scarves as long as they're neatly contained and out of sight."

"It's true" I said. "When I see my belongings in disarray, I feel like I'm trapped in one of those little snowy paperweights with everything fluttering in all directions. I need to feel surrounded by tranquility and order—even if it's only an illusion."

"In the eyes of the world," Etta went on, "what you have might look like clutter; but if it's neat and well organized, it won't seem like clutter to you, and it won't create static in your brain. Of course, it would be far more liberating if you could get rid of all your excess baggage so that you don't have to spend so much time organizing and reorganizing it; but, for now, that's probably a bit too ambitious.

"Remember that button you told us about—the one that says 'I'll see it when I believe it'? Well, I think it's time for you to take that message to the next level. Now that you at least believe order is possible, you need to start seeing it everywhere you look—even if it's only superficial order—so that your belief will be reinforced. Then, you can try to make it real in a deeper way.

"In the meantime, if the objects you have bring you pleasure, I say keep them—but keep them in a well-organized and pleasing state. And the minute they begin to lapse into disorder, nip their descent in the bud. But the visible objects that don't bring you pleasure—your papers, your laundry, your piles of half-finished projects—those are the things to start working on immediately.

"This may sound like a very simplistic approach to a complicated problem, but I really think it will work. At least for now.

"Okay," Etta said, looking at her watch. "Perfect timing. We have exactly three minutes left.

"And, before we conclude, I want to give you a little homework assignment."

I groaned, sounding very much like one of my own students. The semester was barely over, and I wasn't in the mood to hear about homework—not my own or anyone else's. Nevertheless, I dutifully took out my pen and pad.

"Last week at the Botanic Garden . . ."

"I know, I know," I interrupted. "I haven't stopped hearing about it all week. Every one of the Holy Sisters called me to discuss what Yidis has now termed my "'self-esteem meltdown.'"

"Well, it is a cause for concern. If you don't value your own time and space, it's little wonder that your life becomes overcrowded and unmanageable."

"You're right," I agreed.

"So, what I would like you to work on for next time—as an exercise in self-care—is a list of ten things that you plan to do by yourself and for yourself as soon as you've cleared a path through your clutter."

"Would you settle for five?" I offered.

"No," she said emphatically. "And neither should you."

*S*everal weeks later, still not quite ready for a full-blown act of self-care, I settled on a halfway measure—a mini vacation that would be part work and part play. Etta, however, did not consider my all-night preparation for the trip a good example of nurturing myself. And, as I should have expected, neither did Yankel.

"What a nice surprise," he said, looking up from his bagel and coffee. "You're up early this morning."

"Not really," I said, pouring some decaf for myself. "I haven't been to bed yet."

"But it's seven in the morning."

"I know. I was on a roll last night."

"You're going to roll yourself right into an early grave if you keep this up."

"Maybe I am overdoing it a bit," I admitted, "but I was making so much progress packing for my trip to Vermont that I didn't want to break the momentum."

"Your trip to Vermont? Oh, that's right," he recalled. "Now, I remember. You told me the other night—just as I was falling asleep—that you and Annica were going sometime this week. But I thought it was only an overnight stay."

"It is."

"So, what were you packing for so many hours?"

"Boxes of unsorted papers."

"I don't understand. What do your unsorted papers have to do with your trip to Vermont?"

"Everything. They're the major reason I'm going."

"Wait . . . you lost me somewhere."

"Okay, I'll start over again," I offered, eliciting the inevitable silent groan, which basically translates as, "No—please!—anything but that."

Instead, however, he tactfully said, "I'd love to hear the whole story, but I have to leave for work in . . ."—he stopped to check his watch—". . . exactly seven minutes."

"I understand," I said, trying to remember that his rhythm and mine were not always well syncopated, especially at either end of the day. "I'll try to be brief.

"Annica and I were thinking how nice it would be to go on a little spring outing together. Well, it turns out that our friend Fran—remember Fran? She and Louis visited us when we lived in Ellenville?—Anyway, Fran is renting a cottage in Vermont for the summer and invited us to come up. Annica and I loved the idea of a trip together and a day in the country—but, at the same time, we realized that we're both too busy and too chronically overwhelmed to just run off on a little pleasure jaunt for two days. . . ."

"So," Yankel interjected, "you're bringing your papers to Vermont to remind you that you left all this work unfinished at home and, therefore, don't deserve even a moment of guilt-free fun—kind of like a pay-in-advance penance for indulging in forbidden joy."

"That's an interesting interpretation," I replied politely, thinking that it was about as off the mark as you could get. "But, no, I don't think so. We really have a very practical reason for bringing our papers. Annica and I both love being outdoors and hate doing paperwork. We also like communal projects and don't enjoy working in isolation. So, we decided that if we bring a distasteful job to a beautiful place and work on it side by side, we can transform the drudgery into a positive experience—or at least a tolerable one."

"Well, that certainly is a creative approach. But, if you want my opinion, I think you could benefit enormously from some downtime that's a little less productive and a lot more playful."

"Absolutely," I agreed. "And as soon as my last pile is neatly put away, I plan to do just that.

"But, in the meantime, I still have a lot more packing to do. Our plan is to leave bright and early tomorrow morning at the crack of . . ."

" . . . eleven?"

"You're not being very supportive."

"I'm sorry," he said. "But you're so much fun to tease. I can't believe that you're taking this whole clutter thing so seriously."

"Well, wouldn't you like a little more order in your life?"

"Of course, but not at the expense of a summer vacation."

"Well, I'm desperate. Maybe clutter doesn't bother you as much as it bothers me."

"I don't think clutter bothers anyone as much as it bothers you."

"That's probably true—which is all the more reason why I want do something about it right now.

"Etta and I agreed that, at the very least, I should get my belongings to the point where they look organized and pleasing to the eye so that I'll feel motivated to move on to the next level and begin getting rid of the things that I really don't need."

"And what does the rest of your Clutter Committee have to say about all this?"

"Everyone agrees that I should start by organizing my papers because they're completely out of control. They've just about pushed me out of my office at work and at home; they're bulging out of my file cabinets and desk drawers, spilling out the back seat of my car . . ."

" . . . taking over the dining room table," he added, with more than a trace of resentment in his voice, "stacked on every flat surface in the bedroom. . . ."

"Yes, thank you," I said. "I was getting to that."

I could see that this conversation was beginning to tread on highly sensitive ground. Both of us were apparently stuck in the same rut, neither of us wanting to live with clutter—not our own and certainly not each other's—but unable to let go just yet. I approached the problem with anxiety bordering on mild hysteria, while Yankel maintained an impressive level of denial, preferring to keep the focus on my sizable mess and questionable methods of dealing with it rather than examining his own.

"Okay," I said, finishing my last sip of coffee. "I think it's time for me to catch a few hours of sleep before I get back to work."

"Good luck, Pes," Yankel said, giving me a big hug. "I'm sure you'll get it together. I have complete faith in you."

I knew that he really did. And I knew that the Holy Sisters did as well. Now, I just had to muster up a healthy dose of unshakable faith in myself.

This was the summer of the Big Push, and I wanted to give it all that I had and make every moment count. I was determined that, come September, my rocky relationship with the material world would finally be transformed into one of order and harmony. And, in the meantime, if I had to subsist on four hours of sleep a night and consume a trucker's dose of caffeine to make it happen, I was more than willing to do so.

At 11:15 the following morning, I pulled up in front of Annica's building, just off Riverside Drive.

"Hi," I said, with what was fast becoming my standard greeting, "I'm sorry I'm so late."

I went on to explain how I was up half the night packing and then slept through three alarm clocks in the morning.

"It's fine," Annica assured me. "I wasn't ready either, and I was actually relieved each time you called to report another delay. So, it looks like we're both perfectly on schedule—at least with each other."

"Where's all your stuff?" I asked, looking around and not seeing anything on the sidewalk.

She pointed toward the lobby, and as I followed her in, I saw what looked like half the contents of her small studio apartment propped up against the wall.

"I know it's a lot," she said, "but I was feeling so enthusiastic about the prospect of finally making order that I decided to pack every paper I could find and hope for the best."

As we began to squeeze it all into the half of the back seat I had left empty for her, she looked over at my half and commented, "And it looks as if you're just as enthusiastic."

In truth, the volume of our packages was pretty well balanced. She and I had each brought a small overnight case with our clothing and toiletries, an insulated container with snacks for the trip, and dozens of boxes, shopping bags, and backpacks overflowing with papers. It was really more than even the roomy back seat of my 1983 Volvo could handle. In the end, Annica had to sit with a few boxes under her feet and several bags piled on her lap, and I had to resort to using my outside mirrors to see the road around me.

"It'll only be for a few hours," Annica said good-naturedly, as she struggled to free an arm and wrestle the side window open.

Forty minutes later, we had finally completed the ten-minute drive up the West Side Highway to the George Washington Bridge. Having exhausted all our theories of what could possibly cause such a traffic jam in the middle of a Tuesday when it was not rush hour and there was no accident or construction project in sight, we decided to chalk it up to the general clutter of urban life, which, we concluded, was not all that different from our own.

Too many objects in one place at one time apparently clogged the arteries of New York City in pretty much the same way as they obstructed the view in my car and wedged the drawers of my file cabinet permanently open. But, hopefully, all of that would soon be behind us.

Turning onto the Palisades Parkway, we watched the road before us suddenly wrench itself free from the congestion and empty into a clear and open expanse of blue skies and bright sunshine, as the gray bricks of Manhattan quickly faded behind the large trees lining the New Jersey shore of the Hudson.

"A metaphor for our inner journey to freedom," Annica said, apparently delighted that she was able to confer symbolic meaning upon our otherwise disjointed and unproductive morning. Energized by this new perspective, we calculated that, even with our slow start, we could probably still make it to Fran's house in time for an early dinner, which would then give us the rest of the evening and all of Wednesday to work on our papers. Despite the many setbacks, it seemed that we had finally regained our footing and begun to move forward.

And now came the long-awaited highlight of the trip—a solid block of time all to ourselves in which we could explore our complicated relationship with the world of papers. We hoped that this rare retreat from life would provide us with a deeper understanding of the issues. Nevertheless, we approached the moment with a certain degree of apprehension—much as one would a patch of fresh earth at a crime scene—not quite sure just what we would unearth once we began to probe beneath the surface.

"Why don't we start," Annica suggested, "by simply listing all the categories of paper clutter represented in the back seat of the car. Then, we can discuss them in greater detail as we drive."

"That sounds like a good idea," I agreed.

"Okay," Annica began. "At the top of my list is mail. Letters, bills, invitations, offers—anything that requires a response of any sort."

"Newspapers, magazines, and journals for me," I said next. "All the publications that I put aside yesterday to read tomorrow."

"To Do Lists that never got done," Annica added.

And so we continued, back and forth, with barely a pause in between.

"Articles that I want to save but can't figure out where to store."

"Scraps of paper, napkins, and matchbooks with phone numbers scribbled on them."

"Advertisements, Consumer Reports ratings, rebates, coupons—how did buying a toaster ever get so complicated?"

"Greeting cards I bought but never got around to sending."

"Every bit of correspondence I've ever received from the IRS, the Parking Violations Bureau, or the Office of Jury Duty. You never know when they'll come asking."

"Beginnings, middles, and endings of things I plan to write."

"Information I wouldn't have to keep if I were computer literate and could find it when I need it."

"Receipts, warranties, and instructions for every product I've ever purchased."

"Photographs and love letters from all my former lives."

And the list kept growing. We went on for at least twenty minutes and could easily have continued, but we were both eager to begin analyzing the results.

"So, what do you think our problem is?" I asked Annica. "Why can't we just respond to things and move on? What's so difficult about paying a bill, reading a letter, filing a piece of paper, getting rid of what we no longer want or need?"

"Ah," Annica sighed. "If it were only that simple. But each act involves a choice, a commitment, a step in this direction or that. For some people, papers are nothing more than papers. But, for people like us, they're blank canvasses on which we project all of our indecision and anxiety, our fears and insecurities.

"Deciding what to do with, say, an offer for a credit card becomes a major life decision because it forces me to reflect on every aspect of my existence. It brings to the surface all my unresolved feelings about money, my job, where I live, how I live, my plans for the future—everything."

"I know what you mean," I said. "Every piece of paper is really so much more than it appears to be.

"I have two double-size shoe boxes overflowing with requests for charitable donations; and every one of them creates a moral and spiritual dilemma for me—to say nothing of a financial one. My name must have gotten onto some soft-touch list because every week, more and more desperate pleas come pouring in—pleas to help the victims of this hurricane or that earthquake or flood or famine or civil war; pleas to save the whales and the manatees and the Brazilian rain forests; to support world peace, campaign reform, alternative energy, cancer research; to send inner city children to summer camp and to stop offshore drilling and the use of BPA in baby bottles.

"It's all really important and, at the same time, totally overwhelming. I can't say yes to everything, but how can I say no? So, I simply say nothing. And because I feel too guilty to throw out such sincere requests for assistance, I keep them all. Someday, I tell myself, I'll have the time to review each of the deserving causes and respond. Meanwhile, at least I didn't callously discard anyone's cry for help."

"Except," Annica pointed out, "your own. You're the one whose need for help is being ignored as you're trying to dig your way out from under everyone else's request. And I'm in just as deep with my stuff."

"So, Annica," I said, looking around the car, "what are we going to do with all of this?"

"Well," she responded slowly, "I think we need to begin by recognizing that papers are not innocent bystanders in our battle against clutter. They are the most insidious enemy we face—ready at any moment to infiltrate our homes and undermine our attempt to create order. They're not to be trusted for a moment because they will multiply behind our backs and try to crowd us out of our own lives.

"We have to stop them, once and for all, before they take over completely. I'm convinced that every seemingly harmless piece of paper that crosses my doorstep has the potential to mutate into an evil creature that will not hesitate to wreak havoc with my life."

"That certainly is a sobering thought," I had to admit. "All those little mutating creatures waiting to spring into action from the back seat of my Volvo. It sounds like a science fiction movie I once saw that kept me awake for nights."

"It should keep both of us awake," Annica said, shifting the bags on her lap so that she could turn to face me, "because we are definitely at war here."

She was absolutely right, of course. But that provided no guarantee of a change in our behavior. And, so, we continued to discuss the deeper meaning of our resistance to paperwork all the way to the border of Vermont.

As we crossed the state line, we stopped to congratulate ourselves. Despite our significantly delayed start, we had made great time, slowing down only for necessary pit stops and occasional scenic vistas too magnificent to pass up. Now, here we were, close enough to being on schedule that there was no need to rush or seek risky shortcuts. It was, indeed, a sweet moment to be savored.

And, then, quite predictably—although not without a disarming element of surprise—my lifelong adversary appeared. As always, I was unable to recognize him. However, once the damage had been done, I immediately realized that the perpetrator was none other than my own personal demon of undoing—The Great Distractor—come to seduce me with a bit of pleasant diversion.

Called to action, no doubt, by my own complacency and misguided confidence, he always seemed to arrive just in time to deflect me from my goal. Variously disguised as a person, a place, a thing, or a possibility, he inevitably appeared on the scene as I was nearing my destination and my guard had been considerably lowered. Suddenly, with the end so clearly in sight, I would find myself enticed to stop whatever I was doing and follow this pied piper of distraction.

The piper might appear as a friend dropping by for a visit while I was trying to complete a project—or a beautiful flower beckoning from the side of the road during my power walk—or a clearance sale at the bookshop when I was on my way to the hardware store. With his toe in my path, The Distractor would gradually draw me away from my desired objective and reroute my footsteps in another direction. In a different time and place, the new experience would probably have been welcome; but, coming when it did, the effect was to throw me completely and irreversibly off course.

As we drew closer and closer to Fran's house—and to achieving the purpose for which we had come—The Distractor was waiting to greet us, this time seductively cloaked in the ruffled gingham of a Vermont country shop.

"Look, Pesi," Annica said as were leaving the little town where we had stopped for our final tank of gas and cup of coffee. "Isn't that a charming storefront?"

It certainly was. Stenciled vines of pink and blue morning glories trailed their way around the shuttered windows, up and down the stucco walls, and across the trellis overhanging the arched wooden door. A bright yellow sign in the shape of a sunflower welcomed one and all to the Old Vermont Country Shop, est. 1903 by Sam and Martha Shissel, whose sepia-toned photograph hung above the large brass bell.

"Little House on the Overpriced Prairie," Annica fittingly dubbed it after inquiring about the cost of a jar of honey in the shape of a beehive. But we were hopelessly smitten and couldn't tear ourselves away from the rows of calico curtains, homemade maple candy, and flowered aprons with matching sunbonnets.

The real temptation, however, came when we walked through the One-Room Schoolhouse display. Here, piled high on the antique desks, were all the writing supplies of another age. Fountain pens and inkwells, blotters and old slate blackboards, penny postcards and scented stationary in velvet boxes. And several feet away, in reluctant concession to the twenty-first century, were the office supplies of today clothed in their ancestral garb—a calculator shaped like an abacus; a laptop case disguised as a black and white composition notebook; a cellphone holder pretending to be a first grader's pencil box.

"Annica, look," I said, pointing toward a shelf of paper goods on sale. "We could have so much fun getting organized with all these accessories. It would be like playing school when we were kids."

Together, we examined the pastel file folders with mix-and-match labels, the rainbow-colored index cards, and the storage containers painted like our childhood lunch boxes. Thoroughly enchanted by the memories they evoked, we willingly paid the highly inflated prices, which, even with the buy-one-get-one-free sale, were pretty close to outrageous.

All told, The Distraction cost us two hours and $27, plus the cost of the large pizza we had to buy to replace the dinner Fran had prepared that dried up in the oven waiting for us to arrive.

By the time we pulled into her driveway, the sun had disappeared behind the mountains and the night air was developing a chill. As soon as we opened the car door, we could smell the tofu and mushrooms burning.

After a late brunch the following morning, the three of us—still exhausted from our long night—headed for the nearby lake. Determined to make up for lost time, Annica and I sat at the wooden picnic table for close to eight hours, slowly and methodically going through page after page after page. Other than a few trips to the park restroom and two quick walks around the lake to get the kinks out of our legs, we never got up from our bench. Fran brought us lunch, snacks, and several desperately needed cups of coffee.

Annica and I spent the day swinging back and forth between bleary-eyed fatigue and soaring ecstasy. On the one hand, the work was backbreaking and mind-numbing, and we hated every minute of it. On the other hand, the glory of overcoming each oppressive piece of paper was exhilarating. And as the papers began to move from the bags and boxes in the back seat of the car to our pastel-colored files and folders, we beamed with pride. But we experienced the most intense eruption of joy each time we raised a piece of paper high in the air and—with all the fanfare due such a triumphant feat—tossed it dramatically into the recycle bin.

As the sun began to spread its last rays of pink and orange light across the lake, Annica and I were doing a little victory dance around the stacks of paper that would soon be making their way downstream to the Vermont Recycle Center. Of course, the ceremony was largely symbolic because, in truth, we had barely made a dent.

As we were often reminded, there are few tasks in life as slow-moving and thankless as wading through piles of neglected paperwork. But such is the price of procrastination, and Annica and I had come to accept the burden as just another late-pay penalty.

In the end, each of us probably looked over about twenty percent of what we had brought with us and managed to discard maybe half of that. Nevertheless, when we got back into the car, Annica had the passenger's seat almost entirely to herself, and I could see out of all the windows—which was certainly cause for celebration. But, more important, we knew that we had finally triumphed over our own disabling inertia. And as we drove into the dark Vermont night, we agreed that, at the very least, it had been a bonding experience and a vacation we were not likely to forget.

CHAPTER FOUR

Full Steam Ahead

"Man plans, and God laughs."
—Yiddish Proverb

" So, how did your Vermont paperfest go?" Yitta asked, as she and Yidis and Etta and I carried our glass mugs of cappuccino to one of the outdoor tables at Café K. It was a strikingly beautiful day with a gentle breeze blowing, so lovely that even the view from the cafe—one of the least attractive in all of Brooklyn—appeared pleasant on this sunny afternoon.

Despite its proximity to the heavily trafficked intersection of Avenue K and Coney Island Avenue—a distinctly unappealing corner—the cafe held a certain charm for us. Perhaps, it was simply the projection of a belief—apparently common among urban coffee drinkers everywhere—that the seating area in which we gathered could, by sheer dint of our collective wishing, be transformed into a much prettier place than reality would have it. In any case, we found an empty table near the lone tree that had managed to push its way up through a crack in the sidewalk and, at Yitta's suggestion, indulged ourselves in the fantasy that we were dining in luxury beneath a country elm.

"Well," I began, "Vermont is a far cry from Flatbush, and being there really put me in touch with how much I miss mountains and streams and open meadows. But Annica and I brought enough clutter with us to effectively re-create our home environment, so it was almost like never leaving New York."

"In the end, would you consider the experience a success?" Yitta asked.

"It was definitely a successful beginning," I said, sipping my cappuccino and staring off into space for a moment. "All in all, I would say that the trip was a perfect microcosm of my life—a journey undertaken with too much baggage in tow, beset by numerous delays and distractions along the way, but ultimately propelled forward by the unflagging support of good friends."

Unaccustomed to such a succinct and articulate description from me, everyone looked up from their coffee mugs.

"Was that a prepared statement?" Yidis wanted to know.

"Of course," I admitted proudly, opening my pocketbook and pulling out several index cards on which I had scribbled my notes. "It's all here, composed and recorded on the New York State Thruway at 2:00 in the morning. We left Fran's house so late that I had plenty of time on the road after Annica fell asleep to organize my thoughts and weave them into a little sound bite."

"Well, organizing anything is always a step in the right direction," Yitta said encouragingly—but even I could see that was pushing it a bit.

There was a lot to talk about today, so we decided to leave Vermont till later. Over the course of the next few weeks, we would all be going off on our vacations, and everyone had issues coming up for them regarding their trips. Etta suggested that we write about our feelings for ten minutes and then discuss what we had written. Since we were a group not unaccustomed to expressing ourselves, everyone had a pen and notebook handy and was more than happy to spend the next ten minutes being introspective.

Given all the time and energy I had spent over the past few months trying to understand my relationship with clutter, I certainly did not anticipate the sudden coming to light of any previously unnoticed area of concern. However, as was often the case in my life, the slightest hint of complacency on my part seemed to elicit an insight that quickly poked holes in any theory I might have once considered sacrosanct.

And, true to form, as I was writing, a long-held belief of mine quickly began to crumble under scrutiny.

Twice every year—during my summer vacation and my winter break—I traveled to Florida to visit my mother. Hating to fly as I do and loving to drive, I always chose to go by car. Since two and a half days on the road each way with a week of heat and humidity in between was not my husband's idea of a relaxing vacation, I usually made the trip alone. Twice a year, I packed up the Volvo and headed out all by myself for what I considered an exciting journey of solitude.

I loved the freedom, the fluidity of time and space, the absence of rules and regularity. I never found being alone in the car tedious because I filled all those hours on I-95 with stimulating conversation. Not with a friend on a cell phone—I didn't even own one—but in animated dialogue with myself.

Steering wheel therapy, I called it. Having given my conscious mind a relatively simple project with which to occupy itself—that is, navigating the twists and turns of the Interstate—some deeper dimension of my brain, much more closely aligned with my subconscious, seemed to step in and take over. For hours at a time, I would descend into my own private world, coming up only for a breath of air, a tank of gas, or an extra large coffee to go.

The minimalism of the journey, it seemed, provided the perfect antidote to my normally overcrowded existence. Fourteen hundred miles with nothing but myself and the empty road—what could be simpler or less cluttered than that? And, so, for all these years, I had looked upon my trip to Florida as a welcome escape from the complications of my life—a meditative retreat on wheels.

But, as my pen was gliding uncensored across the page, the experience began to emerge in a far less flattering light.

This summer, I was no longer the unconscious clutterer I had been the previous year and for so many years before that. I may not have made it to the other side just yet, but I had certainly learned to regard any acquisitive behavior of mine with suspicion. And when I looked at my free-flowing vacation to Florida, I instantly recognized it as the breeding ground for clutter that it had apparently always been.

The first problem was the trip itself. Whenever I felt the need to stretch my legs or catch hold of my drifting concentration, I turned off the main road into one of the little towns bordering the highway and sought out the local thrift shop. Every town seemed to have at least one, run by the Salvation Army, Goodwill, the local animal shelter, or some other charitable group supporting a cause that anyone would be happy to aid with the simple purchase of a used picture frame or a secondhand flowerpot.

The stimulation of colors and textures plus the thrill of the hunt offered the perfect counterpoint to my hours of introspection and usually succeeded in restoring my attention span. However, a few of these interludes on the way down and, then, a few more on the way back produced enough unexpected treasures to bring my shock absorbers to their knees, especially if one of my finds happened to be a handmade wooden table.

And, then, there was Florida itself—a veritable hotbed of flea markets, thrift stores, and garage sales. In New York, I rarely shopped for anything—new or used—because the experience was simply too unpleasant. But, in Florida, where even low-budget secondhand shops had dressing rooms, piped music, and parking lots, it was such a delight to browse that I went nearly every day and stocked up on whatever I needed for the coming year—as well as whatever I clearly didn't need but felt like buying anyway.

True, I spent very little money on these shopping sprees, but once I got all the new items home, I had to contend with the upheaval they caused when I tried to integrate them with the rest of my densely populated belongings.

Worst of all, I rarely made it to Florida before the end of the summer. I usually tried to leave at the beginning of July, but generally didn't get going until the middle of August. This meant that by the time I returned with all my purchases, the school year was about to begin. And, so, instead of focusing on the new business of the fall semester, I generally spent the first week of September trying to get unpacked from my trip. This would inevitably put me so far behind schedule that I rarely caught up before Thanksgiving.

After our writing time was over, I shared this revelation, and Yidis and Yitta and Etta all agreed that I was indeed heading into a red alert danger zone and should not hesitate to place emergency calls to them from phone booths along the way.

"I know this may sound a bit extreme," Yidis interjected, "but you might want to consider trying a therapeutic fast on your next trip. I mean, total resale abstinence—no stopping and shopping at secondhand stores anywhere."

In response to what must have been my look of alarm at the prospect, Yidis immediately backed down.

"Okay," she relented. "Maybe some other time."

Moving quickly past that poorly received suggestion, we all agreed that I should make every effort to go to Florida as soon as possible, so that by the end of the summer, I would be ready to enter the final phase of my clean-up without having to contend with an onslaught of new items in need of assimilation.

"You know, Pesi," Yitta said, as we were settling into our second round of cappuccino, "I was just thinking that while you're away, you might want to consider keeping a journal. I know I suggest this all the time, but now would really be the perfect moment to start. You could write about whatever comes up during your steering wheel therapy— and you could also record your observations about your mother."

"My mother?" I asked, not quite comprehending the connection. "How did my mother suddenly get into the picture?"

"Well, from what you've told me over the years," Yitta explained, "she sounds like quite an accomplished clutterer herself. This could be a rare opportunity for you to examine the roots of your problem. Who knows?—Maybe you'll find a genetic link."

Yidis rolled her eyes. "Please. I can understand diabetes, flat feet, premature balding—but hereditary clutter? What are we going to hold our DNA responsible for next?"

"How about absentmindedness, poor housekeeping, and love of chocolate?" I suggested.

"You know," Yidis reconsidered immediately, "there might be some merit to that theory after all."

We had a good laugh at the prospect and came up with a host of other issues for which we all would have been only too happy to blame our genes. But even as we laughed, I felt a ripple of anxiety pass through my body, as I tried to imagine what my trip to Florida would feel like with no thrift shops to retreat to along the way.

"*Yidis*," I confessed on the walk home, "I'm not sure just why, but when you suggested that I abstain from all shopping, I got this uneasy feeling that hasn't gone away—and it makes no sense because we both know how much I hate to shop. I think not buying anything new is a great idea; but the truth is I hardly ever buy new things anyway, so it wouldn't be much of a challenge. However, the thought of taking a trip to Florida without being able to visit a few secondhand stores along the way—that feels really upsetting."

"Which just goes to show," she pointed out, "that there's a live wire somewhere in those thrift shop excursions of yours."

"That's probably true," I agreed. "But what do you think it all means?"

"Well, that's what we need to figure out," she said, as we began heading west on Avenue K. "Why don't we take a little detour through the greener side of town and talk about it as we walk?"

And, so, we turned around and headed in the other direction, away from the oppressive buildings that line Avenue K between Coney Island Avenue and the train tracks toward the much leafier section of Midwood that borders on Ocean Parkway.

"What a difference," I commented, as we walked down the wide, tree-lined streets edged with stately homes and well-kept gardens, only a few blocks from the congested working-class neighborhood around the corner.

"Yes," Yidis said, "it's a really pretty section, especially at this time of year; but take a good look at the gardens. Except for a little personal touch here and there, they're almost identical—just what you'd expect, since everyone hires the same gardeners. It's all pink and white impatiens, with an occasional rosebush or flowering hedge. Pleasant, but highly predictable. Which, it seems, is the way most people prefer to live. It's just human nature, I guess. But there's no reason why we have to remain prisoners of our own nature forever.

"Wait—I want to show you something," she said, putting her arm in mine and steering me down a new block. "I know you love gardening metaphors."

We stopped in front of a little stucco house almost entirely hidden from view by two towering homes with meticulously groomed lawns on either side. The tiny yard was lushly overgrown, bursting with early summer vegetables and beautiful wildflowers of every species and color, attracting the attention of quite a few butterflies and birds and humming insects. It looked like a miniature country meadow in high bloom and was unquestionably the most vibrant and exciting garden in the area. And it certainly made a great metaphor for something—although I wasn't quite sure just what.

"I love it," I finally said. "It's so alive and spontaneous—and wildly out of step with everything around it. I can totally relate. But I'm not sure how to apply the message to my issues with clutter. I mean, if anything, this delightful misfit seems to be making a good case for the virtues of unrestrained abundance."

"Maybe it is a bit of a stretch," Yidis conceded, "but I think there's a relevant lesson here. I love this feisty little house because it simply is what it is—no matter who lives next door or what's going on around it. It seems to have found its own voice, and no professional gardener or overbearing neighbor can silence it. And that's my vision for you and for me and for all of the Holy Sisters.

"Now, what does any of this have to do with your trip to Florida this summer? Well, I feel that each time you come close to touching that place of self-acceptance and creative expression, you pull away. There you are, driving down the highway, reaching the deepest levels of consciousness, seeing clear through to your own soul; and what do you do?—You decide to go shopping. I understand that you need a break from time to time, but there's a difference between a break and an escape. Clearing your mind and recharging your batteries are not the same thing as running away from uncomfortable feelings.

"You know, Pesita," Yidis concluded, stopping for a moment to face me, "we'll never be free—like that little house is—until we learn how to deal with our own demons. And you can't do battle with yours if every time they appear, you decide to slip off to the nearest thrift shop."

"You're right," I admitted, "but I'm just not ready to go cold turkey yet. Isn't there a halfway measure we could try?"

"Well, I did think of a Plan B after you reacted so strongly to my suggestion this morning. I knew we were on to something there, or you wouldn't have been that resistant. So, rather than do nothing at all, I figured maybe you would be open to a little writing exercise."

"As long as I can visit my favorite thrift shops, I'm open to anything."

"Great," Yidis said. "Then, how about committing to a thrift shop diary? Whenever you go shopping—and you can go as often as you like—you have to promise to write something about the experience, hopefully something that will shed light on why you went and what you got out of it. And I don't mean the fact that you found the perfect pair of bookends or the Victorian tea set of your dreams."

"Okay," I promised, "I'll do it. Actually, it sounds like it might be fun."

"I don't know if I'd go that far," Yidis said. "But, at the very least, it should be interesting. However, don't be surprised if some really disturbing feelings come up. As a matter of fact, I'm sure you can count on it."

By the first week in July, the car was fully packed and ready to go. I still couldn't manage to make it out of Brooklyn before three o'clock in the afternoon, but—as Yidis pointed out when I called to report my failed attempt at early morning departure—I was leaving for Florida at the beginning of July, not in the middle of August; and, for me, that was a real breakthrough.

As I turned onto the New Jersey Turnpike, I could see that the traffic was getting heavier by the minute, demanding razor-sharp attention from the navigational center of my brain. The rest of my consciousness, however, immediately sailed off on its own, anxious to begin work on the new assignment. I started by reflecting on some of the more memorable items I had purchased from garage sales and thrift shops over the years—most of which had, by now, gone back into secondhand circulation themselves.

There was that handmade bicycle-built-for-two that I stumbled upon at a garage sale during the early stages of a summer romance. The elderly couple who was selling it—reluctantly, it seemed—quickly brightened when they saw that it was going to a young couple in love. However, it never worked very well for us because my new boyfriend was much taller and more athletic than I was, and I had to pedal twice as hard just to keep up. Nevertheless, it made a great conversation piece, especially after we painted it a high–gloss cherry red. We would sing "Daisy, Daisy" as we pedaled along, he waving to charmed passersby as I gasped for breath between verses. As it turned out, neither the bicycle nor the boyfriend endured beyond the summer, but I found myself enjoying sweet recollections of the three of us on the road together.

Then, there was Elsie. She was a large black and white cow with rubber udders. If you lowered her hinged head into a saucer of milk and cranked her tail several times, she would raise her head and emit a heartfelt moo. At that point, all you had to do was squeeze her udders, and milk would begin to flow. She was the barnyard belle of the neighborhood; but, eventually, her hinges rusted and her udders grew stiff, and I had no choice but to send her off to second-hand pasture.

And, of course, there were all those fascinating gadgets that never quite made it as what they were intended to be, but were often wonderful as something else. Like the hand-carved spaghetti twirler that I wound up banging with a wooden spoon for musical accompaniment at folk-singing parties, the bright blue distributor cap that made a great pen and pencil holder, and the antique coffee grinder that never ground the coffee beans fine enough but made a perfect compartment for storing keys.

I could have gone on a lot longer reminiscing in this way about the pleasure of my unique finds and the creative uses to which I put them; the slice of their former lives that they revealed to me; and the memories of my own they came to embody. But I had a job to do on this vacation.

By the time I reached the Delaware Memorial Bridge—already several hours into the trip—I knew it was time to get down to business and tackle the subject in a more serious and focused way. However, I have a tendency to become easily distracted and lose the thread of my own thoughts under even the best of conditions—let alone, on a six-lane highway at the height of rush hour. Therefore, when I really want to come to terms with an issue—as I certainly did at this moment—I often speak out loud to help me concentrate, waving my arms and nodding my head as I go along, in what could easily be mistaken for a full-blown schizophrenic episode.

But thank God for the creation of cell phones. Not that I had one, but since just about everyone else on the road did, the people in the cars alongside me simply assumed that I, too, was speaking into some electronic device. In the past, my dialogues with myself were often greeted by nervous glances from nearby drivers, who, upon noticing that I was having an animated conversation with someone who wasn't there, would immediately change lanes and move as far away as possible.

On this trip, however, none of the passing drivers seemed to attribute my strange behavior to anything other than normal cell phone use, so I took full advantage of the opportunity to speak to myself loudly and passionately all the way to Florida and back. And it turned out to be quite an intense conversation, filled—as Yidis had predicted—with many disturbing insights. But most of that didn't come until much later in the ride.

In the beginning, everything seemed relatively calm and under control, as I tried to compile a mental list of all the reasons why I was attracted to secondhand shops, starting with the most obvious and least interesting of all—the natural desire to save money.

There was, of course, an understandable satisfaction in getting more for less. As one would expect, things were generally much cheaper used than they were new; and the quality was usually superior as well. I could purchase a finely woven, 100 percent cotton L.L. Bean cardigan, slightly worn but in excellent condition, for a fraction of what it would cost me to buy a new polyester and acrylic pullover that was poorly made at a sweatshop in Taiwan. So, on the most basic level, buying secondhand made good financial and ethical sense.

Okay, I told myself, this was a reasonable, if utterly boring, introduction to the subject; but it, in no way, explained any of my deeper feelings. However, when I thought a bit more about the relationship between money and clutter, I realized that I wasn't simply dealing with dollars and cents here.

Spending money involves a decision and a commitment; and for a clutterer, that can be a real problem. Therefore, shopping often becomes a very stressful experience, the difficulties of choosing and committing far outweighing the pleasures of acquisition.

When I walk into a thrift shop, however, the stakes are lowered to such a degree that shopping becomes fun. How serious can an error in judgment be if the garment only costs three dollars?

Who cares if it's the wrong color or doesn't fit perfectly or will only be worn on one occasion? So, I get to do what clutterers love best—acquiring more things—without having to suffer the consequences of making a costly mistake.

Taking that concept a step further, I realized that not only do I feel relaxed shopping in a thrift store but I actually feel liberated. If I want to buy ruby red shoes like Dorothy wore or a floppy straw hat with fruits and flowers on it, I'm free to indulge my wild side or my whimsical side—or a little bit of both. For $1.98, why not?

Of course, many of these items can be found in real antique stores as well; but, there, everyone takes the whole thing seriously. The old washboard lying in the dollar basket at the Salvation Army becomes part of the Authentic Americana Collection at The Antique Gallery, and the price becomes serious as well. And there goes all the joy of shopping.

But in a no-frills thrift store, the joy remains. Not only the joy of the purchase, but the joy of the hunt as well. These shops tend to be small and manageable, with every object placed within arm's reach. There are no escalators, elevators, or labyrinthine malls to contend with. It's just me and the potential treasures. And since I never quite know what I'll find on the next hanger or in the next bin, the delight of unexpected discovery is present at every turn.

As an added bonus, secondhand stores provide guilt-free spending for the socially conscious. There's no self-indulgent consumerism going on here. Every one of these items has already fulfilled the purpose for which it was created. I'm simply offering them a second shot at life. Without people like me, they would be ending their days in the rag pile or the recycle bin. And not only am I helping to avoid unnecessary waste, but I'm also contributing to the worthwhile causes that are supported by the sale of the merchandise.

I stopped to roll down the window and revive myself with some cool air. I was beginning to feel as if I were preparing a public relations presentation for the United Thrift Shops of America. It was all true, of course, but somehow I didn't think this was exactly what Yidis had in mind. Where were the uncomfortable feelings I was supposed to be getting in touch with? And how was this going to give me deeper insight into my issues with clutter?

Then, I remembered that Yidis had instructed me to do this exercise in writing *after* I visited a thrift store—not, in the abstract, before I arrived. Well, it was perfect timing because I would probably sleep in North Carolina tonight, which would get me to South Carolina tomorrow afternoon, just in time to do some research at one of my favorite shops.

I pulled into Florence, South Carolina, at about two o'clock the following afternoon with what seemed a perfect plan in mind. I would limit my thrift store shopping to one hour, with a grace period of fifteen minutes. Then, I would stop for gas and coffee; and during this break, I would jot down a few notes about the experience while it was still fresh in my mind. Back on the road, I would process the whole thing in more depth.

The thrift shop was a bit depleted—they were expecting a new shipment the following day—so I had no trouble making it to the cash register within the hour. However, once I got there, I spotted a Mix and Match Basket on the counter filled with beaded earrings that had become separated from their mates. Most of them were in the basket, the cashier assured me, but it might take some digging to find them and reunite the pairs. No problem, I thought. With my grace period, I still had fifteen minutes left.

At 3:25, I walked out of the store with twelve beautiful earrings, none of which exactly matched each other, but I hoped that would only add to their charm. And, best of all, I hadn't really overstayed my time—or, at least, not by much.

I headed toward the nearest convenience store, where I remembered getting cheap gas and a decent cup of coffee on my last trip. But on the way, I spotted a bright green storefront—you could hardly miss it—with an inviting sign in the window that read: "Grand Opening. Save the Earth Thrift Shop. Free cookies and lemonade."

Always a pushover for southern hospitality and environmental causes, I immediately stepped on the brake and turned into the driveway. Of course, what the sign was really saying to me, had I taken the time to pay attention, was: Beware—Major Distraction Ahead. But I was too busy jumping out of my car and running toward the display of antique rockers on the front porch to notice.

It turned out to be a secondhand shop of rare quality with great bargains and one-of-a-kind merchandise; and when I finally left, two hours later, I was dragging an enormous wooden barrel—which I was certain would make a great outdoor planter—filled to the very top with all of my purchases.

Back on the road, I was overcome with shame. What had happened to my attempt at self-discipline? My commitment to restraint? My one-hour time limit? I could now no longer see out of the rear passenger's window, and the last rays of daylight were beginning to disappear. Was this an act of spontaneity to be applauded—the sort of free-spirited response to the unexpected that keeps life fresh and exciting—or had I, once again, simply overstepped my own boundaries and succumbed to temptation?

After several frustrating hours of trying to understand what exactly had gone wrong, I called Yidis from a phone booth at my next stop in Savannah, Georgia.

"Did you write about it yet?" she asked me.

"No, I didn't," I confessed. "I was too upset after it happened. And, besides, it was getting dark already."

"Well," she suggested, "how about doing it in the motel to-night? Not writing because you're upset is like deciding not to take an aspirin because your head hurts."

"Okay," I agreed. "I'll do it as soon as I stop tonight. But I don't want to spend my whole vacation working so hard. I'm beginning to feel exhausted from all this thinking. It's much more difficult than my usual steering wheel therapy. I just want to relax a little and have some fun."

"Of course," Yidis said. "You're on a vacation—you should have lots of fun. Just don't forget Yitta's advice—Observe your mother and write a little every day."

"All right," I promised. "But I still don't see what my mother has to do with any of this."

"You will," Yidis replied with confidence. "Yitta's never wrong about these things. Just keep looking."

I thought about her comment all the way to Deerfield Beach. Just keep looking. Looking at what? I already knew that my mother was an incorrigible clutterer. Even she knew that. She had been saving things for as long as I could remember. But how would that shed light upon *my* issues?

Her clutter was the understandable accumulation of a woman who had lived through a deprived childhood, the Great Depression, and the limited supplies of wartime rationing. She saved packets of sugar, used tea bags, recycled aluminum foil, and the plastic containers from every bit of margarine, cottage cheese, yogurt, and sour cream she had ever consumed. What did any of that have to do with me?

Still, Yitta was so sure that there was a connection, and Yidis now agreed as well. And although I had no idea what they thought I would find with all this looking, I decided to follow their advice and proceed with a watchful eye and an open mind.

As I drove through the Century Village security gate, I was struck by the same sense of foreboding that I experienced before each visit. Would I find my mother the way I had left her—bright and funny and very much in life—or would she have begun that downward spiral that so many of her neighbors had apparently fallen into of late? Older people, it seemed—much like newborn babies—could become almost unrecognizable in just a few short months, as if the aging process hastened its pace at both the arrival and departure gates.

I ran up the four flights of stairs, knocked loudly, and shouted, "It's me!"—which, I suddenly realized had been my basic doorway greeting ever since I came home from my first day at kindergarten. I wondered if it might not be time for something a bit more age-appropriate, but before I had time to contemplate changing my routine, my mother opened the door, and I saw—with great relief—that she looked almost exactly as she had when I last visited her. A couple of new gray hairs, but still more pepper than salt; a wrinkle or two that I hadn't noticed before; and a slight shuffle when she walked—"Half arthritis, half sciatica, half old age," she explained, in her mathematically creative way—but, all in all, she looked great and far younger than her nearly eighty-three years.

With that worry out of the way, I found myself taking in the contents of the apartment and trying hard not to react to what I saw. It was the cleanest—yet, most densely cluttered—space I had ever seen. All the surfaces were well scrubbed and brightly polished, but there were stacks of paper and tchotchkes of all sorts piled on top of everything. Did it always look like this? I tried to remember. Had the piles actually grown in volume and height, or was I now simply viewing them through a different lens? During my previous visits, I had been so enmeshed with my own clutter that it's possible I didn't see anything unusual in my mother's accumulation. Still, this was not an easy sight to have overlooked.

"It does seem a bit much, doesn't it?" she asked, immediately noticing my reaction.

"Well . . . " I hesitated, trying to find the right words. "I'm sure there's more to it than meets the eye."

"Oh, there is," she assured me. "Clutter is never as simple as it seems. But, then, you've already figured that out, haven't you?"

I wondered how she knew. I hadn't said a word to her about The Project because I wanted to discuss it with her in person, and we had never really addressed her issues with clutter in any serious way. It was simply an accepted fact of life that she lived with a certain amount of excess, around which she kept a very clean and reasonably well-organized home. There just happened to be this baby elephant in the room that everyone who knew her acknowledged and then proceeded to ignore. But this elephant had now grown to full size and beyond and appeared on the verge of taking over the entire apartment.

"While you're getting unpacked, I'll make tea," she offered. "Then, after dinner, we can spend the evening talking about your piles and mine and, of course, playing Scrabble."

I ran to call Yitta.

"You were so right," I whispered into the phone. "For the first time in my life, my mother is initiating a conversation about clutter. What did you do—put a spell on her?"

"Just make sure you write everything down," Yitta reminded me. "You'll have a gold mine at your fingertips by the end of the trip."

My mother and I spoke for many hours that evening and every other evening as well. We settled into a wonderful nighttime routine—an early dinner and light talk, followed by tea and more intense talk, capped off with hot chocolate and a game of Scrabble. And, slowly, I began to understand more about her, more about me, and far more about the relationship that each of us had with our belongings.

"My clutter," she explained one evening, "seems to travel in three different directions. Some of it brings me to the past, some to the future, but most—believe it or not—actually connects me to the present."

That came as quite a surprise to me. I'd always assumed that the bulk of her sizable accumulation consisted of sentimental objects from days gone by or things she was saving for some rainy day to come.

"This coffee table," she said, motioning toward a low piece of furniture with only its four legs showing, "may not have room for a cup of coffee, but it's covered with wonderful memories."

I looked over at all the familiar items that had lined her shelves and countertops for as long as I could remember, before making their final journey from the Bronx to Deerfield Beach twenty years ago. In a prominent position, as always, was the shell-covered jewelry box filled with shell necklaces, bracelets, earrings, and pins that my father had made for her when he was stationed in the Philippines during World War II.

Beside it was a large stuffed mouse with a frying pan in one hand, wearing a chef's cap and a starched apron that said, "Better Mousekeeping Seal of Approval"—a gift from my ex-husband in recognition of Mom's magic touch with food.

"I always liked John," she said, watching my eyes linger on the kitchen mouse. "I'm so glad you two still stay in touch."

Next to that, serving as a paperweight for a pile of old greeting cards, was one of her most beloved objects—a ceramic tea pot with a missing lid in the shape of Mary Poppins, umbrella raised and ready for takeoff, that played a lilting "Chim Chim Cheree" when poured.

And that, of course, was only the tip of the iceberg.

She smiled in satisfaction upon surveying this little sample of her treasures and was then silent for a moment, no doubt reliving a particularly sweet memory or two.

"And these shelves," she gestured toward the china closet, "are my links to the future."

Here, she had photographs of my niece and nephews—Aaron, Leah, and Noah—at various stages of development, along with every birthday card, finger-paint drawing, and popsicle-stick project they had ever sent her.

"But most of these other piles," she said, waving her arms around the living room, "are my attempts at staying connected to the present. I don't get out to see folks the way that I used to, so I keep everyone I love close in my own way. Whenever I read a newspaper or magazine"—and there were dozens of them piled high on either side of her recliner—"I look for anything that might be helpful to someone I know, and I cut it out and save it for them.

"This little pile here is all the coupons that I've collected for my neighbors: half-price meals at Ruby Tuesdays for Rochelle—she and her friends love to eat there; special offers from the Gourmet Pet Supermarket for Honey—you know, your cousin Rita's new kitten that she pampers like a late-in-life baby; senior discount tickets for the Philharmonic that Cyd next door will love—did she ever tell you that she was a concert pianist before she retired?

"And whenever I finish with the advertisements and actually get to read the newspaper—which, these days, is usually several weeks after it arrives—I always keep my eyes open for interesting articles to pass on to all of you."

"Yes, I know," I reminded her. "You saved my life with the information you sent me about mold and mildew when we had that flood last year. And Yankel loved the article about sailing the canals in Fort Lauderdale. Also, thanks to you and *Prevention Magazine*, he's now taking fish oil to lower his blood pressure and cinnamon for his diabetes. And I've shown all my anti-caffeine friends that great story from the *Deerfield Times* about the centenarian who claimed he lived till a hundred because he drank fourteen cups of coffee a day."

"Oh," she said, smiling proudly. "I'm so glad you liked the articles."

"I love everything you send me," I told her. "The only problem is that I keep it all."

"That *is* a problem," she agreed. "And I'm afraid I'm hardly the one to help you solve it. But I can certainly commiserate.

"Anyway, back to my collection . . . I have toys in that box for when the kids come, and birthday and anniversary gifts are over here in this box, and these are scarves that I'm knitting for all my freezing friends back in New York, and here's a stack of old decorating magazines that I thought you might like to look at in case you have to move again . . . ."

"What about this huge steamer trunk," I asked, unable to contain my curiosity. "I don't remember ever seeing it here before."

"You're right," she said, limping over and raising the lid. "Do you remember Esther who lived next door to Ellie? Well, when she died a few months back, her daughter gave it to me. It's amazing how much stuff it holds. I like to think of it as my never-too-late-to-hope chest.

"When I was a teenager, I had a traditional hope chest. Many young girls did in those days. Nobody had much money, so our mothers and grandmothers would slowly collect things for us to start our new homes with when we got married—linens, pillows, blankets, tablecloths—all the things we would someday need when we were finally blessed with the husband and children we hoped for.

"Now, I have a different kind of hope chest. This one is filled with the things I hope I'll be able to use again someday. My set of good china, service for twelve; the wedding band that I'm no longer able to get on or off my finger—arthritis, you know; my favorite pair of red high heels—I used to love to go dancing in them; a basket for my old bicycle, which I recently traded in for a senior tricycle . . . well, you get the idea."

Yes, it was all becoming clear. And with each succeeding conversation, I found myself reaching a new level of understanding, as I peeked more and more deeply into my mother's mind—and, quite unexpectedly, into my own as well.

One evening, she showed me a rainbow prism that one of her coupon recipients had given her as a thank-you present.

"You just hold it up to the light like this," she said, raising it slowly toward the window, "and all these colors come pouring out. It's like seeing a thousand sunsets at the same time."

I suddenly remembered how she used to love sitting by the water in Deerfield Beach and watching the sun slowly disappear beyond the horizon. These days, she could no longer get to the ocean easily, so she had to settle for whatever bit of setting sun she could catch from her fourth floor catwalk, which—with all the new construction going on around Century Village lately—wasn't a whole lot. This little dollar-store prism probably provided as much of a sunset as she could get most evenings, but she seemed perfectly content with that. In fact, she looked almost ecstatic as she watched the colored lights moving across her window; and I instantly flashed to that moment in Etta's office when I had experienced a similar joy watching the crystals reflected on the wall.

A few evenings into my visit, she shared with me the story of her first doll, an experience that apparently colored her relationship with the physical world for many years to come:

"We arrived from Russia in the 1920s," she began, her eyes starting to squint, as they always did when she told a story from long ago, as if she were trying to make out the fine details of an old photograph she couldn't quite bring into focus. "I was only six years old at the time, and we were very poor. But everyone we knew was poor in those days, so it was really no big deal. Four adults and two children sharing a tiny one-bedroom walk-up in East Harlem actually seemed quite luxurious—what, with running water, a flush toilet, and an icebox filled with food.

"Anyway, all the neighborhood children—poor as we were—would look forward to going to the movies once a week at the local theater. For a few hours every weekend, the manager of the movie house would close the theatre to adults and put on a show of cartoons and actions films just for the children. But the best part came when the pictures were over.

"The lights would come on, the movie screen would be raised, and the curtain would open to a stage covered with gift-wrapped toys, sleds, stuffed animals, skates, bicycles—a fantasy land of delights—all prizes for those lucky children who had a ticket stub that matched the one the manager pulled out of his magic drum. But in all the months I had faithfully attended, he never once called my number; and every week I sadly left the theater with empty arms.

"One afternoon, I was feeling so disappointed that I had to try really hard to keep myself from crying. At that moment, I heard the manager's booming voice say, 'I'm going to spin the drum one more time. This will be the final number of the day.'

"And, then, he cleared his throat—I can still remember the sound it made—and called my number. I don't know how I ever got to the stage; but when I did, the manager handed me a large rect-angular box and told me to go ahead and open it. When I finally calmed down long enough to tear the wrapping paper and look in-side, I found a magnificent doll dressed in Scottish kilts, with knee socks to match, and a tam o'shanter on top of her curly blond hair.

"I'd never had a doll before—let alone such a special one—and I had no idea what to do with it. So, from time to time, I would simply open the box, carefully push aside the tissue paper, and stare in awestruck wonder at the treasure inside. Then, I would neatly cover it up and put it away. I was afraid to play with it or even take it out of its wrapping, terrified that something would mar its perfect beauty.

"Every now and then, I would invite a friend to share in the experience, but we were always too intimidated to ever actually touch the blond curls or well-rouged cheeks. Somehow, it was enough for me to simply know that such flawless beauty existed in the world and that I could, from time to time, gaze upon it.

"Eventually, we moved to another apartment; and, in the midst of the upheaval, the box was somehow misplaced. Of course, I was totally brokenhearted—not only because I lost the doll, but because I never really had it to begin with. In the end, however, I found myself strangely relieved. It had been quite a responsibility to maintain her pristine appearance for such a long time, and there was a certain liberation in being freed of that burden. We searched everywhere, but I never saw the doll again.

"Now, here I am, living in a home where everything I love is on permanent display, able to be seen and touched by anyone who passes by. And, as I'm telling you the story, I'm beginning to wonder whether it's not all because of that beautiful doll that I could never quite figure out how to enjoy."

I closed my eyes and sipped my tea, picturing my mother—gentle soul that she is—opening her gift box with great care, delicately working her way through the tissue paper, and staring wide-eyed at the untouched doll from a safe distance. And I could easily imagine how that moment led to this one, where everything she cherished now sat out in public view, bringing endless delight to her and to those of her visitors who were able to see past the cluttered surface.

Saying goodbye a few days later was more difficult than I ever remembered it being. This had undoubtedly been my most emotionally intense trip to Florida and certainly my least distracted. I had spent nearly every waking moment with my mother and hadn't even looked in the window of a thrift shop or ventured anywhere near a garage sale or flea market. Now, as reluctant as I was to leave, I was eager to get back on the road and finally begin to process everything I had experienced. My only regret was that, despite my promise to Yitta and Yidis, I had not managed to write a single word during my entire stay. However, as I turned my key in the ignition, the Universe—no doubt in cahoots with the two of them—was already preparing to rectify that error.

After numerous delays packing my bags and loading my car, I finally made it to the Century Village security gate around three o'clock. Gas, oil, air in the tires, and a final stop at Dunkin' Donuts got me to I-95 close to four. By the time the rush hour traffic had subsided and I was finally able to focus on my own thoughts, I noticed a strange odor beginning to fill the car.

When I stopped to think about it, something had smelled a bit off from the moment I began the trip, but I was in too much of a hurry to pay attention to it. Now, the smell was getting stronger, the temperature arrow on the dashboard inching its way into the red zone, and a thick cloud of white smoke beginning to billow from beneath the hood. I was between exits—which were about fifteen miles apart at this point—so I pulled onto the shoulder and tried to figure out what to do next.

It was really no big deal, I told myself. Eventually someone would see me and offer to help. I tied a white T-shirt with a pink flamingo on it to the antenna and sat there hoping for the best. But the sky was getting darker by the moment, and no one seemed to be stopping. Before long, the wind started to swirl around me, thunder boomed in all directions, and bolts of lightning flashed theatrically across the blackened sky. Within minutes, sheets of rain began to pound my car.

I sat there in a state of mild terror. I was probably safe, I reasoned; but I certainly didn't feel safe. It was just a passing tropical storm, I assured myself, not uncommon during hurricane season in Florida. Truckers kept zooming past on my left; everything to my right was enshrouded in darkness; the sky continued to assault me from above; and the earth beneath my tires was rapidly turning to mud.

Strange, I observed, how the outer world mirrors the inner—or is it the other way around? In any case, this feeling of being powerless over the forces of nature was not unlike the feeling I've frequently had about the chaos that descends upon my life—often as dramatically and unexpectedly as this wild summer storm.

Too bad there was no light to write by in the car, or I might have had something to show for the experience.

Well past nightfall, the rain finally subsided; and, shortly afterward, a patrol car pulled up alongside me. The officer was shocked to find that I had set out on a fourteen hundred mile trip without a cell phone. He gave me a long lecture about the dangers of traveling alone with no means of communication—and I must say he had a point there. As soon as the tow truck he radioed for arrived and carried my car away, the officer dropped me and my duffle bag at the nearest motel, but only after extracting a promise from me that I would buy a prepaid mobile phone before I got back on I-95—which, reluctantly, I did and then proceeded to lose before I made it out of Georgia.

I woke up the next morning with the sun streaming through my window and the sky a cloudless blue, as if the storm the night before had been nothing more than a midsummer night's dream. It turned out that I was in Melbourne (Florida, that is—not Australia—as I had to explain to everyone I called that day), and my car would be laid up for at least twenty four hours and possibly longer because, as Chuck from Melbourne Motors put it, "Them old Volvo parts don't grow on palm trees down here."

"What a gift," Yidis said when I told her. "A forced retreat with nothing to do but write."

And, so, I borrowed a lounge chair from the motel, found a shady tree on the premises, and spent the afternoon with a notebook in my hand, while Chuck combed all of Melbourne in search of a new thermostat for my old radiator.

Yidis was right. The day was a gift. The forced stillness and lack of distraction helped me to focus inward, and I was finally able to begin processing my visit.

Once I began writing, I started to realize just how much my apartment looked like a latter-day version of my mother's—too much stuff in too small an area, resulting in an ever-expanding mess. But, to her, she was simply creating an environment filled with the things she loved.

As she aged and her mobility decreased, her world began to shrink—but not her desire to remain connected to the people, places, and things that were dear to her. The objects with which she surrounded herself gave her joy and hope and comfort. Unfortunately, they also gave her no place to sit or stand or walk. But, then, life is always a tradeoff; and she seemed perfectly content with the deal she had struck with the material world.

I, of course, had grown up at a different time, under a different set of circumstances, with a very different consciousness. Yet, whether through mother's milk or shared DNA or environmental osmosis, her need for physical objects to transport her beyond the physical was clearly my need, too. And her daily challenge to contain it all had apparently become mine as well.

I also realized that not only had her belongings come to mean so much to her but, over the years, she had come to express a good deal of herself through them. Whenever I tried to imagine what it would be like to walk into her apartment if she were no longer there, I immediately felt a sense of her presence emanating from her things.

Both blessed and cursed with an overactive imagination, I began to visualize what it would be like to come to Deerfield Beach one day and not find her shuffling toward the door to greet me. No baby fine hair tickling my nose as I bent down to kiss her— she seemed to be growing shorter every year—and no immediate barrage of loving questions as to whether I was hungry or thirsty or tired, too warm or too cold, dressed properly or in need of a sweater, preferring to rest or unpack or eat first. . . .

Instead, I would have to settle for experiencing her through her things. And I realized that, at that moment, I would probably be enormously grateful that she had paid no attention to me all these years when I encouraged her to thin out her collection of beloved objects.

I could imagine picking up her Mary Poppins teapot and listening to the sounds of "Chim Chim Cheree" over and over again, no longer in touch with how I found the song a bit too cloying for my taste, but hearing only how sweet and harmonious it must have sounded to her ears, and recognizing that her desire for sweetness and harmony in all things probably constituted the basis of her aesthetic and, surely, the driving force in her relationships.

Looking at her belongings was like peering into her world; and, perhaps, someday when that was my only way of connecting to her and to her vision of things, I would be comforted—although probably at the same time, deeply pained—by every object that reflected a piece of who she was.

When I awoke the following morning, I had no desire to write. Not because I had said everything I wanted to say the day before, but, most likely, because I hadn't. There was so much more to get in touch with, but I didn't feel quite ready to approach it just yet. Perhaps I needed the familiar comfort of my kitchen table, the support of Yankel and my friends, the cushion of my own clutter around me. Whatever the case, for now, this was about as far as I could go.

But Chuck wasn't cooperating with my plan. He had not yet found the elusive thermostat, and it looked like I would be spending at least another day hanging around Melbourne.

I had stopped here for coffee on a previous trip, so I was not unfamiliar with the city. I remembered that it had a rather quaint downtown area with several very nice craft stores and thrift shops—definitely the sort of place in which I could easily lose myself for an afternoon. The motel manager directed me to the bus stop, and I headed across town, more than ready for a little escape from myself.

I realized that I couldn't buy very much because I had no way of getting it back to the motel, so I tried to focus mostly on small, light items that would be easy to carry by public transportation. I found a few scarves and T-shirts, a hand-embroidered denim skirt, and four brightly colored Mexican straw hats (two for Yankel, two for myself), which I figured I could carry—Bartholomew Cubbins style—piled on my head.

It was a modest haul, but I had enjoyed the browsing, and the distraction it provided was definitely a welcome release from yesterday's intense emotion.

As I was walking out the door of the last thrift shop still open, I spotted Bewilda lying upon a dusty pile of National Geographic magazines. Someone had carelessly tossed her there face down and tail up, in what seemed a distinctly undignified position, even for a stuffed goose. When I brushed her off and set her down right side up, I was immediately struck by her facial expression. It was so endearing and thoroughly human that I knew at that moment I had to take her home with me.

"How much is she?" I asked the clerk.

Holding her by the tip of one wing and looking disdainfully at her bedraggled condition, the cashier wrinkled her nose and said, "You can have her for a dollar."

"It's a deal," I replied matter-of-factly, restraining my enthusiasm so that she wouldn't feel the need to rethink her decision and raise the price—although I had already made up my mind that I would pay whatever she asked because I knew I wasn't going to leave Melbourne without Bewilda.

There was something about her that felt familiar and comforting, but I wasn't quite sure just what it was until I examined her a bit more closely. As soon as we left the store, I removed Bewilda from the small plastic bag into which the clerk had hastily stuffed her. Fluffing her fur and brushing off the National Geographic dust, I found a manufacturer's tag attached to her tail. The note of introduction from Ms. Noah of the Noah Toy Company read as follows: "Bewilda's crossed eyes are lifted to heaven for help. Her feathers are ruffled, her wings are dragging, but somehow she'll muddle through."

I instantly identified. She was bewildered, overwhelmed, worn out by the challenge of coping with life. She was me with a beak and webbed feet. That familiar look on her face was the one I saw whenever I looked in the mirror—a brave but utterly baffled expression. Life, with all its complicated details and conflicting emotions, was just a bit too much on most days; and, from time to time, I needed to know that I wasn't the only one who felt that way.

"This is really more than I can deal with," those weary eyes seemed to be saying, "but I'm not ready to give up just yet. And maybe—with a little help from above and a hand from my friends down below—I'll manage to get by."

"Keep reminding me, Bewilda," I whispered to her as we boarded the bus, and a group of young children began to point and laugh at the four straw hats piled on my head. "Just keep reminding me."

*B*ewilda and I made great travel companions; but as much as I enjoyed the ride with her, I couldn't wait to get home and back into life.

As I pulled up in front of my house, Yankel came running off the porch to greet me with a huge hug, all the while staring out of the corner of his eye at the barrel in the back seat and Bewilda in the front.

"What's in the treasure chest?" he finally asked, craning his neck to see through the window.

"Oh, lots of wonderful things I couldn't resist buying."

"I can't wait to see them," he said, as obviously ambivalent about the joys of clutter as I was.

"And what's with the chicken?" he said, pointing to Bewilda.

"She's a goose," I corrected him. "And be careful what you say about her—she already knows all the family secrets."

"I'll watch my step," he assured me.

As we unpacked, talking and laughing, I felt enormously relieved to be home. But once we stepped through the front door, I found myself face to face once again with the mess I had left behind—to which Yankel had added a considerable measure of his own. Everywhere I looked, there was a bit too much—and, in many cases, far more than a bit. It was my mother's apartment all over again—more subtle and understated, to be sure—but, in reality, not all that different. I was still happy to be home, of course, but my joy was not without conflict.

The only thing I could think about at that moment was how much I wanted to finally finish this awful job and never see another pile again. The fall semester was starting in just a month, and I wanted my home to be 100 percent clutter-free by then so that I could begin to focus on my office at school. As nuanced and subjective as I now realized the whole issue of clutter really was, I knew that anything I could manage to get rid of—whether it was technically clutter or not—would help to simplify my life dramatically.

As soon as I woke up the next morning, I immediately got to work. I stopped trying to process all of my feelings and new insights and, instead, simply rolled up my sleeves and starting sorting papers and cleaning out drawers.

"Good for you," Yidis said encouragingly. "We'll get back to the psychological dimension after the last garbage bag is sealed and dragged to the curb. That's when I want to discuss the meaning of your mother and Bewilda and the six tables that are still sitting in your garage. But, until then, just keep filling those bags."

Meeting the deadline was quite a close call—as it always has been for me—but after an August of no beaches, no bicycling, no trip to the mountains or the ocean or even the crowded benches of Prospect Park, I finally managed to complete this phase of The Project. All it took was for me to basically stop living—or, at least, stop living a normal life. In the end, however, I had to admit that it was well worth the sacrifice. By Labor Day Weekend, I was as close to having an organized home as I had ever been. Not perfect—not by any means—but near enough to my goal to drink a celebratory glass of champagne with the Holy Sisters.

As if all of this were not enough of a breakthrough for one season, the very next day, Yitta called with an announcement I had been waiting years to hear.

"Pesi," she began, "you won't believe what I'm about to tell you. If you never trusted in synchronicity before, you certainly will now. . . ."

Yitta's news had a long history. One afternoon over lunch more than five years ago, I told Yitta about an idea I had for a book of personal essays. I described the project in detail, and, with characteristic generosity, she gave my idea a standing ovation and even offered to show the budding manuscript to her own agent.

"But, please, Pesi," Yitta said with real concern in her voice, "whatever you do, don't forget to make extra copies of your work. Manuscripts have a strange way of slipping into black holes and disappearing forever. Believe me, I know. I've had at least one of my own vanish into the stratosphere, never to be seen or heard from again."

"Don't worry," I promised Yitta, "the minute the ink is dry, I'll run right out and make lots of extra copies."

Inspired by Yitta's enthusiasm, I headed straight home and began to edit and type all of my handwritten essays. However, between the finicky temperament of my aging typewriter and the endless revisions that I could not resist making, the project took considerably longer than I had anticipated. Whenever I read a page, it seemed that I found something else to add or delete or rewrite entirely.

By the time I was finished, my desk was covered with piles of paper, most of which should have been discarded immediately; but, somehow, I couldn't quite bring myself to do that. It seemed so harsh and so final. After all, these pages were part of my creative process. And, besides, I reasoned, if I read them again, I might just come across an overlooked phrase or image worthy of future consideration. So, instead of separating the rejected from the chosen, I simply deposited them all into one big box and left the entire undifferentiated mess to be sorted through another day.

In the meantime, I ran around the corner to make copies of the corrected essays at the local convenience store. Unfortunately, the mom-and-pop shop had only one primitive photocopy machine—and, that, with a broken collator and a shortage of duplicating fluid. But since everything was running behind schedule, including my long-planned lunch with Yitta, I decided to make do with the outdated copier.

After the barely functioning machine finally cranked out its last gray page, I quickly put together the most legible copies for Yitta and took the rest home—unassembled and blurry—to throw into the box with all the other papers.

Rushing to the end, I made it to our outdoor café just on time and proudly handed the manuscript to Yitta.

"I can't wait to read it," she said, as encouraging as ever. "But as far as showing it to my agent, that may take a little longer. She just told me that she's planning to retire at the end of the year, so it looks like I'll have to find someone new.

"Don't worry, though," she reassured me. "I'll hold on to your work until I connect with another agent. It shouldn't take too long. In the meantime, you did make those extra copies for yourself, didn't you?"

"Oh, absolutely," I said, too embarrassed to tell her what a mess it all was. "Just as you suggested."

A few months passed without a successful lunch date. Yitta was still busy looking for another agent, and I had become quite busy myself moving to a new apartment.

Then, late one evening, Yitta called, her voice awkward with embarrassment.

"Pesi, I'm so sorry. Please forgive me, but I can't seem to locate your essays. Hopefully, I'll find them by the time I get a new agent. In the meantime, I'm so glad you made those extra copies. You still have them, don't you?"

"Of course, I do, Yitta. I'm sure I'll find them as soon as I unpack."

Probably in a decade or two if I'm lucky, I thought to myself.

Eventually, I did stumble upon the box in which all the copies were packed. By then, however, they had already merged beyond recognition with the papers that should have been thrown out in the first place. Now, I would have to sort through the entire mess and carefully study each and every page to find the correctly edited version. Not exactly a dream job.

And, so, the box sat untouched for a few more years and another move. I shuddered at the thought of rereading all those endless revisions in search of the final draft, but I considered it fitting penance for my sloppy ways. And every time I stumbled upon the box, I promised myself that as soon as my life was in order, I would attack the dreaded task and finally resume the writing of my book.

Now, on this Monday of Labor Day weekend, 1999—the morning after completing my eight-month crusade against clutter—Yitta called to say, "Pesi, you won't believe what I found at the bottom of my dresser drawer. . . ."

"Yitta, I don't get it," I finally responded after a long shocked silence. "I spend eight months organizing my house, and, then, the very next day, you discover my missing manuscript in your bedroom two miles away. What do you think it all means?"

"Maybe that God has a strange sense of humor?" Yitta suggested.

We both had a good laugh about that and agreed to continue the conversation over coffee later that evening.

In the meantime, I couldn't stop thinking about the possible explanations. Had my friendship with Yitta created a bond so deep that the space I cleared in my own life produced a corresponding opening in hers? Did the sincerity of my efforts at making order somehow elicit a supportive pat on the back from the Universe in the form of this unexpected gift? Was a lost object being returned to its rightful owner because a proper environment in which to receive it had finally been created? Or was I simply witnessing a less linear version of my mother's oft-repeated observation—"You never know what you'll discover when you finally clean your room"—now raised to the more cosmic level of "You never know what you'll discover in Borough Park when you clean your room in Flatbush."

I really didn't know what to think. Should I view the whole thing as an interesting but essentially meaningless coincidence? A rare moment of serendipity? A genuine miracle? Or was it all perhaps nothing more than the wishful thinking of an insecure writer looking for a sign of encouragement from the Universe?

"Well," Yitta said, when we got together several hours later, "it might very well be a little miracle—but, then again, it could just as easily be a big coincidence. Really, what do we know? But one thing is for sure—whatever it means, it'll definitely make a great chapter for your book someday."

I spent most of the fall semester with my head in one file cabinet drawer or another. Every night, after my last student went home, I sat for hours trying to work on the mess in my office.

The project attracted too much attention to carry out during the day, since I liked to keep the door to my unventilated office open—an act taken by many of my colleagues as an invitation to drop in and see how the work was going. Most were genuinely supportive of my efforts, but there were the occasional naysayers and cynics who found my most recent attempt at organization a source of high amusement.

However, by 11:00 PM, everyone was usually gone, except for a few of my late-night friends who also liked to work in an empty office every now and then. So, I found myself sitting alone at my desk most nights, surrounded by piles of paper and general office miscellanea, hoping that Dan or Paul or Terri or Kevin would drop by for a late-night cup of tea and save me from the tedium of my project.

And tedium it certainly was. I can think of few jobs as monotonous and irritating as this one. Not only was the work oppressively boring, but the glacial pace at which it progressed gave me little hope of ever seeing my labors come to fruition.

There were so many decisions to be made. Each piece of paper required its own response: save it; don't save it; do save it but store it someplace else; save it with all the other papers that you can't decide if you really want to save or not. . . .

Most nights, I left with a splitting headache and a strong desire to forget the entire project. Living with clutter seemed far preferable to this. But the following evening, I always returned. I was in too deep to give up now.

And so it went through September, October, and most of November. And, then, almost overnight, something shifted. As December approached, I was suddenly able to see the end in sight.

My office—although still in need of much work—was starting to look like a real office and not a storage unit.

By the time the semester was over and my birthday came around (both, once again, on December 23), my office was not only free of most of its former clutter, but had been beautifully decorated with pictures and plants and interesting folk art that my students had brought in from around the world. My birthday present that year was the parting comment of a generally skeptical coworker, who stood in visible shock at my office door and proclaimed: "Now, *this* is a miracle of biblical proportions."

And that, I thought, pretty well summed up the events of the past twelve months. Since I had first begun The Project last December, my relationship with the physical world had undergone a series of major changes that, in truth, didn't fall far short of the miraculous.

Now came the best part of all. I was going to go home to my well-organized house, sit down at my uncluttered desk, and try to think about how I had made my way from the chaos of the last year/decade/half century to the order and clarity of the coming Millennium. But this was not a solitary project. Each of the Holy Sisters was going to be sitting at her own desk, working on her version of the coming transition; and on December 30—in preparation for New Year's Eve—we were all going to get together and share our reflections.

Since my home had become a living symbol of actualized potential—"the little house that could," Etta called it—we decided to meet there. Everyone agreed that it provided the perfect setting for a discussion of hope and change, as well as an opportunity for me to show the group what I had accomplished.

Driving back to Brooklyn, I remembered my trip home a year ago. One of the joys of teaching has always been the rhythm that it imposes on my life, the returning cycle each semester of a clear beginning, a well-defined middle, a predictable end. As out of touch with time as I tend to be, the consistency creates a vessel for containing memories that would otherwise surely be lost.

So, as I crossed the Brooklyn Bridge, I reflected on my evening with Barbie exactly twelve months earlier, followed by my desperate cry for help to the Holy Sisters. I thought back—with overwhelming gratitude—to all the pep talks at Café K with Yidis and Yitta and Etta, the late-night conversations with Laya in Portland, the ongoing supply of blueberry muffins from Laurie and soba noodles with seaweed from Atara, the endless advice and help with the details of living from all the other Holy Sisters, the support of Annica and Fran in Vermont, the special time in Florida with my mother, the gentle nudges and good-natured teasing from Yankel every day.

"Yes," I sang loudly through the open window, as the cold night air brushed my cheek. "I get by with a little help from my friends, with a little help from my frie-e-e-e-ends. . . ."

By the time the first Holy Sister arrived, the candles were lit, the wine was chilled, and the homemade desserts were sitting on lace doilies with a dozen long-stemmed roses arched gracefully over them. Since this was our last meeting of the year—and the first we were holding in my house since The Project began—I wanted the setting to be especially beautiful and inviting.

I waited anxiously to see the reaction of each Holy Sister as she walked through the front door. In a matter of seconds, the expression on everyone's face passed from wide-eyed shock to hesitant belief to "Wow—she really did it!"

Once we were seated around the table, ready to drink a toast to what everyone was now calling the last great miracle of the twentieth century, Yidis raised her glass and said, "Pesita, the highest praise I can give you tonight is to say that I am truly speechless."

"A rare moment, indeed!" Yitta observed good-naturedly; and we laughed and clapped and drank joyful toasts to each other.

The plan for the evening was that each of us would share our reflections on the year past and our hopes for the one coming, followed by feedback from the group. Everyone spoke so deeply and so openly that we found ourselves almost immediately behind schedule. By the time my turn finally came—being the hostess, I was the last to go—it was already well past 11:00 PM, and the early risers in the group were beginning to fade.

"I have an idea," I said, as the yawning women turned to me. "Why don't I write up my notes and send everyone a copy? It'll be a great exercise for me, and it will save all of you from having to end the year half asleep. Whoever wants to give me feedback can do it anytime over the next few weeks or at our meeting next month."

Everyone looked greatly relieved at the suggestion; and, in truth, I was relieved myself. Since speaking always involves some degree of tension for me, and since this was such a valuable opportunity for introspection, I felt excited at the prospect of doing it slowly and thoughtfully on paper.

As soon as they were all gone, I made myself a large mug of coffee and headed for the kitchen table. No matter how lovely or comfortable any space in my house ever was, when I really wanted to get in touch with my deepest feelings, I always found myself gravitating toward the kitchen table. I wasn't sure if it was the legacy of generations past—grandmothers and great grandmothers conducting the affairs of life over checkered tablecloths—or the comforting sense of a coffeepot nearby or the memory of moments too spontaneous or intimate for the dining room table. Whatever the nature of the attraction, I soon found myself sitting there, writing journal in hand, ready to reflect upon the year.

As I wrote, a strange process began to unfold. Suddenly, the notes I had jotted down at my desk the week before no longer seemed completely real or honest. Somehow, the kitchen table elicited a very different response from me.

Here, instead of experiencing the satisfaction and optimism that I had felt such a short time ago, I now found myself feeling vulnerable and confused—and I knew it was more than simply a change in mood. Without attempting to reconcile the two states of mind, I simply recorded what I was experiencing in the moment. At the end, I had to admit that the kitchen-table essay—while considerably more ambivalent and troubling—reflected a deeper and more truthful reality.

Several hours later, still unsettled by my own words, I decided to call Laya and see what she thought of it all. Thankfully, she was wide awake and working on her own self-portrait, which she promised to read to me as soon as it was complete.

"My essay is a bit long and rambling," I warned her, but she encouraged me to read it aloud anyway.

"All right," I said, hearing the weariness in my own voice, "but—you know something—all this self-analysis is getting tiresome. I can well understand why the rest of the world is out buying firecrackers and champagne. Okay . . . whatever . . . here goes:

"I used to think I understood what I meant when I said my life was filled with clutter. Now, I can see that it's far more complicated than I ever imagined.

"I've spent the past year, with the help of the Holy Sisters, trying to remove every vestige of clutter from my life. But, with each step I've taken, it's become more and more obvious that this is no simple matter to deal with. What I used to think of as clutter often wasn't, and what I didn't consider clutter frequently turned out to be; and what I now think I know about clutter is probably off the mark as well. If you feel confused listening to this, you can imagine how I feel living it.

"In the end, all I can say is that, for me, clutter is whatever makes me feel cluttered—and that can easily change from one minute to the next.

"But even with that fuzzy definition, I would have to say that, at this moment, I feel I've gotten rid of almost all the clutter in my possession. And what I haven't gotten rid of, I've neatly organized and packed away.

"From that perspective, the year has been a tremendous success. I no longer have embarrassing piles in my house, my office, my car, or any of the other places where the mess has tended to land and multiply. Even my stacks of paper—generally the worst of all my eyesores—have been reduced to a volume that can be respectably displayed or concealed. So, by all reasonable standards, I can now declare my environment pretty close to clutter-free.

"And, yet, I don't *feel* clutter-free at all.

"I used to believe that if I ever managed to remove the excess baggage from my life, order and clarity would instantly take its place. However, apparently the system doesn't quite work that way.

"As I look around tonight at my impressively organized home, I'm overcome by a sense of accomplishment and well-being; but when I close my eyes and gaze inward, I feel as overwhelmed and unsettled as ever. Obviously, there's a disconnect here somewhere, but I can't seem to put my finger on just what it is."

We were both silent for a moment, reflecting on my question.

"What I think is happening," Laya finally said, "is that you're trying to critique the movie before the house lights come on."

"What do you mean?" I asked.

"Well," she explained, "you know, like Yogi Berra says, it's not over till it's over. Just because December 31 happens to be coming around tomorrow doesn't mean that your life has conveniently landed in a nice, neat place waiting to be wrapped up and reviewed. The truth is, you're still in the middle of The Project, and it's much too soon to judge the results. It would be like one of those high wire acrobats pausing midleap to evaluate her performance."

I wasn't sure if she was right or not, but I needed something to get me through the night and into the New Year, so I decided to accept her theory for now and consider myself a work in progress. But in a few days, when all the New Millennium fever died down, I planned to sit quietly in my uncluttered meditation corner and not get up until I understood just why I still felt so cluttered.

CHAPTER FIVE

A Step Back

"It's always something."
—Gilda Radner

On January 2, the phone rang at what was—on a Sunday in our house—a ridiculously early hour. Yankel rolled over and went back to sleep; but the ring had the sharp, persistent tone of an urgent call, so I picked it up and tiptoed down to the kitchen.

It was our landlord calling—a very sweet and considerate man, but, like me, not a particularly succinct communicator. The conversation thus got off to somewhat of a meandering start.

"Happy New Year, Mrs. Dinnerstein."

"Happy New Year to you, Mr. Ziegler."

"How is your husband?"

"Very well, thank you. And your wife?"

"She's good. I'll tell her you asked."

"I hope you received the rent check on time. I mailed it over a week ago, but, you know, with the holiday rush. . . ."

"No, no, it's fine. It arrived on Friday. In fact, it was the last check I deposited this century. Can you believe we're in the midst of such a historic transition?"

"It's quite amazing," I agreed. I didn't have the heart to tell him it was still a year away. Besides, I was anxious to discover why he was calling.

"Ah," he continued, "my grandmother used to tell such wonderful stories about the events she remembered at the turn of the last century. Maybe one day I'll have some of my own to tell my grandchildren.

"And now, Mrs. Dinnerstein, I have good news and bad news. What would you rather hear first?"

"How about the good news. I'm the kind of person who likes to eat the dessert before the meal."

"And, much to my wife's displeasure, so am I. Well, in that case, here's the good news: When your lease is up next month, there will be no rent increase."

"Well, that's always nice to hear."

"But, unfortunately, there's some bad news as well. It looks as if we're going to be selling the house. . . . Mrs. Dinnerstein, are you still there?"

"Yes. . . . I think I am. . . . This is so sudden."

"Well, we didn't put it on the market yet. I wanted to tell you first. You know how the New Year is—it kind of gets you thinking about your life. So, my wife and I started talking about how much we would like to retire a bit early and enjoy some time together in the sunshine. And we don't want to be long-distance landlords, so we're going to sell the few properties we have in New York and head out to Arizona.

"But don't worry—it probably won't happen all that fast. And you can have as much time as you need—we'll put it in the contract. I'm so sorry if this is upsetting for you."

"It's fine, Mr. Ziegler," I said, trying to sound positive. "Just a moment of initial shock there. You've been wonderful—really—and, with a little luck, we'll all be moving on to greener pastures."

I hung up the phone, stood in silence for a moment, and then began to pound my fists on the kitchen counter, screaming, "No, no, no!—It can't be!—Not again!"

I tried to calm down long enough to brew some extra-strength coffee, but I couldn't stop pacing back and forth as I worked.

"How many times can the same thing happen to the same person?" I asked loudly, looking up at the kitchen ceiling. "Isn't there a law of odds or something?"

"Who are you talking to?" Yankel asked, walking into the kitchen and looking around. "I thought I heard shouting. Is everything okay?"

"Well, thank God, no one is dead or in the hospital, but I wouldn't exactly say everything is okay."

I poured a strong cup of coffee into his double-size Sunday mug, figuring he'd be needing it as soon as I broke the news to him.

"Mr. Ziegler called this morning to say 'Happy New Year' and 'By the way, I'm planning to sell the house.' Of course, he's such a sweet soul—he could barely get the words out of his mouth. Obviously, he felt terrible."

"Does this mean we have to move?" Yankel asked, trying to keep his voice steady.

"Unless the new owners are into communal living, I think it does."

He sat back in his chair, rolled his eyes dramatically, and—in his best 1950s William Bendix imitation—proclaimed, "What a revolting development this is!"

But even that well-delivered line—usually guaranteed to get a hardy laugh out of Baby Boomers—barely brought forth a smile from me this morning.

"When do we have to leave?" Yankel asked.

"Well, according to Mr. Ziegler, there's no real rush. They haven't even put the house on the market yet. But who wants to live with an eviction notice hanging over their heads?"

"I'm with you," Yankel said. "I think we should come up with a plan immediately. I'm going to head down to my cave right now and give it some thought. Why don't we meet back here for lunch? Hopefully, by then, one of us will have figured something out."

"Good idea," I agreed. "I'll get to work on it too."

We sounded so focused, so well-adjusted, so perfectly able to cope with adversity—while, in truth, both of us were teetering on the brink of total collapse, each holding it together only for the sake of the other.

As soon as I heard Yankel's footsteps on the stairs to his study, I leaned against the kitchen counter and took a deep breath. I couldn't sustain this upbeat tone much longer. I wanted nothing more than to lie down on the floor and have an undisturbed temper tantrum. But I knew that watching me come unglued would only loosen Yankel's grip; and this was definitely not the time for mass hysteria.

Still, the spectre of moving—even the mere mention of the word—came very close to overriding all other considerations. Moving was the black hole of my universe—the vortex that sucked all my time and energy into its core. Each move—and this would be our eighth in the thirteen years we were married—took at least a year from my life: the time spent looking for a new place, the packing, the moving, the painting, the unpacking, the settling in . . . I was beginning to feel lightheaded just thinking about it.

By the time I called Yidis, I was walking in manic circles around the kitchen table, and I could feel my eye beginning to twitch.

"This is a great opportunity," she said, after hearing my account of the morning's events.

"For what—a psychotic breakdown? Yidis, please, I'm in no mood for New Age aphorisms. This is *not* a great opportunity. This is a terrible disaster—and it's getting to be quite a tiresome one, coming as often as it does.

"I know, I know," I raged on, not giving her a chance to respond. "It's a gift from the universe; a perfect opening for self-growth. Well, I'm tired of all this growing. How about a little peace and quiet for a change? How about a little uneventful stability? Can't I develop my potential without changing my address every year?"

"Pesi, take it easy. Make yourself a cup of coffee. And make me one, too. I'll be there in five minutes."

I must have sounded pretty close to the edge because before I had a chance to change out of my nightgown, Yidis was knocking on the door. And a minute later, she was sitting at my kitchen table, looking very serious and business-like.

"Now, promise me you won't say a word until I finish making my point."

I promised.

"Okay, then, here goes. I think you should buy a house."

I looked at her as if she had just suggested that I go bungee jumping over the Atlantic. She held up her index finger to remind me of my promise.

"Let me explain. It's not that I think you need to own a house. What I think you need to own is peace of mind. If you buy a house, you'll never have to move again unless you really want to. What you'll be buying, in essence, is control over your own life. Can you see my point?"

I was silent for a moment.

"I think I can. But, Yidis, we did have our own home before we moved to Brooklyn. Several times, in fact—in Buffalo and in the Hudson Valley. And we had to move anyway because Yankel got transferred twice, and then he changed jobs."

"But, from what you've told me, that's not likely to happen again. And even if it does, you're not going to leave Brooklyn. Since you've come here, it seems that the only reason you've moved around so much is because of landlord issues. Isn't that true?"

"Yes," I agreed. "Our first landlord died, and our second landlord raised the rent so high that we couldn't possibly afford to stay. And now this."

"But if you had your own home, you would never have to worry about moving again."

"You're right. But how can that possibly happen? We have little savings, marginal credit, and no well-to-do relatives."

"Ah, but you have a Holy Sister with an old friend in real estate. Why don't you put up some fresh coffee, and I'll go call her from the living room."

By the time I ground the beans and heated the milk, Yidis was back with some rather amazing news.

"My friend says that it shouldn't be a problem. You'll almost certainly qualify for an F.H.A. mortgage, which means you can put very little money down and roll just about everything else into the monthly payments. She suggested that you start looking immediately—prices seem to be going up every day—and I totally agree."

And so it was that we entered the New Year thinking only of our impending move. Suddenly, I had no time to worry about clutter—inner, outer, or otherwise. All I could focus on now was finding a new home, getting a mortgage, looking for an honest and competent contractor—an oxymoron if ever there were one—and beginning the dreaded—but, by now, familiar—task of packing.

So much for my well-planned agenda of 2000 AD.

$\mathcal{F}$inding a new home turned out to be the easiest part of the whole process. Since there wasn't a whole lot to look at in our very limited price range, we quickly decided upon an old row house in need of major renovation, but very light and airy and charming. We got an FHA loan, rolled the cost of the upcoming work into the mortgage, and started packing.

It wasn't until we were in the throes of renovation that we began to hear all the horror stories about contractors who deserved their own circle in hell. It soon became apparent that we had hired one of them. However, by the time we realized just how incompetent and ethically challenged the man really was, we were too far into the project to stop and too overwhelmed to deal with all the FHA paperwork that a change in contractor would entail.

For the first six months—the project was supposed to take three—we were still living in our old home, so the inconvenience was minimal. However, once Mr. Ziegler sold the house and we had to leave, things heated up pretty quickly.

All of our furniture and most of our personal belongings landed in a storage facility several miles away because the renovation was still going on. And on and on and on. We lived in this state of chaos—amid exposed beams and pipes, vibrating drills, and circling plumes of dust—for another six months. We slept in the basement on air mattresses, ate dinner at a card table on two folding chairs, and called to each other through holes in the wall. If we hadn't had electricity—and, for long stretches, we didn't—our lives would have been indistinguishable from those of our eighteenth century forebears.

By the time the last worker carried the last piece of sheetrock out the door, the world had already moved into 2001—and into the real Twenty First Century and Third Millennium.

At first, I was elated. I was finally reunited with all of my possessions under one roof—and the roof belonged to me, not to some landlord who might decide at any moment to remove it. But, as I looked around, I realized that, in many ways, I was right back where I had started from over two years ago. I was surrounded by things. The boxes I had neatly packed and labeled were in total disarray after a year of being rifled through in the storage unit every time we couldn't find a can opener or pair of scissors. All of our clothing had to be rewashed; the dishes were piled on every surface in my still-too-small kitchen; there were stacks of books from one end of the house to the other; and all the electrical cords and wires that had become separated from their objects were lying on the floor in a tangled heap. I could feel myself sinking rapidly.

But I didn't succumb. Instead, I called the Holy Sisters—one by one—and asked each of them for advice. I wanted to see the situation from every possible angle.

Surprisingly—or maybe not—they all said pretty much the same thing: You're not back where you started from. Everyone's house looks like this after a move, and especially a move following a yearlong renovation. You're doing fine. Don't count the miles to the finish line; just keep going in that direction. We're all behind you, and soon we'll all be celebrating alongside you.

Yidis, however, had a slightly different perspective.

"The real measure of growth," she said "is when you find yourself in a familiar situation, but you respond in a different way. So, this is a perfect test. You've been here before—in fact, many times before—but, now, you have a deeper level of awareness and a new set of tools. Let's see what you can do with all of it."

Once she framed it that way, I felt strongly motivated to succeed. It would, to some extent, redeem this lost year and hopefully inspire me to return to my work on The Project. Okay, it would be a year late in coming; but, then, so was the new century.

I began immediately—rearranging furniture; unpacking; sorting; organizing; filling closets and cabinets, shelves and drawers; trying to get rid of whatever I had allowed to slip through and pile up during the move. When I needed a little creative stimulation, I hung pictures and curtains and put plants on every windowsill and ceiling hook. And I tried to approach the work with joy and enthusiasm—which, as Yidis continued to point out, was a major part of the test.

Of course, it was a monumental job; and as devoted as I was to completing it, I still had to find the time. Often, that meant only a moment here or there; but, little by little, the moments began to add up. In the end, the work spilled over into the summer months for the third year in a row, but I was more than willing to make whatever sacrifice was necessary to restore things to order before the fall semester began.

By the time the Holy Sisters came back from their summer vacation, I was ready to invite them to a housewarming party in honor of my newly renovated home. But it occurred to me that we had just done that last year—or was it the year before?

"This is, unfortunately, becoming an annual event," I commented. "Some people have birthdays or anniversary parties—I seem to be celebrating a newly organized house once a year."

"Well, making order is always cause for celebration," Etta said. "No matter how many times you do it." And, with that, everyone drank a toast to my latest success.

As the semester got underway, I was feeling so on top of things that I began to think about getting out the manuscript that Yitta had discovered after our Labor Day celebration two years ago. With all the upheaval of recent times, it had remained untouched— and largely forgotten—since then.

"I'll call Yitta first thing in the morning and tell her the good news," I thought, as I got into bed. Then, not wanting to forget, I put a note on my night table calendar, my mind vaguely registering the fact that it was Monday, September 10, 2001.

I'm not certain just when everything began to unravel, but I vaguely recall the ends starting to fray almost immediately. School was closed for several weeks because lower Manhattan was virtually impassable; and the College was right in the thick of it, less than a mile from the World Trade Center.

The first sign that I was not reacting normally was the way I related to time during this unexpected reprieve from work. I did virtually nothing—not nothing as in relaxed vacation, but nothing as in catatonic stupor. However, since the entire nation was in a state of shock and mourning, my behavior did not seem all that strange. At least not at the beginning.

But by the end of November, it was becoming obvious to anyone who was paying attention that something was not quite right with me. And the Holy Sisters were definitely paying attention.

The day after Thanksgiving, a delegation stopped by for an unannounced visit.

"We're really worried about you, Pesi," Laurie said, handing me a plate of chocolate chip cookies. "I stopped by several times, but no one answered when I knocked."

"You haven't returned my phone calls for weeks," Myriam said. "That's so not like you."

Yidis and Yitta and Etta were there as well. We had managed to stay in touch with each other during this period; but, even with them, my contact of late had been sporadic and mostly by telephone.

We were having this conversation in the vestibule of my house, which was barely large enough for three people. After a minute or two, I had no choice but to invite them in. I braced myself and waited for their reaction.

They hadn't been here since my housewarming party in August, and they were obviously not prepared for the sight that awaited them. The beautiful, well-ordered home they had oohed and aahed over then had been transformed into a scene straight out of Armageddon.

There was a moment of silence, followed by several sharply inhaled breaths.

"Pesi, are you . . . depressed . . . or . . . something?" Yitta asked, barely able to form the question.

Looking around, I could well understand her reaction. It would likely be the response of any normal person entering the ruins in which we were standing.

"No, not really," I answered honestly. "I'm not depressed, but I'm obviously not okay either."

I couldn't find seven clean mugs in the kitchen, and I was all out of paperware, so I served everyone coffee and tea in irritatingly small styrofoam cups that had to be refilled several times. I pushed aside the piles of paper on the dining room table and removed the stacks of newspaper from the chairs. Thank God for Laurie's cookies—they added the only touch of civilized dining to the experience.

"So," Myriam asked, "what do you suppose all of this means?"

"I'm not really sure," I said. "But I think I'm having an extended reaction to the events of September 11."

"Well, you've certainly done a great job of re-creating Ground Zero here," Yidis observed. "The place definitely looks like a bomb hit it."

And, indeed, it did. In fact, that was exactly how it felt as well. Everything seemed to have exploded in an instant, shattering my fragile order and stability, and tossing my home once again into a state of spiraling chaos.

"Why don't we take a few minutes to reflect on this," Etta suggested. "Each of us was deeply affected by what happened on 9/11, and I think we would all benefit from writing about how our lives have changed since then. Does ten minutes seem like enough time?"

Everyone nodded, but at the end of the ten minutes, no one was finished, so we agreed to keep going for another ten. This was obviously an issue that we all needed to process on a much deeper level than any of us yet had. In fact, it hit such a sensitive nerve that we agreed to continue writing at home and meet the following week to share our thoughts.

As soon as everyone was gone, I went to the kitchen table and continued to write. In fact, I couldn't get myself to stop. It was all I did—and all I wanted to do—for the rest of the Thanksgiving weekend and for the entire week that followed. And for the first time since September 11, I could feel the fog beginning to lift and my forgotten thoughts and feelings coming back into focus.

But why had the mess returned? I kept asking myself. Was it simply because, after the trauma of 9/11, I was unable to muster the effort to keep it at bay? Or did the clutter itself provide something that I needed—now, perhaps, more than ever?

Suddenly the desire for an answer became overpowering.

"I'm looking for a ruthlessly honest therapy session," I said to Etta's voice mail. "Any idea where I might find one?"

She called me back immediately.

"Ruthless is not my preferred style," she said, "and I know it's not yours either. I usually resort to it only with my most desperate clients."

"Well, you saw my house," I reminded her. "Wouldn't you say I qualify?"

"I hate to think of you that way," she replied, "but you're probably right. Are you free to come over now?"

Twenty minutes later, Etta and I were sitting in her office—which had recently been repainted a different and even more beautiful shade of peach—trying to get to the heart of my problem.

"Let's try a little exercise," Etta said. "I'll start a sentence, and you complete it with the first word or phrase that immediately comes to mind. Then, repeat it with a different ending four more times. Don't worry if they seem to contradict each other—that's the whole idea. But it's got to be spontaneous—no thinking or censoring."

"Let's begin with an easy one: My first cup of coffee in the morning makes me feel . . . "

I repeated the sentence, each time ending with a different word: " . . . awake . . . alive . . . happy . . . sleep-deprived . . . addicted."

"See how revealing it can be?" Etta said. "The important thing is not to try and direct the answers. As much as possible, just let them come from your subconscious."

She started off with a few neutral statements and then gradually came around to the more provocative ones:

"Clutter makes me feel . . ."

" . . . out of control . . . suffocated . . . strangled . . . comfortable . . . protected."

"Living in an orderly and uncluttered environment gives me . . . "

" . . . peace of mind . . . a positive self-image . . . a sense of well being . . . the feeling that I don't really belong here . . . no place to hide."

"Right after 9/11, I . . ."

" . . . had nightmares every night . . . lived in terror of the next attack . . . was afraid to cross the Brooklyn Bridge or the Battery

Tunnel to go to work . . . stopped cleaning my house . . . watched the piles return."

"Now, when I'm in my own home, I feel . . . safe again . . . overwhelmed by the new mess . . . embarrassed . . . isolated . . . like I want to do nothing but write."

Etta sat silently making notes on index cards for a few minutes, while I admired her freshly painted peach walls, noting that the color was close enough to the previous one to provide the comfort of the familiar to her clients, while still creating a space that felt new and exciting.

"I want to read a few of your answers back to you," Etta said, sliding her glasses down the bridge of her nose and looking over the tops at me. "When you put the statements together, I think you'll find an interesting pattern emerging. Listen to this," she continued, sliding the glasses back up and reading from her notes: "Clutter makes me feel comfortable and protected. Living an orderly life gives me no place to hide. After 9/11, I stopped cleaning my house and watched the piles return. Now, I feel overwhelmed but safe again."

"That *is* interesting," I said, leaning forward in my chair. "Do you think I've brought this mess back in my life because it provides me with an escape from all these uncomfortable feelings?"

"Yes," Etta said. "Actually, I do. On September 10—no doubt, a rare moment in your life— you were living virtually clutter-free; and it was a wonderful, liberated feeling. But when September 11 came around, you were left standing naked with no place to run. There were no more cushions of clutter, no endless busywork to lose yourself in, no piles of mess to crawl behind. It was just you— exposed and vulnerable—and all those terrifying feelings. Either you had to allow yourself to experience them or re-create a mess in which to hide. Unfortunately, you chose the mess."

"I guess I did," I had to admit, "but I don't have to choose it again. I mean, I can decide right now to make a different choice."

"Absolutely," Etta said. "That's what therapy is all about."

"Okay," I said. "Can we meet again in a few days?"

"Of course," Etta said. "As often as you want. What did you have in mind?"

"Well, since you and the Holy Sisters dropped in on me last week, I've been writing nonstop. Now, I'd like to think about what you just said and write about that, too. But before I read it to everyone next week, I want to read some of it to you privately and get your feedback."

"That sounds like a great idea," Etta said. "Why don't you call me as soon as you finish writing, and we'll set something up?"

As I was leaving the room, I suddenly turned back—doorknob therapy, Yankel called it—and asked Etta, "Do you really think there's hope for me? I mean, am I going to be like one of those people on a perpetual dieting roller coaster who gets fat and thin and then fat again? I'm starting to feel like the cluttered version of that—messy and then neat and then messy and then neat. . . . "

"Pesi," Etta said, putting her arm around me, "I have total faith in you. And, right now, the switch to that roller coaster is the pen in your hand. If you can write yourself into a place of deeper understanding, I think you'll find a way to control the ride."

I ran home and immediately pushed the dirty dishes on the kitchen table to one side. More motivated than ever, I reached for my notebook, determined to penetrate the mess that surrounded me. But the words were no longer coming, as if someone had accidentally tripped the cutoff switch.

In place of the thoughts and feelings that had been flowing so effortlessly onto the page for the past several days, there was now nothing but a dull buzzing in my brain, as my mind started to tick off all the things I should have been doing instead of trying to write: making dinner; returning phone calls; watering the plants; correcting homework; attacking my new accumulation of clutter . . . and the list of Things in Need of Immediate Attention by a Responsible Adult went on and on. I hated that guilt-inducing voice more than any of the other noisemakers in my head—all of which seemed to be activated by my desire for quiet reflection.

Rather than supporting my attempts at silence and self-awareness, these inner voices always seemed determined to direct my attention outward. I used to think of them as the voices of my conscience, come to keep me dutifully on track; but I had since begun to regard them as little more than my personal Demons of Distraction—here for the sole purpose of deflecting me from my higher goals.

Instead of trying to negotiate with them in order to reclaim my time—"I promise I'll only meditate for ten minutes and then get back to work"; "Just one more paragraph before I do the dishes"—I decided to finally stand my ground and refuse to surrender.

I sat back down at the kitchen table, and on a fresh piece of paper I wrote the title, "Demons of Distraction and the Journey That Never Was." And for the next two days, no matter how much guilt or shame they tried to provoke, I said no to their demands. Instead, I kept writing—stopping only to prepare food (which I ate with a fork in one hand and my pen in the other), sleep a few hours, and show up to teach my classes.

As soon as I finished the essay, I called Etta; and, that evening, on the way home from work, I stopped at her house to read to her what I had written.

"Etta," I said, as we climbed the stairs to her office, "I've come to the conclusion that of all the relationships I've ever had in my life—including marriage—the most complicated one, by far, is the relationship I have with my clutter. And the more I write about it, the more complicated it seems to get. But I feel like I'm finally beginning to crack the code."

"That's very exciting," she said, settling into her chair. "Tell me more."

I took out my notebook and began to read:

"I've always loved the concept of a journey; and, for most of my adult life, I believed I was on one—a journey of discovery, a quest for truth, a path leading to something beyond myself.

"Now, however, I can see that what I've been engaged in most of these years was really more of a battle for control with my own sweet-talking demons. And rather than scaling the heights of spiritual consciousness, I'm afraid I've been spending most of my time simply trying to survive in the trenches.

"At first glance, my tempters might appear relatively benign. After all, they do not entice me to drink, drug, overeat (except occasionally in the presence of chocolate), gamble, or indulge in illicit affairs. All they do—these Demons of Distraction—is encourage me to fill my life with more than it can possibly hold. And, in the process of trying to fit all of this physical and mental clutter into my narrow world of time and space, I've lost the thread of my journey.

My search for meaning has been diverted over and over again by the constant struggle to deal with the by-products of my own excess.

"Yet, the voices persist; and, despite my best intentions, I usually succumb.

"'More, more . . . ,' they whisper in my ear, as I mindlessly overbuy, overbook, and persistently overextend myself. 'The universe is constantly expanding, and there's so much more out there waiting for you. . . .'

"However, what is clearly missing in this universe of infinite expansion is a small empty space in which to meet myself, unencumbered and alone. Not me doing or possessing or creating. Not me with my projects, my errands, my endless lists. Me, in silence, simply being.

"This is the experience that the seekers of my generation have meditated, hiked across the Himalayas, and sat by the ocean at sunrise to achieve: that moment of perfect stillness in which we can connect to ourselves and to the Source of all creation. It is also the experience that we have cluttered our lives and distracted our minds and bodies to avoid, for it is here, in this quiet, unfilled moment, that our desire to break free slams into our final wall of resistance.

"Yet, most of us, unable to bear the distance or the intimacy, the darkness or the light, choose, instead, to simply fill the space. We fill it with objects and activities. With complication and obsession. With wine and brownies and late-night TV. With consuming relationships and endless conversation. They all succeed well in blocking the way.

"I myself prefer piles. Piles of paper rising off my desk and piles of laundry sitting on the floor; piles of boxes in every corner waiting to be packed or unpacked; piles of things I don't know where to put or how to manage with or how to manage without. Piles that protect me from life and prevent me from living.

"They give me something to park in the middle of every landscape, a few notes of static to disrupt each symphony, so that no moment can ever be completely mine without first tithing a few seconds of guilt to the piles that lie in waiting.

"These piles provide my volume control on life. When the colors become too bright, the connections too deep, the truth too starkly naked, the piles materialize in my mind and instantly deflect my attention. You have work to be done, they remind me. There's a mess looming somewhere. . . .

"Thus, the wedge is driven, and I'm no longer one with the experience. The intensity dial has just been lowered a few notches to a more manageable level of less-than-total involvement, and everything is now safely diffused. My pain has a cushion, and my passion, a slow leak. Life has, once again, been neutralized and restored to a pleasantly dull finish.

"But that well-padded, dimly lit world no longer calls to me. I want to experience the full measure of joy and beauty and intimacy—and, on occasion, even darkness—that human existence has to offer, with no veils or filters to shield me.

"And that, I now realize, will probably never happen until I confront my Demons of Distraction, standing guard at the exit gate to make certain that I'm too preoccupied to ever contemplate escape. I want to know how they've managed to keep me in this cluttered prison cell all these years, convinced that I am free; how they can take me so far from myself and make me believe that I'm home. And, perhaps, with understanding, their power will finally be diminished; and the long-delayed journey—to myself, to freedom, to God—can begin to move forward at last."

"Pesi," Etta said when I put down the notebook and looked up at her, "I think your roller coaster will soon be making its last trip—and I have a feeling your Demons of Distraction will be riding in the back seat."

When the Holy Sisters got together a few days later, we all seemed a bit out of sorts, obviously unsettled by last week's writing exercise. Apparently, none of us had realized just how deeply we were affected by the events of September 11. And as psychologically aware as the Holy Sisters generally were, most of us had nevertheless turned to our unhealthiest behaviors for comfort.

"This is beginning to sound like a Twelve Step Meeting," Etta commented, as we went around the room, telling our tales of overeating, out-of-control shopping, compulsive cleaning, manic exercising, obsessive reading of romance novels, and, of course, my own descent into chaos and clutter.

When it came my turn, I read an abridged version of what I had shared with Etta the other night and added the following observations:

"Just yesterday, the president raised the national terror alert from yellow to orange, leaving only red between us and the unthinkable. At a time like this, my struggles with dirty laundry and mounting paperwork seem laughable. And the fact that it's gotten worse—that my piles have grown higher and my disorder spread farther—makes me feel even more foolish. Is this how I cope with a world-threatening crisis—by hiding behind a wall of clutter?

"Yet, what am I to do? What are any of us to do? We're all seeking shelter from the storm; and whatever has given us comfort in the past is, naturally, what we turn to first. In my case, that happens to be the warm embrace of my own mess.

"After 9/11, clarity—the goal I've always claimed to be pursuing—was the last thing I wanted. Cool, sharp-edged clarity offered me no solace. I was in the market for something softer, more gentle, more soothing—and, of course, I found just what I was looking for in the enveloping fog of my clutter. It was the ultimate distraction; the perfect escape.

"Now, however, I feel ready to move on. The problem is, on to what? The world is every bit as terrifying and unpredictable today as it was on September 11—just a bit more familiar.

"The entire planet, it seems, has gone mad; and there doesn't appear to be a whole lot I or anyone else can do about it. Of course, we can easily nurture the illusion that we're doing something; but, in truth, most of our efforts probably fall somewhere between ineffective and ridiculous.

"It reminds me of those shelter drills we endured in elementary school during the Cold War years: 'Everyone under your desks at the sound of the siren, and don't forget to cover your head with your hands.' Even in the third grade, we raised a skeptical eyebrow. Why were we doing this? To shield us from nuclear fallout? To hide from the invading Russians? To protect us in case the building collapsed in an atomic explosion? No one seemed able to explain the point of it all. But, perhaps, taking an action—any action—was simply its own point. To do something fed our fantasy of being in control—even if an eight year old could see that what we were doing bordered on the absurd.

"Nevertheless, it seems to be hardwired into our human nature to take an action—no matter how small or insignificant or utterly irrational. And now that the initial shock and horror of 9/11 have passed, I've been trying to decide what my next action in our newly destabilized world should be.

"As I sat here thinking and writing, an old folk tale that I heard many years ago came to mind. . . .

"There once lived a young man who wanted only to make the world a better place. He had no desire for wealth or glory, but only to serve others by spreading the light of truth.

"At the age of twenty, he set out by foot to find enlightenment and share it with the world. He traveled from village to town and from town to village, seeking wisdom and passing it on to everyone he met. He did so for ten years, but then realized that the world was simply too large a place to be transformed by one man.

"And, so, at thirty, he narrowed the focus to his own land and tried only to educate his fellow countrymen and encourage them to follow a spiritual path. Unfortunately, that was also beyond his reach.

"As he approached forty, he decided to concentrate all of his energy upon changing the consciousness of his own village, where his family had lived for many generations. Yet, even here, he had little impact upon anyone.

"By the time he entered his fiftieth year, he began to feel that if he could simply alter the lives of a few of his close friends, his mission would be fulfilled. However, once again, he met with no success.

"At sixty, he drew an even smaller circle and tried only to influence his own children and grandchildren, but none of them were interested in following in his ways.

"At seventy, he turned to his devoted wife of many years and shared with her his deepest insights. She listened attentively but, in the end, she, too, remained the same as she had always been.

"Sadly, the wise man concluded that he had spent his entire life traveling in the wrong direction. Finally, at the age of eighty, he reversed course and focused on changing himself, for he now understood that only by changing himself could he begin to change the world.

"And that's pretty much the way I'm looking at the situation today. It all feels so surreal and so far beyond my reach, beyond even the reach of my imagination—international terror cells headed by bearded men in long robes, threatening to release medieval plagues and biological poisons into my subway system and my water supply. What can I possibly do about any of this from my little corner of the universe here in Brooklyn?

"Well, in the end, I'm doing the only thing I can that gives me any control over my life and the world around me. I'm filing my papers and folding my clothes. I'm returning my phone calls and sweeping my floor. I'm doing whatever it takes to bring order and harmony to my life and hoping that this order and harmony will somehow spread to the people around me—and maybe even ripple its way across the ocean to some remote cave in Afghanistan."

$\mathcal{I}$ spent the first two weeks of December trying to organize my latest wave of clutter—which, thankfully, turned out to be nowhere near the monumental task I had anticipated. Most of the new mess was on the surface, and it didn't really take all that much work to restore everything to the relatively neat and orderly state it had been in before my 9/11 setback.

And just in time, too. My birthday was coming around once again, and that always filled me with a renewed desire to get my life back on track.

The following week, Yidis, Yitta, Etta, and I made a plan to meet for brunch at Café K. Many of our dates were loose and spontaneous, but this was not one of them. With the semester ending and the holidays coming, life was more hectic than usual for all of us; and it was no simple matter to find two hours when each of us could manage to get away.

"We'll meet at 11:00 AM sharp," we agreed. "Everyone is on a tight schedule, so let's all try to be on time."

And I did try. I tried extremely hard.

I laid out my clothing the night before; got my exams ready to bring to school, so I could go straight to work afterward; packed dinner and snacks for the evening ahead; and even made certain that my keys and my gloves were sitting on the dining room table waiting for me. I intended to leave my house by 10:30 so that I could make the nine-minute walk to Café K with plenty of time to spare. I wanted to be there early enough to greet Etta—who was usually the first to arrive—as she walked through the door.

Now, with such meticulous planning, what could possibly have caused me to arrive at 11:40? I asked myself that question over and over again as I ran breathlessly down Avenue K. Everything had been moving along so smoothly—until, all of a sudden, it wasn't.

One minute, it was 10:00, and everything was right on schedule; and, then, the next thing I knew, it was 11:30, and I was really late—as if some giant cosmic vacuum cleaner had suddenly sucked ninety minutes out of my earthly allotment of time.

It's true that I got a few unexpected phone calls, and a neighbor stopped by to collect money for a family of poor orphans in the community, and I cut my finger peeling an apple and had to search all over the house for Neosporin and a Band-Aid—but could all that have taken an hour and a half?

In any case, I found myself once again in dramatic—but unsuccessful—pursuit of time, like a Keystone Cop chasing the village hooligans down Main Street. And it's not like I have a casual attitude toward the subject. I'm certainly not one of those latecomers who saunters nonchalantly into a room, totally oblivious to the fact that everyone there is yawning and tapping their feet and growing more impatient by the moment. If anything, my attitude is the complete opposite. I come running in, huffing and puffing, apologizing profusely, and feeling genuinely contrite for having been so inconsiderate. Nevertheless, the effect is exactly the same: Everyone is still sitting around waiting for me.

At least in this case, Yidis and Yitta and Etta were all enjoying each other's company in a warm and pleasant café (not that anyone would ever risk meeting me on a chilly street corner); but, still, I felt terrible.

"I'm so sorry," I said, before I even sat down. "Please forgive me."

"Of course," they said. "But what happened?"

"I don't know," I answered honestly. "I really have no idea what went wrong. But, please, keep talking. I'll go look for the waitress."

When I returned with my cappuccino and muffin, everyone stopped and asked me again: "What happened?"

Usually, there was a string of mishaps to relate—lost keys, a dead battery, my forgotten lunch, a missing shoe. . . . Today, however, there was no tale to tell. Where those ninety minutes had disappeared to would apparently remain forever an unsolved mystery.

But as I was giving my order to the waitress—who looked like she had consumed a few croissants too many—I suddenly remembered my old friend Patt, who also had that well-rounded look. And although I hadn't seen Patt in close to thirty years, and she really had nothing to do with what happened today, as soon as I thought of her, everything started to fall into place.

"I'm not sure just why I was late this morning," I said to the Holy Sisters, "but I have a feeling it's connected to an old friend of mine.

"Patt," I explained, "was my closest and most overweight friend in junior high school. That's Patt with two t's, as she always reminded us. Compared to your average seventh grader, she was positively voluptuous—although I'm sure she would have been considered well-endowed in any setting.

"But Patt was not at all pleased about this and was even more unhappy about the extra pounds she carried with her in less desirable locations, especially when the boys in our class began referring to her as Fatt Patt with four t's. So, she did what most overweight women did in those days—she purchased an extra-large girdle. Now, the problem with girdles is that, like everything else in the universe, they pretty much conform to Newton's Third Law of Physics—or is it his Second?—well, whatever. Anyway, loosely translated, Newton's law states that for every bit of fat you try to constrain, an equal bit of fat will pop out someplace else.

"Well, the girdle succeeded in flattening Patt's stomach, but it pushed the unwanted fat up to her midriff, where her long line bra took over and moved it along. In the end, with no place left to go, the rising fat finally popped out between the two D cups of her bra and created what appeared to be a third breast. Poor Patt. It just kept getting worse."

Suddenly, we all began to laugh, as if we were watching a video of Patt's rising cleavage, and the moment of climactic eruption had just appeared on the scene. A few minutes earlier, I had noticed out of the corner of my eye that the two women at the table next to us had stopped speaking and were listening to our conversation—for which you could hardly blame them, considering how close the tables were—so, I now turned to include them in our group laugh, which made the moment feel even more like it was taking place in my junior high school locker room.

"Of course," I continued, "you may be wondering what any of this could possibly have to do with the fact that I arrived forty minutes late today, but I really think there's a connection here. Patt's dilemma seems to represent my own. My clutter, like her fat, is constantly being compressed here and concealed there and shunted from one spot to another—but, in the end, it always manages to pop out someplace, usually where it's least desired and most inappropriate.

"Now that I've removed most of my clutter from the physical world, it seems to have taken up residence in the world of time. It's as if I've traded an overcrowded house for an overbooked calendar. So, instead of having too many things to put away and no place to put them, I now find myself with too much to do and no time to do it. But, one way or another, it looks like that pound of fat is here to stay.

"And that, I believe, is why I was late today and why there's a very good chance I might be late again tomorrow."

After this long and winding description of my most recent insight, I finally took my first sip of cappuccino, which I always drink as hot as humanly possible. Now, however, it was barely tepid; and I was forced to admit to myself that I had been paying no attention whatsoever to how long I was speaking.

I took this latest victim of my time blackout and quietly poured it into a nearby potted plant, which I could swear perked up at the caffeine infusion. *Would I ever develop a normal awareness of the passage of time?* I wondered, as I watched the cold coffee soak into the soil. *Would I ever get a grip on my life?*

When I looked up, there was a strawberry shortcake sitting on the table with fifty-three candles burning. Then, the waitress brought me a fresh cup of steaming cappuccino, which I made certain to drink immediately. *You know,* I thought to myself, as everyone—including the waitress and the two women at the next table—joined together to sing "Happy Birthday" to me, *this might turn out to be a pretty good year after all.*

*Y*idis knocked on my front door early the following morning, as Yankel was leaving and I was still sitting at the kitchen table in my bathrobe.

"I couldn't wait," she explained. "I have something really exciting to show you."

She handed me a large manila envelope.

"This," she said, "is your birthday present—and the beginning of your new life."

In large block letters, the envelope said TWELVE STEP LITERATURE.

"But Yidis," I immediately protested, "this is for addicts. What does it have to do with me? I'm not an alcoholic or a drug abuser. I may have a tendency to accumulate clutter, but I'm not addicted to it."

"Just look at the material," she said. "And try to keep an open mind."

I unfastened the envelope and removed a packet of multi-colored pamphlets, each with a different title and a heading that said Clutterers Anonymous (CLA).

"I've never heard of Clutterers Anonymous before," I said, flipping through the pamphlets: Recovery from Cluttering; Declutter Your Mind; Decluttering Resentment. It all sounded pretty repetitious to me.

"I haven't heard of it either," Yidis said. "Apparently, it's not one of the better-known Twelve Step Programs; but, based on what I've read here, it sounds like just what you need. One of my clients told me about it and brought me these pamphlets. I read them last night, and I was really impressed. I think it could change your life."

"How?" I asked, curiosity overriding my skepticism.

"Well, it takes your process to the next level. I mean, we've been saying for years that we want to understand why you keep re-creating clutter. I know you've learned a lot about the positive things that attract you to it and the negative habits that keep you trapped there and even some of the deeper reasons why you can't seem to move on; but I don't feel that we've really gotten to the darker side of it—you know, where your desire for abundance might just border on addiction."

"I'm not sure I understand," I said, wondering whether I was really confused or just being resistant. "But what do you think I should do?"

"I think you should read the literature and go to a meeting."

"Go to a meeting? By myself?"

"You don't have to speak if you don't want to. You can just go and listen and drink a cup of coffee. They always have coffee at these meetings."

"Well, that's good to know. But what do they do there besides drink coffee?"

"They generally have a speaker, and, then, they go around the room and everyone who wants to has an opportunity to share. My client said that at the meeting she usually attends, they begin by placing a large black garbage bag in the center of the room, and everyone deposits something they want to get rid of. But don't let that mislead you. The primary purpose of Clutterers Anonymous—and they tell you this right on the first page of the Welcome Pamphlet— is not to learn how to be more organized or productive, but to understand what your clutter is about on an inner level and how it's connected to a Higher Power.

"Pesita, I really believe it's the next step on your journey. You have all these amazing insights, but they don't hold together. The Program will give you a structure and a philosophy; and it will connect you to a community of fellow clutterers.

"And with the help of the people you'll meet—and, of course, with the support of the Holy Sisters—this could be the beginning of a whole new chapter of your life. And what better time to start than your birthday and the New Year?"

"Okay," I agreed. "I'll do it. I'm not totally convinced, but I'll give it a try. Can you get the information for me?"

"Here," Yidis said, handing me a list of meeting times and locations. "I already did. I knew you'd say yes."

"Because you know that, in the end, I always follow your advice?"

"No, because I believe that, in the end, your desire for truth always wins out."

CHAPTER SIX

Another First Step

"Denial ain't just a river in Egypt."
—Mark Twain

After several weeks of stalling, I finally walked into my first meeting of Clutterers Anonymous five minutes after it began. It was one of the few times in my life that I actually arrived somewhere late by design. I had decided—with considerable reluctance—that I would go to the meeting, but only to the meeting. I wasn't interested in engaging in conversation with anyone before or after.

I wasn't sure just why I was feeling so much resistance, but I couldn't seem to shake the feeling. Part of it, no doubt, was my extreme discomfort with the concept of clutter as an addiction. I liked to think of my relationship with clutter as my own freely chosen and personal way of relating to the world. Dysfunctional, quirky, overwhelming at times—but mine. Seeing the relationship as a compulsive force over which I had no control was too unsettling a prospect to consider.

My arrival time was perfect. The speaker was just beginning, so I was able to slide into my seat without interaction. All I had to do for the next twenty minutes, I assured myself, was sit back and listen.

"Hi. My name is Lisa Marie," the speaker began. "And I'm a grateful member of Clutterers Anonymous."

"Hi, Lisa Marie," everyone responded in perfect unison, like the well-rehearsed chorus in an ancient Greek drama.

Lisa Marie took a sip of coffee from her styrofoam cup, leaving a bright red outline of her lips on the rim. Her nails were the same shade of red, and so were her sling-back heels. Her dress was too tight, her hoop earrings too large and shiny, and her heavily-applied mascara a throwback to another era. Yet, there was something wise and self-contained in her demeanor that stood in stark contrast to her overstated appearance; and it definitely intrigued me.

"It feels really good to be here," she said slowly and deliberately, as if she were taking a moment to actually experience the feeling. "I've been in Program for many years, but today is the first time I've ever been the main speaker at a CLA meeting. And it's definitely where I need to be right now.

"I want to begin by telling you about my name because it really says it all. My mother named me Lisa Marie not because she particularly liked the name, but because she was a devoted Elvis Presley fan, and he had named his daughter Lisa Marie. Even as a kid, it made no sense to me. My mother doesn't name me after an accomplished person or a family friend. She doesn't even name me after a famous star. She names me after a star's unknown daughter. Like that's her highest aspiration for me.

"And that pretty much sums up my childhood. Humble beginnings and low expectations all the way.

"But, thank God, I was so screwed up that I found my way to the Program at a very early age. I started in OA [Overeaters Anonymous] when I was still in my teens. And since then, I've moved on to margaritas, marijuana, nicotine, sleeping pills, and now clutter. But sugar is still my drug of choice.

"Then, one day, about a year ago, I'm rushing to get to a meeting, and I bump into an old friend of mine. I mean really bump into her, like I almost knocked the poor girl over.

'Hey, Lisa Marie,' she says, 'where's the fire?'

'I'm late for a meeting,' I tell her.

'You mean one of those Twelve Step meetings you're always running off to?' she asks; and I nod yes. 'You want to know what I think?'

"Actually, I don't; but she goes ahead and tells me anyway.

'Well, personally, I think you're addicted to those meetings.'

"Whoa. That stopped me dead in my tracks. Not because it was really true, but because it definitely touched upon something that was. Here I am, late as usual, and running, running, running to get to a meeting. And what does my Higher power do? He arranges for me to hear that what I really need is a meeting for my addiction to running to meetings."

Everyone began to laugh—one of those knowing laughs whose subtext reads, "If you really get this joke, you're part of the club." I, of course, not being part of the club, understood the humor only on the most superficial level; but, even on that level, I had to admit it was pretty funny.

"Of course," Lisa Marie continued, "I immediately realized that it's not the meetings I'm addicted to—it's the running. Which, I can now see, is just another way of creating clutter in my life. And that's why I ran to this meeting today."

Everyone laughed again, and, this time, I joined in a little less self-consciously.

"Well, anyway, the next day, I called my sponsor and told her about the conversation.

"'Can I come over now to talk about it with you?' she asked.

"'Why don't we meet at Starbuck's?' I suggested.

"'I think I'd rather come to your house, if that's okay with you,' she said. Which is her polite way of insisting that she wants to finally see my place.

"So, an hour later, she's walking through the front door of my tiny one-bedroom apartment, and I'm sitting on the couch, chain smoking my way through the first pack of cigarettes I've touched in six months.

"Since I moved to this apartment two years ago—right after my ex and I broke up—I hadn't invited anyone in. It was like my private sanctuary, and I wanted to keep it that way. But it was also a bit of an embarrassment. Not because it was a mess—I'm much too compulsive for that—but because it was the most over-organized collection of clutter you've ever seen.

"I had all this stuff left over from my marriage and my five-bedroom house that I couldn't possibly keep, but I wasn't ready to let go of just yet. So, I put everything in bags and boxes, with obsessively detailed labels of the contents on each, and stacked them neatly throughout the apartment. They lined the hallway and circled the furniture. They were under my bed and pressed against my walls and climbing up the sides of every doorway. Very neat and orderly, but—judging from the look on my sponsor's face—grounds for a mental status test.

"'What is all this?' she asked, looking around in shock.

"'You're my sponsor,' I reminded her. 'I was hoping *you* could tell *me*.'

"And, so, she did. And I'll never forget her words.

"'Lisa Marie,' she says 'you've talked about this apartment many times. But I didn't really get it until I saw the place with my own two eyes. Being in your home is like taking a tour of your brain. Now, suddenly, all the pieces are starting to fit together.'

"And, as the cigarettes are piling up in my ashtray, she tells me what she sees.

"'You've built a fortress here. No one's getting in, and you're certainly not getting out. It reminds me of what they did along the coast a few years ago when we had that big nor'easter. They lined the shore with sandbags to prevent the water from flooding the land.

"'Well, you've certainly got your sandbags well stacked up here. No unwanted feelings are ever going to get past all that stuff. It's like your own personal Wall of China. Too bad you've walled in as much as you've walled out.

"'Now, if you want my opinion, I say it's time to finally tear down that barricade and begin to exchange your sandbags—and all the clutter in them—for some real serenity.'"

Lisa Marie went on with her story, which was followed by the comments and stories of others, but I was no longer paying attention. All I could think about from that moment on was how much I wanted to trade my sandbags for serenity, how I wanted to create a natural boundary inside myself instead of an artificial wall of clutter on the outside. As soon as the meeting was over and everyone had recited the closing prayer, I jumped out of my seat and ran over to Lisa Marie.

"Hi," I said, without really thinking about what I was getting myself into. "My name is Pesi, and I'm a brand new member of Clutterers Anonymous. Would you like to be my sponsor?"

I felt a little like I had in the second grade when I asked the boy who sat next to me on the school bus if he wanted to be my valentine. Fortunately, Lisa Marie's response was a bit more encouraging; and I was, by now, somewhat better equipped to handle rejection—which this may well have been, although I wasn't completely sure.

Lisa Marie didn't actually say no, but she didn't exactly say yes either.

"Why don't you come to a few more meetings, and then we can decide," she suggested. "I'm not the easiest sponsor in the world. I'm into tough love—do you know what that means?—and I only work with people who really want to work the Program. I have no patience for self-pity and whining or for people who think they're coming here to learn how to organize their linen closets. The Twelve Steps are all about changing your attitude and changing your life—nothing less than that."

I knew I wanted her as my sponsor—even though I didn't know exactly what that meant—so I agreed to see her again at the next meeting, which I was sorry to learn would not be for an entire week. Because CLA was a new and relatively small program, there weren't many meetings available, and most of them were at times when I wasn't free. But there was a lot of literature to read—not just Clutterers Anonymous literature, but Twelve Step Literature in general. So, I spent the following week trying to learn all that I could about recovery.

*A*fter the next meeting, Lisa Marie suggested that we go out for coffee. The diner she brought me to—the only one in this non-Starbucks neighborhood open till midnight on a weekday night—was apparently the official Twelve Step coffeehouse; and as we spoke, the phrases and slogans of the Program could be heard reverberating through the heavily caffeinated air. . . . "first things first" . . . "just for today" . . . "act as if " . . . and—my very favorite— "easy does it—but do it." ·

"So, Pesi," she said, after depositing her glossy red signature on her coffee cup, "you heard my story—or at least part of it—last week. What's your story?"

I tried to give her the abridged version, but the abridged version of a clutterer's story is generally not all that abridged. Nevertheless, she was an intensely focused listener—so focused, in fact, that it made me nervous; but it also kept me on track. And, in the end, I would have to say that I spoke with noticeably more clarity and precision than usual. Nevertheless, it was still one long, drawnout tale of a tangled life that only a fellow clutterer could endure and even appreciate.

The following week, we repeated the same ritual. After the meeting, we returned to the same diner—same table and same order, as well—but, this time, Lisa Marie wanted me to explain to her why, in my opinion, I create and re-create clutter in my life. A far more challenging task than the mere retelling of my life story.

However, I tried. I began with some of the lighter and more positive conclusions I had come to over the past few years. But without the details, they sounded, for the most part, like simpleminded platitudes. And if I really had the issue as under control as I was making it seem, why was I attending a program for addicts?

In an attempt to redeem myself, I tried to move to the next, slightly more introspective level: I was disorganized by nature; I tended to procrastinate; I could be easily distracted and thrown off course; life chronically overwhelmed me, and I didn't know how to cope; I couldn't make decisions; I had poor boundaries. . . .

Lisa Marie was beginning to look bored. I could hardly blame her. It sounded like I was writing an article on clutter for the *Ladies Home Journal.* She was waiting for some honesty and some real depth, and I was inundating her with psychobabble and fluff. And I couldn't figure out why. I was certainly capable of answering her question on a deeper and more insightful level—so, then, why wasn't I?

After speaking nonstop for the past ten minutes, I now fell mysteriously silent. All I could think of was how ridiculous I must have sounded and how Lisa Marie—or, for that matter, anyone worth having—would never want to be my sponsor.

Then, it began to dawn on me that what I was really feeling beyond—my own insecurity and awkwardness—was a paralyzing sense of fear. I was, I suddenly realized, afraid of everyone and everything that now stood before me.

Lisa Marie scared me. The Program scared me. All those strangers sitting in a circle, baring their souls to one another and talking about their Higher Power, scared me. And, most of all, I scared myself. Who knew what I would find if I started poking around in my psyche the way they poked around in theirs?

I could think of nothing more disturbing at the moment than the image of Lisa Marie running her blood-red nails through my thoughts and exposing my most well-protected feelings. Why would I voluntarily subject myself to this?

Suddenly, I was no longer filled with anxiety. In fact, I felt greatly relieved at the prospect of Lisa Marie saying that she did not want to be my sponsor. I would thank her for considering my request and leave the diner before she had time to feel sorry for me and change her mind. Then, I could walk away from all of this in good conscience, knowing that I had tried my best to connect with the Program and find a sponsor, but it simply hadn't worked.

Instead, Lisa Marie leaned across the table and—with unexpected gentleness and concern—lightly touched my hand and said, "Pesi, are you all right?"

Once again, I felt vulnerable and ill at ease.

"No," I blurted out, "not really. I'm scared. Of you and of the Program and of what I might discover about myself. But please," I continued—startled by my own words—"can you be my sponsor anyway?"

Lisa Marie smiled and reached into her pocket. She pulled out a business card with a picture of a spiral staircase on it. Handing it to me, she said, "Call me anytime."

In the language of the Twelve Steps, I guess that meant yes.

*L*isa Marie liked her coffee black at room temperature with no sugar. I preferred mine light and sweet and as hot as I could possibly drink it. We almost never approached anything in quite the same way. Neither our methods nor our conclusions seemed at all compatible. Yet, she was the best sponsor I could ever have imagined.

A glance at our clothing made it all perfectly clear.

Lisa Marie favored a well-tailored look, with strong lines and sharp angles. She was fond of geometric shapes, especially bold stripes and jungle patterns; and black and white and red was her favorite color combination. Most of her shoes had pointed toes and spike heels. Her nails were always perfectly manicured and polished to a bright red sheen. She appeared, at all times, to be ready for either a wild night on the town or a high-level business luncheon.

My closet, on the other hand—which still occasionally had its annex on my bedroom floor—was filled with long flowing garments that never seemed to fit quite right, probably because they had been purchased—without benefit of label or proper elastic—from a secondhand store. I preferred colors that melted into one another or patterns with lacy backgrounds and little flowers. My shoes were usually round toed and soft bottomed, better suited for a mountain trail than a city street. And my nails had not been manicured or polished since my Sweet Sixteen—and, even then, only under duress.

Without a doubt, we made quite an odd pair. Nevertheless, despite our contrasting styles, we were both compulsive clutterers. Like two patients with radically different symptoms of the same disease, we wore our affliction with as much divergence as our garments.

Lisa Marie happened to be an extremely neat and orderly clutterer. All of her personal belongings were assembled with the same attention to detail and definition that she displayed in her wardrobe. However, when it came to any item beyond clothing, practicality trumped physical appearance at every point. The aesthetic quality of her living space seemed of far less importance to her than its potential for storage. Whatever she kept in her three little rooms was neatly bagged or boxed, clearly labeled, and carefully arranged for easy access. But her tiny apartment looked more like a well-stocked warehouse than a home in which guests might feel comfortable.

I, on the other hand, was an organizationally challenged clutterer, far more interested in creating beauty and a welcoming environment than in maintaining a smoothly functioning system of order. Even when my excessive belongings were displayed in what appeared to be a well-thought-out manner, they were rarely able to be retrieved without some degree of difficulty. Items I needed to reach daily often sat upon the highest shelves—attainable only by the step stool that was usually to be found at the other end of the house—while my most rarely used possessions frequently rested comfortably at eye level. If the lines and the colors harmonized well together, I was perfectly willing to sacrifice ease of use for visual appeal. And keeping my mess out of everyone's sight—particularly my own—was generally a higher priority than designing a convenient structure for storing it.

So, Lisa Marie and I found ourselves off to a somewhat rocky start, with her natural tendency toward clear boundaries rubbing up against my poorly defined edges. Nevertheless, we tried to rise above it all.

"Despite our differences," Lisa Marie assured me at the beginning of our first official sponsor-sponsee conversation, "I'm sure we'll do just fine once we get into the work. But, before we can do that, you have to be willing to admit that you're powerless over clutter and that your life has become unmanageable. And you have to really mean it."

"I already realized that last week when I read the literature."

"Good," she said, "but now you have to admit it out loud. And you have to really mean it."

"Okay," I repeated. "I'm powerless over clutter, and my life has become unmanageable. And I think I really mean it."

She tried to stop herself from laughing. "All right, I guess that'll do for now. So it looks like you've just taken your first step toward recovery. Congratulations! You'll never be the same."

"I certainly hope not," I replied. "After fifty years of living buried in my own mess, I'm definitely ready for a change."

"Great," she said, "but, remember, it's not just your life that's going to change—it's you. Most of us want everything *around* us to be different—the circumstances we face, the way people treat us, the environment we live in—everything but us. Nice idea, but it doesn't work that way. As we say in the Program, things don't get better; we do."

"Well, I can't wait to get better," I said, feeling energized by the challenge.

"Then, start with this," she said, handing me the same yellow booklet entitled *Spiritual Timing* that Yidis had given me a few weeks earlier.

"I already have it," I told her.

"You may have it," she said, "but it looks like you didn't get it."

"What do you mean?" I asked.

"I mean that you've been late to every meeting so far. I think you should read it carefully before we get together next week."

"Okay," I agreed. "Do you think it'll help me to be on time?"

"I don't know about that," she said. "But, at least, it will help you to understand why you're not."

Spiritual Timing. An interesting term—although I wasn't quite sure just what it meant. However, if both Yidis and Lisa Marie were offering me a booklet bearing that title, I could only trust that it was something I needed to know more about.

Nevertheless, it was 2:00 AM before I finally managed to sit down at the kitchen table with a cup of peppermint tea and my reading glasses. Needless to say, I should have been in bed by then. When it came to sleep, my timing appeared to be anything but spiritual. In fact, as far as my body was concerned, my handling of time probably qualified as passive abuse—and, sometimes, I wasn't so sure it was all that passive. Which was exactly why I felt compelled to stay awake and read the booklet.

I was immediately struck by the simple and profound truth expressed in the very first sentence: "All clutter wastes time."

Not space—the obvious victim—but time.

The second sentence went on to explain: "Unnecessary objects and unhealthy relationships take maintenance."

And further: "Because we believed our problem was poor time management, many of us consulted experts. We hoped they'd show us how we could gain more time by becoming more efficient, but this proved counter-productive. . . .We filled the time 'saved' with even more activities, and the result was less time."

I sat up straight in my chair, suddenly wide awake and focused. Finally, someone had accurately described my twisted relationship with time—how more was less, and no amount was ever enough. This booklet was definitely talking about me. Yet, I was now being included in something much larger that called itself "we": "What we lacked was not time, but spiritual timing. In turning our life, our will, our day over to our Higher Power, we . . . cooperate with that timing."

I read and reread the booklet many times, wishing it were a work of multiple volumes, rather than the equivalent of two type-written pages. Nevertheless, there was more in those two pages than I could really absorb in one sitting. It began by listing many of the different forms that time clutter takes, most of which were well represented in my repertoire of daily behaviors: overdoing and overachieving; being a perfectionist; wanting to try everything for fear of missing something; always being available to others and neglecting personal needs; creating information overload in order to keep up with every new development; and leaving no unfilled moment to confront deeper issues and negative thoughts.

The booklet then touched on some of the reasons why we choose a lifestyle of unrelenting busyness and how we can move beyond it. There were so many thoughts to savor that I took out a pack of index cards and began to write some of them down:

"Our lifelong problem wasn't time scarcity; it was lack of spiritual connection."

"An overloaded schedule . . . is equivalent to hoarding. . . . It insures that we'll always be distracted."

"When we're rested, available, and receptive, wondrous things happen."

"Our Higher Power is now our time manager."

By the time I saw Lisa Marie the following week, the booklet and the index cards were already dog-eared and well-worn, and I had committed just about every quotable statement to memory. And to demonstrate that I was—as they say in the Program—walking the walk as well as talking the talk, I made it a point to arrive ten minutes early for the next meeting.

"That's great," Lisa Marie said afterward when I elaborated on my reaction to the booklet, "because time is one of the most challenging issues a clutterer faces. Or, at least, let me speak for myself here. My physical mess is right out there in your face. No one can miss it. And even when I'm in the throes of denial, it's pretty hard to ignore.

"But my relationship with time—it's subtle and slippery and easy to conceal. The perfect place to hide when I'm not in the mood to confront my life or myself."

The waitress came with our coffee, so we stopped talking for a moment while we engaged in our preparation rituals. Lisa Marie reached for her cup and dropped in an ice cube—which the waitress knew to provide—and then watched in fascination as I began the delicate process of adding a little sugar and a little milk and then a little more sugar and a little more milk until the surface was a perfect creamy beige.

"Why do I always feel like I'm watching a Martha Stewart demonstration?" she asked, starting to laugh.

We continued laughing together—as we often did now—having finally gotten over our initial awkwardness with one another. I still felt intimidated by her at times, but, more and more, that was giving way to my appreciation of her depth of Program wisdom.

"You know," she said, several sips into our coffee, "when I joined OA, I was about thirty pounds overweight. And for the first few years, I bounced back and forth between taking the weight off and putting it back on. You know, the old yo-yo effect. But ever since then, I've kept it off. So, you would think that, by now, I could consider myself 'recovered.' But I can't.

"I still weigh and measure my food every day and call it in to my OA sponsor. It's the only way I can keep my eating disorder under control. And that's what I think you need to do with your time issues."

"Weigh and measure my time? How do I do that?"

"Well," she said, looking over at my bare wrists, "you might begin by getting a watch."

"I already have lots of watches," I assured her. "They just need repairs or batteries."

"Well, I want you to get a new watch—one that works—and that has a special feature. Actually, any cheap electronic watch can probably be programmed this way. Every hour, on the hour, the watch should make a little beep. I want you to consider that beep a wake-up call from your Higher Power. It's reminding you to stop, check in with yourself, pay attention to the fact that one hour has passed and another is about to begin. Then, you can take a few seconds to think about what you want to accomplish in the next hour and ask your Higher Power to help you with it."

"Am I going to have to walk around with my watch beeping every hour for the rest of my life?" I asked, suddenly beginning to feel trapped. Was I really such a hopeless addict that I had to weigh and measure every minute of my day?

"You know, Pesi," Lisa Marie said, "I want to tell you about my old Honda. It was a real classic, so I kept it for years even though it had lots of issues. One of them was that the gas gauge didn't work properly. When the tank was actually full, the gauge would read half empty. And if the needle would drop even slightly below the halfway mark, the warning light would begin to flash. It was obviously not a reliable instrument by which to measure my fuel supply.

"Well, it seems that those of us with clutter issues have similar gauges, so we continue to put more into the system than it either needs or can hold. It's all a miscalculation, of course, but what can you do when your instruments don't work properly?"

"Buy a watch with a beeper, I guess."

"That's right," Lisa Marie said. "And I suggest that you start using it immediately—just for today, of course. In Program, we don't talk about doing things for the rest of our lives—or even the rest of the week—or we would never do anything at all. Whatever we do, we do one day at a time."

"Okay," I agreed, "I'll start beeping—just for today—one hour at a time."

After each meeting, Lisa Marie and I would go out to the local diner for a cup of coffee. Since we lived in different neighborhoods, this was the most convenient time and place to get together; and the rest of the week, we stayed in touch by phone. One Tuesday night, we decided to drive a few extra miles and go to a more upscale coffee shop in Park Slope.

Although it was not exactly a long-established tradition we were departing from, the change in routine nevertheless felt a bit disturbing to me. There was something about the old diner, with its worn linoleum and vinyl seats, that had very quickly come to feel familiar and safe. Tonight's coffee shop was much prettier and more fashionable, with tree trunk tables and beautiful plants, dozens of hot and cold beverages to choose from, and a staggering number of desserts—most of which, we were assured, were free of all traces of wheat, dairy, eggs, sugar, and anything remotely unnatural or un-healthy. But the café was almost empty—even in Park Slope, who could afford $3.50 for a cup of regular coffee?—and the high ceilings and unfilled space made me feel a bit too exposed.

Lisa Marie, however, seemed to have no difficulty making herself comfortable in the new environment. Not wanting to make a fuss, I tried to situate myself so that I would see only her and the large ficus tree in the corner. A lovely young waitress brought us our coffee—Lisa Marie's being too weak with no ice cube, and mine too strong and not hot enough. And they didn't even have half and half or full-fat milk. After several gracious but unsuccessful attempts by the waitress to remedy the situation, Lisa Marie suggested that we say no more and simply practice acceptance. I wondered if I would ever internalize the tools of the Program the way that she had.

"I want to talk to you about something," Lisa Marie said when we were finally settled in. "Do you remember that conversation we had before I agreed to be your sponsor—the one about your reasons for creating clutter?"

"Of course, I do," I said. "I still feel embarrassed just thinking about it. I sounded like such an idiot—I can't believe you didn't simply get up and walk away."

"It wasn't really all that bad," she assured me. "I've heard worse."

"I was too nervous back then to think straight," I said, remembering how muddled my mind had felt.

"Well, do you think you might be ready to talk about it now?" Lisa Marie asked. "I mean, if we want to move forward with our work, I think it's really important to understand just what you get out of having all this clutter in your life."

I now realized that what Lisa Marie had been asking me that night was not why I'm attracted to clutter, but why I allow clutter to make my life unmanageable. Or, for that matter, why I allow *anything* to make my life unmanageable.

"Let me think about it for a minute," I said.

While Lisa Marie went to survey the dessert counter, I grappled with her question. It's not that I hadn't considered it before, but I wanted to try for a deeper level of understanding tonight.

By the time she returned with her doughnut, I had stumbled upon a new insight.

"You know, sitting here by myself in this empty diner for the past few minutes has made me feel very uncomfortable. Not because of the question you asked—although I'm sure that's part of it—but mostly because I feel unprotected with all this wide open space around me. The ceilings are too high, the tables are too far apart, and there's hardly anyone around to fill in the gaps.

"And as I was getting in touch with that feeling, it occurred to me that empty space always seems to affect me this way. So maybe that's the beginning of the answer to your question.

"I guess I'm looking for protection from the emptiness—or from whatever is on the other side of it that I'm afraid to confront. Being busy all the time and surrounded by my own mess seems to provide just the cushion that I need. There's always this little cloud of dust around to kick up whenever things get too intense. Clutter might make my life unmanageable, but it also does a really good job of pushing away all the things I'm trying to avoid. Maybe when I'm finally ready to face whatever they are, I'll be ready to let go of my clutter as well."

I wasn't sure if I had really answered her question, but I couldn't think of anything else to say, so I busied myself flagging down the waitress for a free refill that I had no intention of actually drinking. Meanwhile, Lisa Marie stared out the window, apparently lost in thought.

Suddenly, she turned around in her chair and looked directly at me.

"Pesi, do you know what I think it is that you're most afraid of and will go to just about any lengths to avoid?"

I shook my head no, not having the slightest idea of what she was about to say, but sensing that it was probably something I would prefer not to hear.

"I think what you're trying to run away from is nothing less than God—or your Higher Power—or whatever you want to call the spiritual force in your life."

I nearly choked on my gluten-free muffin.

"Lisa Marie," I said a bit too loudly. "That's completely crazy."

I could hear my words echo throughout the room. It was the first time I had ever disagreed with her, and it felt a little scary.

"All I've ever wanted in life is to have a close relationship with God; and if that hasn't happened, it's only because my issues with clutter have gotten in the way. And now you're saying that the very thing I've spent my life pursuing is what I'm really trying to run away from? That doesn't make any sense at all. It's totally insane. Why would you think I've created a wall of clutter to separate me from God rather than from my own thoughts and feelings?"

"I don't think that at all," she said. "I'm sure you *are* trying to hide from your own thoughts and feelings. Most of us are, or we wouldn't be addicts to begin with. But, in your case, I believe it goes beyond that. More than just trying to escape from yourself, I think you're trying to escape from the Higher Power that you've created."

"That I've created? What do you mean?"

"Do you have *Spiritual Timing* with you?" Lisa Marie asked.

I rummaged through my handbag and managed to find the well-worn booklet. She opened it and read aloud a sentence that I must have read a dozen times myself, but had no recollection of having ever seen before: "We may have created a Higher Power in our own image—a being who is preoccupied and unreachable, except in emergencies."

"Do you really think that's what I've done?" I asked, suddenly feeling very unsure of myself. "Have I created a Higher Power with whom I can't have a relationship because He's as inaccessible as I am?"

"Well, let me put it like this," Lisa Marie said, her voice becoming more gentle as she saw how shaken I obviously was. "I think the God you really believe in is a God of infinite love and compassion. But the Higher Power you relate to on a day-to-day basis seems to resemble *you*—or, at least, the dysfunctional you—a whole lot more. Essentially, a kind and well-meaning God, but too busy most of the time to be bothered—so hey, kid, you're on your own.

"Naturally, you're ambivalent. You want to be close, and, at the same time, you want to be as far away as possible because it's all very confusing, and it definitely doesn't feel safe."

And confused I certainly was. The only clarity I had at the moment was that I desperately needed a cup of coffee. An extra large cup of very hot coffee with real cream.

"Lisa Marie," I finally asked, "how about going back to our regular diner and continuing the conversation there?"

"Good idea," she said, tossing her uneaten spelt doughnut into the trash can. "I was just thinking the same thing myself."

*M*y last visit with Lisa Marie and our follow-up phone conversations left me feeling more unsettled than ever. And, so, I was really grateful that the next meeting of the Holy Sisters was coming up in just a few days. Of course, if I had had more Program experience, I would probably have realized that I shouldn't have been discussing Lisa Marie's comments with anyone other than her. But I didn't fully understand the ways of the Twelve Steps yet, and I was sufficiently distressed by what she was suggesting to want the insight of those who had shared my spiritual journey for so many years.

To be perfectly honest, I knew exactly how I wanted them to respond. I was hoping that the entire group would speak with one outraged voice and tell me that Lisa Marie was clearly mistaken here. A wise and caring person, we would all agree—but one hundred and eighty degrees off the mark on this one. After all, sponsors— even great ones—are human and fallible; and this was obviously one of Lisa Marie's rare but significant lapses in judgment.

Despite my obvious bias, I tried to present my conversation with her in a fair and objective light. She said, I said—just the facts. But when it came to presenting her conclusion, I could no longer maintain my neutral stance.

"And Lisa Marie thinks—can you imagine?—that I've created all this mess around me in order to avoid having a real relationship with my Higher Power. Talk about confusing cause and effect. I explained to her that the only reason my spiritual journey has been derailed so many times is because I'm too busy dealing with my clutter to stay on track. Yet, she's convinced that it's the other way around—that I'm so conflicted about wanting to be close to God that I make sure to keep myself in a state of perpetual chaos."

I was certain that the Holy Sisters would be as indignant as I was and immediately leap to my rescue and defend the sincerity of my spiritual quest. Instead, in a rare display of unified dissent, everyone in the room basically gave me the same unwanted advice: Go to meetings. Stick with the Program. Listen to your sponsor.

I couldn't believe it. My closest friends were now telling me that I had spent years in total denial about my relationship with God. Here I was, thinking of myself as a devoted seeker of truth, when, in fact, I had probably spent most of my life running in the opposite direction. And if they weren't exactly saying that, they certainly weren't disagreeing either.

In the end, I felt I had no choice but to acknowledge defeat and surrender.

The following day, I called Lisa Marie and reluctantly admitted to her that I was more powerless over clutter than I had realized. Not only had my life in the physical world become unmanageable, but my spiritual life was apparently falling apart as well.

"That's great," she said with sincere enthusiasm. "Now you can really get to work on your First Step."

"Get to work?" I asked. "Didn't I already complete it?"

"As we say in the Program," she reminded me, "change is a process, not an event."

(Lisa Marie seemed to be in possession of an infinite number of these ubiquitous slogans. When I asked her how many there actually were, she told me, "As many as you need." I should have known.)

And, so, as the Holy Sisters advised, I committed myself fully to following the Program and listening to the unfailingly wise advice of my sponsor. I showed up every Tuesday night for our weekly CLA meeting, checked in daily with Lisa Marie, kept in touch with other members of the Program, participated in phone meetings whenever I could, and read the literature every day. I considered myself a model addict in search of recovery.

I made my bed every morning, never left dishes in the sink overnight, put away whatever I took out, and made sure to get rid of at least one item every day. That was pretty much the definition of abstinence in Clutterers Anonymous. I also bought the beeping watch that Lisa Marie had suggested and purchased a day planner with an elaborate system of record keeping. (Actually, she wasn't too happy about that. Anything that appeared overly complicated was suspect in her mind. "Keep it simple" was probably her most frequently quoted slogan.)

But with all this dedication, I hadn't even made it to Step Two yet. When I complained about my lack of progress, Lisa Marie reminded me that "getting a step" was a deeply complex experience.

"If you don't really internalize each step," she warned, "you're building your recovery on sand. And you're on your way to becoming a dry drunk. That's someone who may not be actively using—or, in your case, cluttering—but who still thinks like an addict."

By now, we were already well into April; and spring recess, Passover, and Easter were just around the corner. Lisa Marie and I agreed to revisit the issue of my Second Step when we returned to our normal routine. In the meantime, Yankel and I decided to visit our friends in Buffalo for Passover. And, in truth, I was only too happy to finally get a break from all this introspection.

The long drive upstate took us through the Southern Tier, where the mountains were still dotted with frozen snow. Route 17 has always been one of my favorite roads, especially at this time of year when half the towns we passed through were still in winter, while the others were beginning to awaken to spring. It was like traveling in and out of a time warp.

A week in Buffalo was just what I needed—seeing old friends, sharing communal meals, walking along the Niagra River, and forgetting all about my complicated issues with clutter. By the time we drove back, the snow on Route 17 had completely melted, and the daffodils and forsythia were already displaying their colors. It seemed as if we had been gone for months.

"Doesn't it feel like a fresh beginning?" I asked Yankel, as we watched the world being renewed through our car window.

"Absolutely," he agreed. "I can't wait to get home and see what's coming up in the garden."

As we piled our suitcases and shopping bags on the front porch, we looked around at our Brooklyn neighborhood in bloom. It was really quite a lovely sight. Not exactly the Hudson Valley that we both loved or the Finger Lakes we had just passed through, but a place of beauty in its own right.

Blinking at the sudden change from bright sunlight to the muted darkness of our foyer, we pushed open the inner door leading to the living room. As soon as our eyes made the adjustment, we stopped dead in our tracks, neither of us able to fully take in the sight before us.

A huge chunk of the ceiling had collapsed, and the living room and dining room were filled with wet cement, broken furniture, and the metal and glass remnants of our antique chandelier. We were both speechless until Yankel managed to say—with his usual perfect timing and deadpan delivery—"What a revolting development this is—once again!" At which point we both sat down on our duffle bags and began to laugh and cry.

Now that I was finally beginning to understand why I pursued clutter, I was more anxious than ever to understand just why it pursued me. Wherever I moved—and I certainly moved with uncommon frequency—pipes soon burst, roofs leaked, toilets overflowed, and basements filled with water. As a result, I'd spent most of my adult life in a state of upheaval—stalked, it seemed, by one little catastrophe after another.

Things had quieted down of late, but I always lived in dread fear of that first drop of water. I could never listen to a relaxation tape of a mountain stream or a babbling brook without running to check my faucets and my pipes. The sound of running water had long ago ceased to be a bridge to tranquility.

And now this. The insurance company surmised that a pipe in our second-floor bathroom had been leaking slowly for a long time, until one day—fortunately, a day that we were not sitting at our dining room table—the ceiling collapsed from the accumulation of moisture, bringing the chandelier and the wooden molding down with it.

On the one hand, it was a miracle that we were far away and spared any harm. On the other hand, we now had a huge mess on our hands and faced a major renovation that included plumbing, electrical work, construction, and painting. But more than the enormous headache of it all, I found myself deeply disturbed by the spiritual implications.

Why did this keep happening to me? The disasters were rarely caused by my own negligence or lack of awareness. And they seemed to occur whether or not I was actively engaged in creating order, as if my personal interaction with the material world had no bearing whatsoever on the way it responded to me. Was I drawing this chaos to myself in some mysterious, metaphysical way, I wondered—because I craved the distraction or the drama? Or could it all be one meaningless coincidence that I felt compelled to extract meaning from?

"I hear your Higher Power knocking," Lisa Marie said when I discussed it with her. "I don't know what it means or why it happened; but when your ceiling collapses, how can you not take it as a call from above? I think it's definitely time to start working on your Second Step."

It was Yidis, however, who really connected the dots and pointed me in the direction that they seemed to be leading.

"This is—what?—your forty-seventh flood since I've known you?" she said, as we walked through the disaster area that was now my dining room.

We climbed over the piles of plasterboard and bags of cement and made our way to the kitchen, which was still relatively intact and functional—although it probably wouldn't be for long, since it shared a common wall with the dining room.

"Not exactly my forty-seventh," I said, as I looked around—still in disbelief—"but you're probably not too far off.

"Yidis,"—I suddenly stopped and turned to face her—"what am I going to do? I don't think I can live through another renovation. All that noise and all that dust. It's such a colossal waste of time and energy, such an invasion of my privacy, such a violation of my space. I just want to run as far away as I can."

"And that's exactly what I think you should do," she said.

"Really?" I asked, a bit startled. "You don't think I should stay and try to be transformed by the experience?"

"Of course not. I'm into growth, not toxic poisoning. There's nothing transformative about inhaling paint fumes and carpenter's glue."

I could feel my spirits lifting.

"Okay, that's great. Do you think we should go to the mountains or to the ocean? Or maybe we could take a road trip out west and visit B. J. and Laya in Portland."

"That's not exactly what I had in mind," Yidis said. "I was thinking that you should spend some time in Israel."

After all our years of friendship, I could still never predict what she was going to say. And this was certainly no exception.

"Why Israel?" I asked. "I mean it would be great to go to Israel, but why now in particular?"

"Well," she began, "do you want me to start with the spiritual, the practical, or the wild and outrageous?"

"How about the wild and outrageous."

"Okay. You need to do something truly wild and outrageous to break the pattern. Instead of slipping into your usual routine—which is either to stick around and get sucked into the chaos or leave but stay close enough to micromanage the whole thing—you need to go somewhere far away that you've never been before. Somewhere exotic, yet familiar; somewhere you can lose yourself and find yourself at the same time.

"Israel is perfect because you have friends there, and you already have a connection to the land; but it's like nothing you've ever experienced before. It'll be intense and exciting—but gentle."

"Did you ever think of writing travelogues?" I asked.

"No," she said, "but I'll consider it if you say yes."

Actually, I was pretty close. The idea was sounding better and better by the moment.

"Okay," she continued. "Now on to the practical. You need to go *someplace* while they're kicking up all that dust, so why shouldn't it be someplace wonderful? After all, you've just been through a trauma—even if happens to be a trauma that you go through on a regular basis—and victims of trauma deserve special treatment.

"And now for the spiritual. Isn't it time for you to finally resolve this whole chicken-and-egg issue between your Higher Power and your clutter? I mean, which really did come first—did your clutter get in the way of your relationship with God, or did you create all that clutter to avoid the relationship?

"In Israel, it'll just be you and your Higher Power. There won't be any clutter to distract you, so maybe you'll finally be able to sort the whole thing out."

"And, if not, maybe I can find a friendly Kabbalist to help me."

"You never know," Yidis said.

No, I thought to myself, *you never do.*

CHAPTER SEVEN

A Detour

"He who would travel happily must travel light."
—Antoine de Saint-Exupery

Yankel loved the idea—touring the land, visiting the holy sites, sailing on the Kinneret, and not having to spend the summer smelling polyurethane and listening to the sound of a drill. And, so, the plan was immediately set in motion.

The plumbers would fix the leak, but the rest of the work would not begin until we were gone. A friend of ours who needed a place to stay would move in and keep an eye on the construction. I wouldn't be there to supervise it personally—which I found more than a bit disturbing—but, at Lisa Marie's suggestion, seconded by Yidis and Yitta and Etta, I agreed to work on letting go.

If everything proceeded according to schedule, by the middle of June, we would be on our way to Ben Gurion Airport in Tel Aviv.

There was, however, one major kink in the plan that still needed to be worked out—and that was my pathological fear of flying. I had always been highly acrophobic and almost never traveled by plane. I also suffered from severe motion sensitivity, which made the thought of being in the air for all those hours even more disturbing. And although I wasn't actually claustrophobic, I wasn't crazy about the prospect of long periods in confined spaces either.

Everyone offered his or her own physical and psychological remedies to get me through the experience: prayer, meditation, wrist bands, relaxation tapes, hypnosis, desensitization therapy, E.F.T. tapping, acupuncture, acupressure, Chinese herbs, and a host of drugs and supplements. Lisa Marie proposed reciting a combination of appropriate slogans: Let go and let God; Turn it over; Feelings aren't facts; I can't. . . . He can. . . . I think I'll let Him.

In the end, I chose Dramamine, the Book of Psalms, and a stack of index cards with Program sayings and other spiritual quotes. In addition, the Holy Sisters prepared a package of what they called "airplane letters"—their own brief notes or lengthy letters to me expressing love and support, advice, blessings, and whatever else they could think of to inspire and distract me during the flight.

Miraculously, everything moved forward with remarkable ease. Until it actually came time to pack.

Packing has always been a source of extreme anxiety for me. It seems to awaken all of my deprivation fantasies and instincts to hoard. No matter where I'm heading off to—and it's usually a destination in close proximity to urban civilization—I am seized with an irrational fear that I will not be able to acquire whatever it is that I need.

Before we leave on any trip, Yankel expends a great deal of effort trying to convince me that I really don't have to take most of what I'm packing because wherever we're going, they're sure to have—fill in the blank—and, if not, we can probably live very well without it. To which, I always respond that I'll feel so much better if I know that I have enough Band-Aids, lotions, chocolate kisses, organic coffee, crossword puzzles, books to read and notebooks to write in, rain gear and sun gear—and, of course, extra blankets and pillows and a large box fan to drown out unfamiliar noises. In general, it's a losing battle for him; but since we typically travel by car, my overload simply adds a bit more sag to the chassis. Most of the time, we never even remove the extra boxes from the trunk.

But packing to go overseas presented a whole different set of problems. There were now weight and space restrictions aboard the plane to consider, as well as our own limited ability to drag all that excess baggage from one location to another.

"Shouldn't a journey to the Holy Land be undertaken with as few material possessions as possible?" Yankel asked, in a last ditch effort to lighten our load by appealing to my sense of spiritual purpose.

"Absolutely," I agreed. "And what we have here is my version of as few material possessions as possible."

I left what I considered the simplest category of items to pack for last, which was my collection of summer clothes, consisting mostly of oversized T-shirts, sun hats, denim skirts, and Indian cotton dresses.

Every fall, during the first few weeks of the semester, I would wash all my summer things and pack them away in plastic containers for the following year. At the end of the spring semester, I would do the same with my winter clothes. It was one of my more successful organizational strategies and always left me with just enough room in my crowded closet for the coming season.

The evening before our flight, I laid out all the plastic boxes on the bedroom floor alongside my open suitcases, ready to complete the final phase of packing. But as I began to sort through the contents, it immediately became obvious that I had skipped a critical step in the process. Somehow, I had managed to put away all my summer clothes the previous year without first washing any of them. Of course, in retrospect, this was perfectly understandable. In the aftermath of September 11, the storage of my summer wardrobe had not been a topic that ranked high on my list of immediate concerns.

Tonight, however, the issue had suddenly become one of critical importance, since it now appeared that I had no clean clothes to take on my trip. And since I wasn't about to spend the entire night at the local laundromat or in a friend's basement, there was little I could do to remedy the situation. In addition, I discovered—to my further horror—that I had no clean socks or underwear to bring with me because, with all the excitement of the past month, I had never made it to the laundromat.

As I sat in the middle of the floor, surrounded by mountains of indisputable proof that I was not on the winning side in my battle with clutter, I started to think about my long and tangled history with laundry. This did not seem the ideal moment to turn my attention to such a subject, but I could hardly restrain myself. The sudden realization that all the garments I needed for the spiritual journey I was about to embark upon were unwashed and not suitable for immediate use was simply too ill-timed a development to ignore.

My relationship with laundry had always been a highly complicated affair that had become even more complicated in recent years—a relationship too intimate to share with outside help, yet clearly too overwhelming to handle myself. It was nearly impossible to convey the full complexity of the situation to those who saw laundry as little more than a mildly unpleasant fact of life, while, for me, it was one of the most insidious forms of clutter I had to contend with—one with which I seemed permanently locked in a losing battle of wills.

In addition to the practical implications of the stand-off, the struggle was deeply symbolic as well. Here, in this pile of dirty laundry, my disdain for the menial tasks of the physical world collided with my love of its sensory pleasures, and my tendency to procrastinate banged heads with my desire for perfection.

If I did not care so much about the gentle touch and sweet smell of freshly laundered fabric against my skin, I could, no doubt, have found a simpler way of dealing with the problem—one that did not involve my personal supervision at every step. And if I were not such an unrelenting purist, I might have considered trading in my cotton for polyester and my handwoven wool for a synthetic blend, which would also have eased the burden of the task. But even with all that, I'm not so sure the situation would have been significantly improved. My resistance—both to doing the job myself and to hiring someone else to do it—apparently had far deeper roots than I could yet grasp.

It was an issue that seemed to elude me on every level, until, one day, purely by chance—or, perhaps, not—I stumbled upon a near-perfect solution.

I was single at the time and living in the Hudson Valley, driving back and forth to Manhattan, and frequently spending the night with friends in the city to avoid the two-hour commute each way. By the time I made it through the front door of my rented cottage on Thursday night, my To-Do List for the weekend generally consisted of little more than Take a Walk by the Stream, Sit in the Sun, and Read a Good Book. Needless to say, doing the laundry rarely made it to the Top Ten—or even to the list.

Then, one day, driving down Main Street in Saugerties, I happened to notice a laundromat with a large sign in the window announcing that it was open 7 days a week, 24 hours a day. I couldn't imagine why. Who in this sleepy little town was intending to do their laundry at four o'clock in the morning? Suddenly, a bell went off in my brain. Here, at last, was the answer to my prayers.

The next night, I hauled in my three-month accumulation of dirty laundry. Finally, I could do it all in one place at one time without incurring the wrath of every laundry washer in Ulster County who had the misfortune of showing up at the same time that I did.

As I ran around the laundromat—pouring a cup of bleach here, tossing a few capfuls of liquid detergent there, attempting to coordinate fabric softeners and rinse cycles—I tried to understand how this simple task of daily living had gotten so completely out of hand. But the truth is, it didn't really matter anymore because I had now found a solution. Not a perfect one by any means—it required an enormous supply of clothes and bedding and towels to bridge the gap between washings and a large amount of storage space to keep the growing piles out of sight—but it would certainly do until something better came along.

Now, I could finally lay the matter to rest. Instead of thinking of myself as a chronic procrastinator, I felt reborn as a woman with a plan—a somewhat unconventional plan perhaps, but a plan nonetheless. Instead of continually promising myself that I would get the laundry done tonight/tomorrow/Sunday morning/next weekend and then feeling like an irresponsible adolescent when I didn't follow through, I now had a system in place. Four times a year, I would simply plan for an all-night vigil at the laundromat.

Best of all, I would always be in control of my own laundry. I would never again have to deal with the scratchy towels and jasmine-scented bedding that I had to endure whenever I broke down and used a laundry service. Nor would I have to continually obsess about when and where and how to deal with the rising piles. At last, there would be peace of mind—and all it would take was four all-nighters a year and a Ball jar filled with quarters.

The system worked beautifully for quite a while. Occasionally, the three months stretched to four; but, most of the time, everything went according to plan.

And, then, I met Yankel.

Wonderful as he was in so many ways, he unfortunately failed to appreciate my innovative approach to laundry. In his eyes, a night spent in a 24-hour laundromat did not qualify as the fine example of creative problem solving that I considered it to be. He couldn't quite decide which half of the issue was worse—allowing the laundry to accumulate in the first place or attempting to deal with it in the middle of the night—but, clearly, he was not pleased with either.

"Why don't you just do what I—and most normal busy people—do, and drop off your dirty clothes at the laundromat on the way to work. Someone there will wash them and dry them and fold them for you, and you can pick everything up on your way home."

"But it never comes back quite right," I tried to explain. "Things shrink and wrinkle and smell funny. One time, my favorite embroidered blouse unraveled; and, another time, a silk scarf disintegrated entirely. They don't know how to deal with delicate items, and I don't like the way they handle the rest of my things either. It just feels too weird and disconnected to have a complete stranger touching the things that touch my body."

"Okay," he conceded, "this is obviously not a simple issue here. But we need to come up with some sort of a plan right away, or neither one of us will have any clean clothes to wear to work Monday morning. So, why don't we try it like this: You wash your own personal laundry and whatever else you like; and I'll bring my personal laundry and anything you want to give me to the laundry service in town. You can do yours in any wildly complicated, offbeat way you like; and I'll continue to do mine in the dull but efficient manner that has served me well all these years. What do you say?"

"It sounds like a great idea," I responded. "His and hers laundry—the secret to a happy marriage."

"But, please," he continued, "just one thing—promise me, no more all nighters in godforsaken laundromats."

"I promise I'll try" was the best I could do; but I really meant it.

I decided to begin by tackling the pile-up part of the problem. If I didn't have so much laundry to contend with in the first place, I reasoned, I would not have to take over the entire laundromat on each visit and could, therefore, undertake the project during normal daylight hours. This was not an easy change to make, however, since I was still commuting to Manhattan from the Hudson Valley several times a week and wasn't in any one place for all that long.

To simplify the process and keep me from becoming overwhelmed, I came up with what I called my "one handkerchief a day" plan. According to this system, each morning, as I walked out of the house, I would carry a small bag with yesterday's laundry to my car. In this way, whenever I passed a laundromat and had a little free time—at home, near school, or on the road—I could chip away at the accumulation, several machines at a time.

At first, things seemed to be working quite well. Every day, I added a few more socks, a dirty washcloth, another T-shirt to the laundry bags in my trunk—until, little by little, the trunk began to bulge. It also began to sag because this new plan called for a large variety of laundry supplies to be on hand at all times. Suddenly, my trunk was filled with bottles of detergent (one for heavy-duty loads, one for regular cold-water wash, and one for woolens and other delicates); two types of bleach (one for whites, one for colors); a can of stain remover; and several extra-large containers of unscented fabric softener. All of this seemed unquestionably necessary, since I certainly wanted my efforts to result in a product that would be exceptionally pleasing to the senses.

There were admittedly a few glitches in the operation, such as the fact that the detergent froze when the temperature dropped below thirty-two degrees, and, on one occasion, the bleach leaked all over my trunk and ate a huge hole in the carpet. But, basically, the system functioned well—except for the fact that I rarely got to the laundromat. I had, of course, succeeded in removing the pile of offensive laundry from my bedroom; but I now had a pile of offensive laundry in my car.

When the trunk finally refused to receive one more dirty dish towel, I was forced to resort to the back seat, thus bringing my plight into public view once again. Friends and passersby began to inquire about the growing piles, so I decided to attempt camouflage; but that only served to arouse the curiosity of the local street people, who finally decided to check out the concealed goods for themselves. When I came out of work late one night and found the contents of my laundry bags strewn across the rear seat—with a few rather personal items missing and a pair of pantyhose dangling from the rearview mirror—I decided it was time to abandon Plan A and proceed to Plan B.

The goal of Plan B was to beautify the act of doing the laundry so that this distasteful chore might be transformed into a pleasant and uplifting experience which I would actually anticipate with joy. From the dreaded task that laundry has always been, I hoped to elevate it to a welcome interlude of quiet reflection in my otherwise unquiet day. This would, of course, require the setting of a very special laundromat; but in the Hudson Valley, such places did exist.

I began an exhaustive study of local laundromats, visiting all the potential candidates in what I considered a reasonable range, which was basically a forty-minute drive each way. Not something I could handle on a daily basis, but once every few weeks definitely seemed manageable.

The winner was located at the outer edge of the acceptable range, but well worth the trip, I felt, because of its special qualities. Besides the lovely scenery en route, this laundromat possessed a spectacular feature not found in any other—a large picture window overlooking an open meadow surrounded by the Shawangunk Mountains. In addition to the magnificent view, the spacious laundromat was extremely clean and well organized and did not seem to be frequented by the type of people likely to suffer from untreated toenail fungus or chronic incontinence.

For the next year, once every few weeks, I triumphantly carried several medium-size bags of laundry to the car and headed for my mountainside laundromat. Aside from the hour-and-twenty-minute commute round trip, even Yankel had to agree that the time spent actually doing the laundry seemed quite reasonable.

At the conclusion of a quiet afternoon spent reading and staring reflectively at the mountains and the meadow, I would begin to prepare for the trip home, carefully hanging my gauzy cotton dresses and lacy fabrics on plastic hangers to dry so that they would neither shrink nor wrinkle, rolling my socks into compact little balls, and neatly folding my outstandingly soft sheets and towels. Then, I would carefully place everything in plastic milk crates and begin the drive across Route 209 to Ellenville, confident that this was my final rite of passage into adulthood.

But, of course, life—or, at least, my life—never seems to go on for long without change or challenge. And, one day, just as Yankel and I were comfortably settling into our new routine, he was offered a promotion that required moving and, then—when things didn't work out—moving again.

The laundry gradually began to slip in priority, surrendering its position to the packing, unpacking, and repacking of boxes. Before I knew it, the mountain of dirty clothes had once again begun its manic climb to the sky. But this time, there was no quaint laundromat with a big picture window down the road to rescue me. We had now arrived in Brooklyn, the heartland of repulsive laundromats.

A slight reprieve was granted to me when I stumbled upon an old-fashioned, family-operated laundry with a distinctly out-of-town flavor in Staten Island. However, it was only open during normal business hours and couldn't handle more than a month's accumulation of my laundry at one time. In addition, the $7.00 bridge toll and the response of my new Brooklyn friends—"You're going *where* to do your laundry?!"—soon shamed me into seeking a more socially and financially acceptable solution.

Then, one day, it dawned upon me that although my affliction might not be commonplace, surely I couldn't be the only person in Brooklyn with this problem. Outside the city, most people have their own washing machines; but here in Brooklyn, there must be a whole community of dysfunctional laundry washers with whom I could commiserate and perhaps even form some sort of support group.

I began an informal survey of neighbors and other acquaintances, designed to detect potential laundry hoarders.

"What do you do here in Brooklyn when your laundry begins to pile up?" I would casually inquire of everyone I met.

"Oh, I never let it pile up!" was the most common and least credible response I received.

"I wash it by hand every night in the kitchen sink and hang it to dry in the bathtub."

"I use a laundry service."

"My cleaning lady does it once a week."

"It's my husband's job, and he's always on top of it."

"That's disgusting. How could anyone let their laundry pile up?"

I could see that no one here was ready to come out of the closet.

Then, finally: "I take it home to my mother."

Ah, now there was an honest answer. And a promising solution.

Unfortunately, my mother didn't have her own washing machine; but she did live in a condominium with the laundry room for her half of the floor right next to her apartment. And since it was a retirement community in which many of the residents lived alone and were there only several months of the year, I reasoned that the machines would not be used all that often. In the course of a one-week visit, if I did several washes a day—which did not, even by normal standards, seem excessive—the job would be done before it was time to come home.

Now, it was true that my mother lived fourteen hundred miles away in Florida. However, since I drove down to visit her twice a year anyway, I saw no reason why I couldn't simply bring my laundry with me. True, a return to the semiannual system would be somewhat of a step backward, but considering the struggles of life in New York City, it seemed a justifiable concession. And as a fill-in between visits, I could make a few trips to Staten Island. Even Yankel had to admit that, in the context of urban living, my approach to laundry probably qualified as a positive survival strategy.

The main difficulty with the new plan was finding a way to smuggle all that laundry into my mother's apartment without calling undue attention to myself. Life is relatively quiet and uneventful in Century Village, and unusual activity of any sort was bound to arouse the curiosity of neighbors. Therefore, I arranged to show up well after dark and, under cover of night, stealthily drag my black garbage bags full of laundry onto the elevator and across the catwalk to my mother's fourth floor condo. I quietly carried bag after bag after bag past the darkened windows of the neighboring apartments, confident that I had spared my mother any potential embarrassment.

However, by 9:00 AM the following morning, the phone calls were beginning to come in: "Is your daughter moving in with you?" . . . "She certainly brought a lot of stuff for a one-week visit." . . . "How many guests did you say were coming?". . .

"Well," my mother would try to explain, "my daughter always comes with a few extra things. You see, she's a college professor, so she carries a lot of books with her and all of her papers to grade. And she's a kosher vegetarian, so she has to bring her own pots and pans and dishes, and most of her own food, too. And she frequently ends up staying a lot longer than she expected because her car is old and doesn't work so well all of the time. . . ."

Undeterred by the public humiliation, I persisted, successfully washing and drying every bit of the dirty laundry I had brought with me. After two or three such visits, the neighbors got used to my odd behavior, and I began to think I had found another good solution to the problem.

Then, one summer, my mother announced that she was coming to New York for a visit, which meant only one trip to Florida that year. My supply of clothing and household items could barely hold out for six months—and, then, only by resorting to hand washing and Staten Island as a backup. An entire year was definitely out of the question. When my mother began to extol the virtues of northern summers, I feared my latest method of laundry management was in serious jeopardy. In the end, her intentions never materialized, but I took it as a sign that it was time to come up with a more reliable alternative.

In the end, however, the problem solved itself. When our landlord sold the house we were living in and we decided to buy one of our own, the new home we purchased came with a washer and dryer already installed in the basement. True, the two old Maytags were probably twenty years old, but they still seemed to be churning out clean clothes.

So, for one glorious year, we lived a life free of laundry drama. But, then, the washing machine began to agitate more and more slowly, until, one day, it no longer agitated at all. The local repairman tried his best to restore the machine to life, but it was apparently beyond fixing. And by this point, we had already piled so much of our unsorted clutter into the tiny basement that it was virtually impossible to carry the broken machine out or to bring a new one in. Then, September 11 was upon us, and who cared about matters of such little consequence anymore?

Tonight, however—surrounded by these familiar piles of my unwashed belongings—I had begun, once again, to care very much.

As I sat on the floor, lost in my remembrances of laundry crises past—and not quite ready to confront this most recent one—I thought I heard a faint knock at the door, followed by Yankel's footsteps on the stairs.

"It's 11:00 PM—who could be coming to visit at this hour?" I heard him say, with the slight edge in his voice that usually indicated he had either gone past his bedtime or his threshold of patience—or, in this case, probably both.

A moment later, the door to my bedroom opened, and there stood my Holy Sister Shaindel.

"You made it," I said, wondering why I had ever doubted that she would. Somehow, Shaindel always seemed to make it—even if we were the only two people left standing when she did. Despite her demanding job and her house full of children and guests and extended family, she never failed to show up when I needed her. And I certainly needed her now.

"Shaindel, I have a little problem . . . " I began to explain, as she looked around at the mess that stretched from one end of my room to the other.

But she needed no explanation.

"Do you have any clean clothes here?" she asked, already sufficiently experienced in dealing with my laundry issues to recognize a genuine crisis when she saw one.

"Not for a hot Israeli summer," I said.

"How about socks and underwear?"

I shook my head no.

"What time are you leaving?" she asked

"We have to be at the airport by one o'clock tomorrow. Our flight"—I had almost forgotten about *that* issue—"takes off at 3:00."

"Okay," she said, picking up an empty plastic bag from the floor. "Give me all your socks and underwear. I'll run home right now and put them through the washer and dryer. I should be back in about two hours. Is that too late for you?"

"For me? No, of course not—but what about for you?"

"For me?!" She said, beginning to laugh. "For me, there's only too early and not late enough."

The next thing we knew, we were both sitting on the floor between the piles of dirty laundry and laughing as if we had nothing better in the world to do. Two unrepentant night people, overstimulated by exhaustion and the total absurdity of the moment.

"And don't worry about the rest of the stuff," she said. "You're not going to some third world country. Israel has electricity and running water and plenty of laundromats. When you're there, you'll find one and wash whatever you need. Don't try to deal with it now. Just stuff it all into a bag, and keep going. With any luck, you might even get to bed tonight."

By the time Shaindel returned with my pile of clean, neatly folded laundry, I had already thrown everything I needed into one oversized suitcase, leaving just enough room for the newly washed socks and underwear. And I had managed to squeeze every bit of my unsorted dirty laundry into a huge duffle bag, which—I discovered when we got to the airport—exceeded the allowable weight by over fifty pounds. At that point, however, I was willing to do just about anything to keep moving forward. Whatever it would cost seemed a small sum to pay for my sanity and the few hours of sleep I actually managed to get.

When we arrived at the airport, everyone was complaining about the extra security restrictions and the added fees for over-weight baggage that had recently been tagged on; but since I didn't really know what security was like before September 11, I was per-fectly content to go along with it all. Yankel, meanwhile, went off to argue with a supervisor about the charge for the excess weight of my duffle bag.

Standing at the ticket counter alone—now, only moments from the flight—I began to feel the first wave of panic. However, before I had a chance to work myself into a full-blown attack, I was suddenly distracted. I looked up and saw several dozen pink and purple balloons bearing my name, all moving steadily in my direction, like a Walt Disney production of Macbeth, with Birnam Wood marching in technicolor toward Dunsinane. I wondered if I was having a mystical experience of some sort or the beginnings of an anxiety-induced hallucination.

It turned out, in fact, to be neither. The Holy Sisters—to my utter surprise and delight—had shown up bearing the unexpected balloons to send me off with bright colors and memorable pag-eantry. They were also carrying goodbye gifts; but, realizing how unlikely it was that I would have a millimeter of unused space in any of my bags, they had brought me only tiny objects that I could easily stick in my handbag or in the pockets of my jacket. And each gift was accompanied by a special blessing.

Etta gave me a cassette that she had recorded specially for my trip—one side with Irish folk music that we both loved, and the other side with a guided meditation that she created to relax me through takeoff and landing. It was accompanied by her personal blessing: "You should go in peace and come in peace, and your journey should always be filled with music."

Laurie handed me a bag of individually wrapped chocolate brownies and a map of Jerusalem. "It should be a sweet trip, and may you find everything you're searching for."

Atara presented me with an envelope of magnificent photographs she had taken in Israel on her last visit: "I bless you that your eyes should see beauty and holiness wherever you look."

Judy gave me a little box of earplugs: "To help you tune out the world and tune in to yourself."

Yitta offered me a pocket-size notebook and a fold-up pen: "May your words flow like the waters of the Kinneret."

And Ruchama handed me a copy of *Clutter's Last Stand*: "For inspiration, advice, and comic relief."

Just as they announced that it was time for my flight to begin boarding, Yidis placed a gift-wrapped cell phone in the palm of my hand. "Here. It's a gift from all of us—a hot line to the Holy Sisters. I bless you that the lines of communication should always be open between you and everyone you love, and especially between you and your Higher Power."

We all gave each other one last hug, and I ran toward the boarding gate, where Yankel was pacing up and down beside our overweight luggage.

CHAPTER EIGHT

Ancient Stepping Stones

"Where is God to be found?
In the place where He is given entry."
—Rabbi Menachem Mendel of Kotsk

Thanks to repeated doses of Dramamine and a week of long days, short nights, and unremitting stress, I was so exhausted by the time I finally crawled aboard El Al that I pretty much slept through the entire flight. Every now and then, I would wake up in a panic, certain that the plane was about to spiral into the ocean; but, then, I would remember Lisa Marie's advice and keep repeating, "Feelings aren't facts . . . feelings aren't facts . . . feelings aren't facts . . . just let go and let God . . . "

The plane landed in Tel Aviv the following morning at about 8:00 AM. Raezelle, Reizl Malka, Leah, and Elana—old friends and Holy Sisters who were now living in Israel—came to greet us at the airport. Amid hugs and kisses, bouquets of flowers, and a bilingual brouhaha at the baggage pick-up counter, it finally began to sink in that I had survived the flight and was actually here. But it didn't become totally real until we stepped out of the terminal and looked up at the Mediterranean sky radiating its iridescent blue light in all directions.

The next thing I knew, I was lying on the grass—right there at the airport—and kissing the ground. Not one to make a spectacle of myself in public places, I couldn't quite understand my own reaction. Later in the trip, however, when I looked at the photographs my friends had taken, I could see that I was obviously overcome with joy to finally be touching the ground of Israel—and, no doubt, overcome with relief to be touching any ground at all.

The high point of my arrival, however, came an hour later when we drove through one of the gates leading to the Old City of Jerusalem. Surrounded on all sides by a thick stone wall (a relatively recent sixteenth-century addition), the Old City was originally built by Kind David in 1004 BC and was home to both the First and Second Holy Temples.

Today, all that remains of the original Temple is the Western Wall, which Judaism regards as the holiest site on earth and which, according to tradition, will never be destroyed because the Divine Presence continues to dwell there. Built of massive stones—some weighing hundreds of tons—the Wall has managed for thousands of years to withstand invading armies, deadly earthquakes, and the ongoing battle for political sovereignty.

In recent times, the Old City—barely one square kilometer in size—has been divided into four sections: the Jewish Quarter, the Muslim Quarter, the Christian Quarter, and the Armenian Quarter, each filled with deep religious significance for its inhabitants.

As we entered the Old City, the street washers had just begun to pour water onto the narrow cobblestone walkways in preparation for the Jewish Sabbath, which would begin that evening at sundown. Watching the ancient stones of this walled city shimmering in the morning sun, I was overcome by the profound beauty of Jerusalem. The sages of the Talmud had said thousands of years before that ten measures of beauty were given to the world, and nine of them went to Jerusalem. I now understood what they meant.

It was my first love affair with a city; and like most first loves, it was passionate and consuming and, at times, almost more intense than I could handle. We were barely acquainted with one another, and, already, there was an unsettling intimacy between us. Everything unknown seemed strangely familiar; each new experience, a memory come alive.

I remained endlessly fascinated by its braided rhythms. The Old City of Jerusalem was, at the same time, exuberant and subdued, bustling and utterly still; a self-contained world at the center of the universe, vibrating with tension, yet totally at peace with itself.

The Old City, I had been warned, did not yield itself easily. Like many of its inhabitants, it was covered in veils. Yet, perhaps sensing my desperation, it did not behave toward me like a guarded lover. Instead, it flung open its gates and allowed me to wander freely through its hidden gardens and secret paths.

I spent my first Friday night at the Western Wall—also known as the Holy Wall or, in Hebrew, the Kotel. Jerusalem, like Manhattan, is a city that never sleeps. But, unlike Manhattan, it is not fueled by its own adrenaline. There is a natural ebb and flow of spiritual energy here that moves through the day and into the night, and those who are sensitive to its rhythms rise and recede with it. Friday evening at sunset, that energy reaches its peak; and the Kotel is filled with worshippers seeking to connect with God at the moment when the Divine Presence—the *Shekhinah*, in Hebrew—descends and spreads its light upon the world.

Time, in Jewish tradition, is more sanctified than space; but if there is an earthly intersection of the two, it is surely here in this place at this moment, where it is said that heaven meets earth and, for twenty-four hours, steps beyond its own boundaries.

As the last rays of the sun streaked bands of golden light across the Old City, Yankel and I made our way to the Holy Wall. We separated at the partition that divides the men from the women—a separation based, at least in part, upon the mystical concept that during prayer, male and female energies should not commingle, in order to channel the desire for intimacy toward union with the Divine.

Before entering, I stood on the side and looked at the women in the courtyard, as they began to say the special prayers welcoming the Sabbath. They seemed to have come from all places and all times, as new as the moon whose rebirth is celebrated here each month and as ancient as the stones upon which we were standing.

The range of their relationship to tradition was perhaps best reflected in the diversity of their headwear. In response to the Biblical precept that married women should not expose their hair in public (hair being considered a vehicle through which spiritual and sexual energy are transmitted), some accepted the ruling without reservation; some disagreed with the interpretation and chose to ignore it completely; and others tried to find their own level of comfort somewhere in between. The injunction to cover one's hair was treated variously as a religious obligation, a spiritual opportunity, a restriction to be rebelled against, a mere suggestion, and a modern irrelevancy—all of which made for quite a collage of possibilities, each well represented in the courtyard.

Among the uncovered heads—where I myself would once have stood—there was everything from purple punk to aging-hippie gray, with moussed blonds and curly brunettes well represented. The fully covered heads—among which I now counted myself—were amply clothed in oversized hats, wigs, snoods, shawls, and flowing scarves of cotton, silk, and rayon. The partially covered middle-of-the-roaders had on small caps, lace doilies, little handkerchiefs, and everything shunned by both the fully covered and the uncovered.

The men's section was no less complicated. There were Orthodox men in black hats—hamburgs, fedoras, and borsalinos—each indicating a particular affiliation; Chassidim in *shtreimels* and *spodeks* (wide fur hats—yes, fur in June); and everyone across the religious spectrum (Orthodox, Conservative, Reform, Reconstructionist, Renewal, and Unaffiliated) wearing yarmulkes made of black velvet, white cotton, traditional satin, and handwoven Moroccan wool; crocheted *kippahs* in all sizes and patterns; intricately embroidered skullcaps; rainbow rasta hats; berets; and baseball caps.

It was a clutterer's fantasy—a kaleidoscopic explosion of colors and fabrics, spanning all ages and nations, cultures and beliefs.

Yet, for all our diversity of expression, most of us had probably come with pretty much the same basic desire to welcome the Sabbath, draw closer to God, and share the experience with those around us.

As I would later learn, on every day of the year other than the Sabbath or a special Holy Day, the courtyard was also filled with throngs of beggars who would repeatedly ask the worshippers for a few shekels to help them get by until better times were upon us. In the merit of the charity given, the holy beggars would bestow their blessing upon the worshippers.

It was a daily ritual—deeply touching to some, chronically irritating to others—but one that I would personally come to cherish as an integral part of the Kotel experience. A reminder of sorts that, in this imperfect world of ours, caring for the needs of others was not a burdensome obligation to be discharged every now and then in some grand philanthropic gesture, but a godly act to be savored slowly, day by day, shekel by shekel, one holy beggar at a time.

On the Sabbath, however, when all forms of money were forbidden, there were no holy beggars with whom to interact. This, of course, had the immediate effect of creating a quieter and less congested environment. As a result, I was able to navigate my way to the front of the courtyard with relative ease, but, sadly, with diminished opportunity to help a sister in need—an act no doubt as spiritually meaningful as the one I was off in search of.

Slowly making my way across the courtyard, I tried to imagine what it would feel like to finally press my face to the stones that held the tears and supplications of millions of people. Was it all still there, I wondered—thousands of years of pain and hope and unwavering faith? Could any physical object—even the Holy Wall—contain so much emotion and such intense spiritual longing?

As I drew closer to the Kotel, I passed rows of women in various modes of prayer. Some were swaying intently, their arms outstretched and their palms facing upward; others stood rod-straight and perfectly still. There were elderly women, hunched over the worn pages of their prayer books, and young girls, their eyes closed and their heads tilted toward heaven. There was silence, and there was singing; self-contained meditation and wildly ecstatic prayer. I inhaled deeply, wanting to absorb all of it and make it my own.

When I finally reached the Kotel, a few women standing directly in front of me seemed to sense that this was my first visit. They graciously stepped back and allowed me, not only to come close to the Holy Wall, but to have a bit of space around me on either side.

I smiled gratefully at them and then turned toward the Wall, bracing myself for the feeling of cool stone against my cheek. Cool was not a sensation that I generally liked. Other than on a day when the temperature was in the nineties or I was running a high fever—neither of which was the case today—I took no pleasure in anything cold. I liked my hot beverages steaming hot, and, in the case of thirst-quenching drinks, I preferred them at room temperature with no ice.

As I took my final step forward, I suddenly noticed all the bits of paper that had been stuffed into the Kotel's many cracks and crevices—handwritten, tearstained notes from all corners of the world, beseeching God to bless the writers with health and happiness, loving marriages and good children, peace and prosperity and a long life in which to enjoy it all.

I wondered if my own requests were still there. Over the years, friends going to Israel had deposited many of my desperate pleas for clarity and order and spiritual guidance in these very spaces. And, now, I was here, at last, to offer my prayers in person.

Careful not to dislodge any of the notes, I slowly raised my hands to the Wall and placed my cheek against the smooth rocks. But there was no sensation, as anticipated, of a cool assault upon my skin. Instead, my cheek was gently greeted with the unexpected warmth of stones left baking all day in the Jerusalem sun.

To me, this was not simply an act of nature that I had over-looked in my calculations. It seemed, instead, that my Host—in a gesture of extraordinary kindness—had made certain to perform the spiritual equivalent of heating the guest towels before I arrived. It was, after all, my very first visit; and I needed, perhaps, to feel fussed over a bit and personally welcomed. Now, as the warmth penetrated my skin, I felt certain that I was standing in the presence of such pure love that no person or object or distracting thought could ever come between us again.

I returned to the Kotel at midnight that night—and just about every other night during the entire month that we spent in the Old City. Midnight was said to be a particularly auspicious time to connect spiritually at the Holy Wall, and I clearly needed all the help I could get.

The timing actually worked well for me. I was generally awake at midnight anyway and never experienced the jet lag that everyone had warned me about. Or maybe I did but never identi-fied it as jet lag.

Being as out of sync with time as I tended to be, it was not uncommon for me to lose an entire day or night every now and then. However, I generally considered whatever adjustments I needed to make to get back on track nothing more than simple realignments—the sort of thing a chiropractor would do to get a kink out of my neck, or a repair shop to get all my tires moving in the same direction again.

It was necessary to reset my inner clock so often that I had come to regard the process as my own personal form of daylight savings time. Now that I thought about it, I had probably lived my entire life in a revolving state of jet lag, but I had never realized—until this moment—that there was actually a name for it.

In any case, midnight at the Kotel was a perfect fit.

Most nights, I set out alone, relishing the solitude of my five-minute walk through our tree-lined courtyard, out the arched gate, and across Misgav Ladach Street. Sometimes Yankel came with me, especially during the first few days when he was seriously jet lagged himself and had trouble sleeping. But, after that, I was mostly on my own, which was just as well because it gave me the freedom to come and go as I pleased.

That first Friday night at the Holy Wall, I was overcome with a new sense of hope and possibility; but a week later, I found myself stuck in the same place I had always been. All the things I was certain would never again disturb my connection to God had returned in full force to block my way once more.

Standing at the Kotel, surrounded by more holiness than I had ever felt in any one place at one time, I found myself strangely and uncontrollably distracted. During the day, it was people praying too loudly, tourists snapping pictures, birds hovering overhead (reincarnated souls, some said, but their interminable flapping drove me crazy nonetheless), cell phones chiming and vibrating, heavy perfume triggering my allergies . . . The world seemed like one hyperactive mosquito, hell-bent on destroying any concentration I could summon.

Even at midnight—as much as I loved the Holy Wall at that magical hour—I was never able to be fully present. The distractions were more internal, but no less bothersome. My mind flitted back and forth between the things I needed to do the next day, the places I was hoping to visit, the thoughts and feelings I wanted to record in my journal, the decisions I had to make about the renovation back home, and, of course, the fate of that duffle bag filled with dirty laundry that had traveled halfway across the world to park itself right in the middle of my meditation.

I couldn't quite believe my own inability to focus on anything spiritual. Here I was in the Holy Land at last, in this city of breathtaking beauty, standing at one of the most sacred places on earth—and all I could think about was tomorrow's errands and the color of my new kitchen in Brooklyn. And I called myself spiritual. Who was I kidding?

My friends, of course, begged to differ. They had all sorts of creative theories about my current inability to connect to God, but none of it convinced me that I was anything less than a spiritual charlatan. All these years, all that soul-searching and desperate longing—and now that I had finally taken the ultimate step on my journey, I couldn't concentrate long enough to repeat a three-word mantra.

I was beginning to think that Lisa Marie was right. Perhaps my search for God had been no search at all, but a convoluted act of self-sabotage, conveniently designed to prevent me from ever reaching my destination, while providing me with the illusion of being on a sincere quest. And maybe my clutter was really part of that design and not an obstacle to it at all.

When I finally got Lisa Marie on the telephone and described my current struggle, along with my most recent insight—which was basically a restatement of her own theory—she was silent for a moment and then responded with genuine concern in her voice.

"Don't give up, Pesi," she said. "You know, we say in the Program that *trying* to pray *is* praying. We're responsible for the effort, not the outcome. So, no matter how distracted or unworthy you feel, your job is just to keep on trying. And, sooner or later, you *will* get a response—even if it looks nothing like what you expect."

"*I* think you should leave," Yidis said when I talked to her later that day.

"Leave?" I responded. "I just got here."

"I don't mean leave Israel," she explained. "Just the Old City. And only for a few days."

"But I love it here more than anyplace I've ever been. Why should I leave? The fact that I can't focus and connect spiritually is obviously *my* problem. It has nothing to do with the Old City."

"Of course," she agreed. "But because the Old City is such a special place, it might be contributing to your problem. I mean, all that holiness can be a little intimidating. Trying to pray at the Kotel could be giving you performance anxiety—kind of like walking down the aisle at your own wedding. It's such a highly charged moment, and there's so much pressure to make the experience beautiful and memorable that sometimes we just freeze and can't feel anything.

"The way I look at it, there's nothing that kills peace and joy as surely as oversized expectations. Which is probably why vacations cause so much stress. And this is so much more than just a vacation. But, hopefully, in a different environment with fewer expectations, things will start to flow more naturally."

"You're probably right," I agreed. "So, where do you think I should go?"

I was certain that she would suggest a healing spa at the Dead Sea or a beachfront resort in Eilat or Netanya.

"I think Tsfat would be perfect," Yidis suggested.

"Tsfat?" I responded, totally surprised. "But that's just as spiritually intense as Jerusalem."

"Well, yes and no," Yidis said. "Yes, because there are all these holy sites there, and people come by the thousands to pray at them; but no, because there's more open space and access to nature. It's not enclosed the way that the Old City is, and it has a freer energy. They say that Jerusalem is fire and Tsfat is air; and, right now, I think you could use a deep breath of fresh air.

"I know there are a lot of places you can go just to relax—and Tsfat certainly isn't one of them—but you're here on a spiritual journey; and I think that sitting in a mud bath or sunning yourself on the beach isn't going to make you feel as peaceful as finding what you came looking for. You can do all the rest of it on your next trip."

"Well, we were planning to go to Tsfat at some point anyway," I said, "so I guess we might as well do it sooner rather than later. But how should we get there—it's about four hours north of Jerusalem, isn't it?—and where do you think we should stay?"

"It's been quite a few years since I was in Israel," Yidis said, "and things have changed a lot in that time. Why don't you call Raezelle—she really knows her way around. She met you at the airport, didn't she?"

"Yes," I said, recalling the excitement of that moment. "With Leah and Reizl Malka and Elana. It was a wonderful Holy Sisters' reunion."

"You know," Yidis suggested, "Raezelle has a driver's license, and she speaks Hebrew pretty well. I bet she could rent a car and organize a little trip."

It was a great idea, and I called Raezelle immediately. Within a few hours, we had a plan in motion: Raezelle, Leah, and Elana had been talking for months about going camping in the Banias—a beautiful nature preserve with hidden caves and magnificent waterfalls—which was slightly north of Tsfat; but they had no means of transportation. If we all shared the rental of a car, they could drop us off in Tsfat for a few days, go camping, and pick us up on the way back. Of course, they wanted to spend time in Tsfat as well, but they could do that on their own, making the trip by bus. This was a rare opportunity to go someplace that really required a car.

I couldn't believe how easily the whole plan was coming together. Leah even had a friend who knew a great place to stay in Tsfat—a lovely guesthouse with a balcony overlooking the hills of Meron, where Rabbi Shimon bar Yochai (author of the Zohar, the primary text on the mystical tradition of Kabbalah) had been buried in the second century. And it was walking distance to every place we wanted to go—the ancient synagogues and study halls, the cemetery where many Kabbalists and holy rabbis were buried, the Artists' Quarter, and all the felafel stands and espresso cafés in town. It couldn't have been more ideal.

But it was.

This little guesthouse actually had a washing machine right outside our front door. When I called to make the reservation, the owner assured me that it was nothing fancy, but a good old solid machine.

"It's the only one on the premises for our guests," she told me, "but since it's on your front porch, no one will use it while you're here."

"This is a miracle," I proclaimed.

"Yes, it's nice to have something for wet towels and bathing suits," she replied, obviously having no idea that anyone who sounded as normal as I probably did was planning to bring a fifty-pound duffle bag of laundry from Brooklyn. "We don't have a dryer here, but we do offer the Mediterranean sun free of charge. And it's the best dryer in town."

Now, I was really beginning to get excited. A trip to Tsfat, the ancient birthplace of Kabbalah. I tried to imagine what it must have been like there in the sixteenth century, when bearded mystics in long, flowing caftans walked the cobblestone streets, seeking to unlock the deepest mysteries of the universe. Soon, I would be walking those same streets—wearing freshly laundered garments above my new Israeli sandals.

I got out my suitcases and started to pack immediately.

The following morning, Raezelle, Leah, and Elana pulled into the parking lot of the Old City, driving the minivan we had rented for our trip. Yankel and I, unfortunately, were nowhere to be seen. The Holy Sisters waited patiently until we finally arrived, short of breath and dragging two oversized suitcases and my bulging duffle bag—a full twenty minutes later than we had agreed to meet.

"What happened?" they asked, sounding more curious than upset.

"Oh, it's a story," I assured them. "We'll tell you on the way."

Once we were on the road heading north, Yankel and I took turns explaining how our morning had unfolded.

The Old City, it seemed, maintained its special timeless quality—at least in part—by not allowing too much of the twenty-first century to pass beyond its gates. There were, of course, little food markets, bookstores, gift shops, and the ubiquitous felafel stands—but not a whole lot more. This was all fine with me, except for the absence of two significant items whose omission impacted directly upon my life.

First, there was not a single laundromat in the entire Jewish Quarter. Apparently, most people either had their own washing machine, used the machine of a friend or neighbor, or brought their laundry out of the Old City to be washed—none of which seemed like reasonable options for me. (Yankel, in an amazing stroke of good fortune, met an old friend who generously offered to wash his one small bag of laundry for him. However, no one I knew had a washing machine, and I wasn't about to spend an entire day dragging my duffle bag by bus to downtown Jerusalem.)

Secondly, the Old City did not allow cars. There were no roads, no parking places, no gas stations. You could bring your car as far as the parking lot just inside the city walls, but no farther. So, even if you were one of the fortunate few who actually owned a car, you still had to travel everywhere in the Old City by foot. And no matter where you went, your foot did not step upon a normally paved street, but on a roughly hewn cobblestone path.

Now, all of this was delightfully quaint and charming, unless you had to actually transport something from Point A to Point B—something like two oversized suitcases and a fifty-pound duffle bag. Since our apartment was probably a good half mile from the parking lot, up and down stairs in the main plaza, and through a few winding alleys, we realized that we had a major challenge on our hands. On the way in, the cabdriver—for a well-earned tip—had piled all of our bags on a dolly and brought them to our front door. This time, however, we seemed to be on our own.

One of our neighbors suggested that we ask Boris for help. He was a local handyman and recent immigrant, always in need of a few extra shekels.

"No worry," Boris assured us when we explained—in the simplest English possible—just what our dilemma was. "I send my son tomorrow morning at 8:00 with wagon, and he brings all bags to parking lot—only cost you forty shekels—no worry."

But the following morning, we found ourselves with no handyman, no handyman's son, no wagon, and plenty to worry about. Both of our suitcases had wheels, but they were quite old and not designed for cobblestone streets—especially not mine, which was overloaded and in disrepair to begin with. A few feet from our front door, one of my wheels fell off; and then, a block later, another one; and, finally, a third. The suitcase—far too heavy to carry such a distance—had to be dragged the rest of the way on one wheel, along with the duffle bag, which was wearing dangerously thin from all the friction. I only prayed that we made it to the parking lot with the bag intact and no dirty laundry scattered across the plaza. And, so, we inched our way forward, beneath the already-blazing Jerusalem sun, pushing and pulling, dragging and rolling all of the things that, at the time we were packing, seemed absolutely essential to take on a three-day spiritual retreat.

After Yankel and I finished telling our tale and I closed my eyes to rest, I began to see the cobblestone streets of the Old City as the perfect metaphor for my own path through life—a richly textured but somewhat complicated road to follow, surrounded by beauty and holiness on all sides, but impossible to navigate with the extensive baggage I was carrying with me.

I was so exhausted after the morning's adventure and the previous night's packing that I fell asleep and missed most of the scenic ride that I had spent a whole day looking forward to. When I finally awoke, we were already climbing the hill to Tsfat, and I could see Mount Meron rising in the background.

There is a color that can only be described as Tsfat blue, which winds its way through this mysterious city like the thread of the same color that is woven into a Hebrew prayer shawl. It is a rich and resonant blue that evokes the sea, the sky, and the egg of a robin—which is, of course, no coincidence, since the color is obviously meant to remind us of God's presence in nature and beyond.

Local mystics say it is the color of heaven; and the holy city of Tsfat—already well on its way to the Upper Worlds (resting, as it does, at the highest elevation in the country)—has chosen to wear this celestial shade at all times and in all seasons to remind everyone who passes through to turn their thoughts toward the heavenly realms.

Tsfat blue appears in all the places that you would most—and least—expect to find it. Synagogues here have used it for centuries to adorn their walls and woodwork and ceilings; local artists and craftspeople splash it freely throughout the work they exhibit in the galleries and outdoor markets of the Artists' Quarter; residents paint it on their doors and gates—and businesses, on their storefronts; and even the ancient cemetery, where many of the holiest rabbis and Kabbalists are buried, proudly displays it upon the graves of some of its most illustrious inhabitants.

When we arrived at our guesthouse, I was overjoyed to find the entranceway painted in just that shade of blue. And not only the entrance to the courtyard, but our own front door and the wooden shutters on our windows and the wrought iron railing on the stairs leading up to our apartment. I imagined myself spending the next three days blissfully floating in a sea of Tsfat blue, reluctant to ever return to the world of earth tones again.

However, as we were standing in the courtyard admiring all the lovely touches, it suddenly occurred to me that we would actually have to *climb* that steep and winding staircase with the beautiful blue railing in order to reach our front door—and there was no one around to help with our oversized luggage, since we had apparently arrived at what was the Tsfat equivalent of siesta time. But, somehow, with Raezelle, Leah, and Elana pushing and Yankel and I pulling, we managed to get all our bags up the steps—by which point, Yankel and I were pretty much ready for a siesta ourselves.

When we awoke, we sat out on the balcony overlooking Meron and ate the zatar bread dipped in lemon hummus and olive spread that we had purchased on the way in from the Yemenite café in town. And, then, to make our meal official, I prepared two cups of Moroccan coffee with steamed milk and ground cardamom. As we leaned back in our chairs, our feet resting on the blue railing, our arms dangling in the warm sunshine, we both agreed that it was hard to imagine life being much sweeter than this.

Later in the afternoon, we took a walk to the Old City— which, like the Old City of Jerusalem, was filled with cobblestones and holy sites. But there seemed more to buy here and definitely more to eat, as if the otherworldly nature of this place had to be grounded in a greater level of physicality to keep it from drifting off into the Tsfat blue sky. I could totally relate to that need because I was beginning to feel a bit off balance myself from the sudden infusion of so much spiritual energy. And, yet, it was a dream come true.

We stopped for a bite at Mystic Pizza—"How could you not?" Yankel said when he saw the name—and walked home along the western edge of Tsfat, as the sun was beginning to set over the Upper Galilee. Tomorrow, we were planning to visit the cemetery and a few of the ancient synagogues. And I was hoping to find some time to go off by myself and try to connect with that elusive Higher Power of mine.

We returned to our room just in time to catch the most dramatic moments of the sunset from our balcony. As the last flaming rays of purple and orange filled the sky, we opened the bottle of cabernet we had picked up in town, lit a candle, and sat in silence watching the sky darken and the stars come to life. I could see why so many artists had settled in Tsfat. And even if you weren't an artist to begin with, I could see how you might fast become one here.

By ten o'clock, Yankel was beginning to yawn. Actually, so was I, but I tried to resist the urge. We were only going to be here for three nights, and I had enough laundry for at least six washes, which meant that I had to average two a night in order to have time and space for everything to dry in the sun before the next batch was ready. I knew I would never manage to get the laundry done before we went out in the morning, so this was really my only opportunity.

"Are you actually going to use that thing?" he asked, pointing at the largest and probably oldest single-load washing machine either of us had ever seen—clearly the product of another era. "I bet it's been here since the days of the Second Temple. Does it work on electricity, or are we supposed to stand here and blow on it or something?"

"Only when you want to dry the clothing," I said, trying to keep it light.

"Speaking of which, where *is* the dryer?" he asked, looking around.

I pointed up at the sky.

"You're joking, of course," he said hopefully.

"No, I'm not. My mother dried our clothing that way, and so did her mother and her mother and probably your mother as well."

"My mother did not," Yankel assured me. "We lived in a high-rise co-op in Astoria. People didn't do that sort of thing there."

I decided it would be wise to end the conversation at this point. He was obviously overtired, and so was I; and it did not seem the ideal moment to discuss the merits of his mother's apartment-size dryer in Queens versus my mother's backyard clothesline in the Bronx.

"I'll be in soon," I said, as he kissed me goodnight. "I'm not ready to go to bed just yet, so I might as well do something useful. And just think—by this time tomorrow, I should finally have some clean summer clothes to wear."

"If it doesn't rain," he called over his shoulder—a possibility I had never even considered.

But I quickly put it out of my mind, preferring to dwell upon the ancient Chassidic teaching, "Think good, and it will be good." And, so, with good thoughts in my heart and a pile of laundry in my arms, I walked out into the fragrant mountain air of Tsfat.

I have often wondered just what it would take to move a seemingly normal person to the brink of madness; what confluence of events could create a violent explosion in an otherwise peace-loving soul.

I received an unexpected education on the topic that first night in Tsfat.

Shortly after Yankel went to sleep, I started to prepare my first load of laundry. This meant sorting everything in the duffle bag and combining it with the new additions from my suitcase. As expected, it all added up to six loads, divided according to category and color. I took out the detergent, bleach, and fabric softener, which thankfully had not leaked all over my clothing. By 11:15, I was ready to begin.

I decided to do my least delicate whites first because I wanted to add a lot of extra bleach, since I had no idea who had used the washing machine before I arrived. I could only hope it was someone who believed that cleanliness came in a close second to Godliness.

The machine made more noises—and far stranger ones—than any washer I had ever encountered and took about twice as long to complete a cycle. However, I was so pleased at the prospect of having one less pile of dirty laundry to contend with that I sat patiently through the seemingly endless rounds of swishing and churning. After what must have been well over an hour, the machine finally sputtered to a stop, and the red "Finish" light came on.

I immediately removed the wet laundry and began to hang it on the wooden rack beside the machine. I didn't want to go overboard, however, and make the beautiful courtyard look like a Fluff and Fold annex, so I took whatever seemed like it would dry quickly and hung it in the apartment. I figured I could always move things around in the morning.

The second load was really the most important—all the light-colored T-shirts and cotton tops that I needed for the hot summer days here. And, so, I tried to push the faded dial onto what looked like the gentle cycle with the temperature set at cold water only. By now, I was feeling pretty comfortable with the operation, so I loaded the machine, paid little attention to its strange noises and sporadic twitches, and sat in the cool night breeze reading a book on the holy sites of Tsfat.

About ten minutes into the wash cycle, the vibrations became so intense that I feared the onset of an earthquake, until I realized that nothing but the washing machine was shaking. Within a matter of seconds, the machine—behaving as if it were suddenly possessed by a dybbuk—had what I can only describe as a grand mal seizure. I'd never seen anything quite like it before. When my washer in Brooklyn died, it went out with a quiet whimper; but, apparently, in this land of heightened intensity, even the machines passed on with a soul-wrenching cry.

At first, I was too stunned to react. Then, in a matter of minutes, I moved through all five stages of the classic response to death. I went from denial to anger to bargaining to depression to acceptance; but I quickly returned to anger.

"How could God do this to me?" I asked aloud, as I plunged my hands into the icy water. Each item was soaking wet, which was bad enough—but also full of soap, which was even worse. Over the course of the next hour, I carried all the dripping laundry into the kitchen sink, where I washed each piece by hand, wrung it out as thoroughly as I could with frozen fingers, and—too upset by that point to care about aesthetics—draped it across the Tsfat blue railing to dry.

Then, I sat down on the ground and slowly began to unravel.

However, even as I was losing control, I stopped to point out to myself that, in the larger scheme of things, this was utterly ridiculous. People were suffering with terrible illnesses, dying in wars, watching their children go hungry, being oppressed and tortured and unjustly imprisoned—and, here I was, making a fuss about having to wring out a few wet T-shirts. Of course, it was just that sort of dismissive thinking that had, no doubt, led to this moment to begin with.

The world is—and, sadly, always has been—filled with terrible tragedies; and most of humanity suffers far more than I do. An important fact to remember when I succumb to self-pity and lose my perspective. But am I not entitled from time to time to bemoan my own misery, no matter how it pales alongside the misery of others? Does my paper cut have to be compared to someone else's gaping wound? If something causes me discomfort, I would like to believe that I have the right to complain about it—and even, on occasion, to briefly whine—without feeling guilty.

I say all of this in hindsight. As I sat on the floor that night, I had no such awareness. I simply swung back and forth between feeling angry at God that, no matter what I did, my life seemed to be enshrouded in mess and, then, thinking that I had no right to be feeling such anger because my life was basically so good. There I was, crouched on a cold cement slab, sobbing, feeling totally abandoned by God—and telling myself that I was not even entitled to my own spiritual breakdown.

But, finally, I couldn't take it anymore. Entitled or not, I began to tell God just what I thought of the way He was handling my life—fully expecting, at any moment, a flash of lightning to come out of the indigo sky and send me and all of my wet laundry off to the next world.

"This isn't fair," I began in a whisper, but I could hear my voice growing louder and more agitated as I went on. Fortunately, there were no other guests within earshot, and Yankel was sound asleep two rooms away.

"All I want—all I've ever wanted—is a little peace and quiet so that I can feel more spiritual. I know it's my own fault that I have so much clutter and that I make everything so complicated, but I've really been trying to change all that. And I'm sorry to say that I don't feel you're helping me.

"Every time I turn around, you seem to send me another little crisis that creates more clutter in my life. Each one is really no big deal, but all together, it's more than I can handle. Moves and floods and leaks and more moves and more floods and collapsed ceilings and broken washing machines. I just can't take it anymore. No matter what I do, my world is always in chaos.

"How can I get close to you when you keep putting all these obstacles in my path? Here I am in this holy city, trying—as always—to find you; and, instead, look what I have to spend my time dealing with!

"I know I usually choose the most roundabout way of getting things done, but I'm really trying to simplify my life. And, still, everything I do seems to become one huge mess. Did this washing machine really have to die right now, with all my wet, soapy T-shirts in it? Would the earth have fallen off its axis and life as we know it come to an end if the machine had died the following week—or, at least, at the end of the spin cycle?

"Do you want to know what I really think?" I said, my voice rising even higher now. "I think that you don't care about me at all, that you're not interested in having a relationship with me, that it wouldn't bother you one bit if you never heard from me again. So, if that's how you feel, then I give up—and who cares if my laundry is clean or dirty or piled in one big heap right in the middle of this stupid blue courtyard?"

And, with that, I proceeded to take each piece of wet laundry—one by one—and throw it violently at the washing machine, until the entire porch was covered with bleached socks and snowy white towels and every pastel-colored T-shirt I owned. I had to admit that, at the end, although I felt like a complete lunatic, I also felt freer than I could ever remember having felt before.

I could hear Yankel gasp as he opened the front door to check the weather the next morning. I was standing at the kitchen counter making coffee, not at all in the mood to discuss the events of the night before.

"Pesi, come here—This is terrible!—What happened to your laundry? Was there a storm here last night after I went to bed?"

"I guess you could say that," I responded calmly, not bothering to explain myself further.

"Well, what happened?" Yankel persisted, never having seen me quite this way before.

"I'll tell you about it some other time," I said evasively. "Right now, I need a few hours to myself. Why don't we meet for a late lunch at that Yemenite café, and then we can walk around the Artists' Quarter together? I think I'd rather leave the cemetery for tomorrow."

Yankel, taken aback by my strange behavior, seemed ready to agree to just about anything.

As soon as he was out the door, I called one of the car services listed in the local directory and arranged for a cabdriver to pick me up in twenty minutes. I stuffed all my laundry—wet and dry, dirty and clean—into the duffle bag and packed the detergent into a canvas tote. For a few extra shekels, the driver was only too happy to load all my bags into his car, drive me to a laundromat in town, carry everything in for me, and return to pick me up several hours later. Why, I wondered, had I never thought of anything like this before?

The whole trip went so smoothly that I had an hour to spare before I was due to meet Yankel for lunch. It would have been a perfect opportunity to take a stroll on the outskirts of town and have that long-overdue conversation with my Higher Power. But after my outburst the night before, I felt too embarrassed to even consider the possibility. I sat and meditated instead. It wasn't a great experience either, but observing my breath created far less stress than facing the Master of the Universe after I had spent the night hurling wet laundry at Him. I wondered if this was how the ancient Israelites felt the morning after their episode with the Golden Calf.

On our last night in Tsfat, as we walked back from our dinner at Mystic Pizza, we talked about what an amazing few days it had been—and, yet, how anxious we both were to return to the Old City. Tsfat, as beautiful and holy as it was, had simply not opened its gates and received us with the same loving welcome that Jerusalem had. And, unlike most places in the world where people choose their cities, in Israel, it often seemed to be the cities that did the choosing.

As we walked, I decided to tell Yankel a little bit about my fight with God. I wasn't ready to discuss it in great detail just yet, but I felt I had to say something.

"So, what do you plan to do now?" he asked when I finished my story.

"I don't know," I answered. "I feel like I need a therapist from the other world."

"Well, you've certainly come to the right place for that," he said."

Yes, I suddenly realized. I probably had. "Any idea where I might find one around here?"

"No, but I bet my sister knows someone."

"When is she coming back?"

"Well, I spoke to her a few days ago, and she said she was planning to return later this week; but, of course, you never know."

We both smiled at the image of his sister—the eternal free spirit—coming and going as the cosmic forces moved her.

"I can't believe that we totally missed each other," I said. "Our planes practically crossed in the air—we landed in Tel Aviv just as she was leaving for New York—what timing! Anyway, I'm glad she'll be here soon."

"Well, we'll see . . ." Yankel said, never quite sure what might happen when it came to the arrival of either his sister or his wife.

few days after we drove back to Jerusalem, Yankel's sister called to say that she was on her way back as well. The Old City had been her home since she left Brooklyn in the mid-'90s, and, like us, she couldn't wait to return.

The next afternoon, Yankel and I climbed the many winding steps leading to her rooftop apartment with a large bouquet of pale pink roses in our arms. (She always had at least one pale pink wall somewhere in her home, so it seemed a good choice.) We stood by her front door for a few minutes before knocking, waiting for our breathing to return to normal and admiring the newly painted sign that said, in finely scripted Hebrew and English calligraphy, BRACHA DIN—JEWELS OF JERUSALEM.

Bracha, whose name (pronounced Brah-kha) means blessing in Hebrew, was a sister on many levels. She was Yankel's sister by birth and, of course, my sister-in-law by marriage; but she was one of my most beloved Holy Sisters as well. I couldn't wait to see her and hear all about her life and her new adventure with gemstones.

Entering Bracha's apartment was a bit like stepping from the workweek into the Sabbath. You were immediately transported to a place of almost magical serenity. It felt as if every object were radiating holiness and light, and the rooms themselves seemed filled with prayer. Wherever Bracha lived, her home always exuded that quality; but, here, in the Old City, there was something much deeper and more affecting about the tranquility she had created.

In addition to the beauty of her antique lace and delicately woven fabrics, she now had precious and semiprecious stones, pearls, crystals, and hand-blown glass beads neatly displayed throughout the apartment. They dangled from hooks in her windows and stretched across the arch of her doorway. They sat in baskets and bowls and glass jars on tabletops and shelves. Bracha explained that on their way to becoming necklaces and bracelets, earrings and pins, the stones were absorbing the energy of the Old City, making them truly into Jerusalem jewels.

We spent the afternoon catching up on all that was new with each other and with our family, friends, and Holy Sisters. Then, we talked about how much we loved being in the land of Israel and especially in the Old City; and Bracha told us about her latest attempt to share the beauty of the land with everyone who passed through.

"I've been taking people on retreats to some of the most exquisite places in Israel," Bracha explained. "Like the Negev Desert, the Judean Hills, and the ancient tunnels beneath the Old City. I call these trips 'quiet tours' because in the silence of these holy places, you can hear the voice of your own soul and the soul of the land."

I wanted to know more about these special places, but I could see that Yankel was beginning to get tired and hungry. So, we all went off to eat at Bonkers Bagels—one of the Old City's few concessions to the modern world—and then Bracha and I took a long walk together while Yankel headed home for a nap.

"Bracha, I need your help," I said as soon as we were alone. And I proceeded to tell her about my unsuccessful attempts to connect with God here in Jerusalem and Tsfat and everyplace else, grateful that she already knew the background to the story and was familiar with all my issues concerning laundry and clutter and the general mess of my life.

"How can I help?" she asked when I finished describing the problem.

"I think I need to talk to a Kabbalist. Do you know of anyone here?"

"I know of a few," she said, "but I'm not sure that's really what you need. I mean, it's always nice to talk to someone who understands the Higher Worlds, but it seems to me that what you're really looking for is a wise, compassionate person to help you connect the physical and the spiritual in *this* world. Of course, if that person happens to study a little Kabbalah on the side, all the better."

"Okay," I agreed. "That's good advice. Can you think of anyone who fits the description?"

"Actually I can," Bracha said, after giving it a moment's thought. "But you have to be willing to set aside your expectations."

"What expectations?" I asked.

"The ones we all have about what a spiritually evolved person looks like and sounds like."

"I don't think I have any expectations about that."

"Well," Bracha said, not sounding convinced, "it might not be conscious, but most of us have some image in our mind. It probably comes from all those New Age magazines we still read in bed late at night."

"Maybe you're right," I admitted, recalling an article I had just seen about a yoga teacher in Sedona who dressed only in white to keep her energy pure. I remember thinking to myself how holy she looked—when, in fact, what did I really know?

"All right," I promised, "I'll try my best to keep an open mind. So, who's this person you're thinking of?"

"Her name is Tova," Bracha said, "which means good in Hebrew, and she is very good. She's a deep and wise soul who just knows things."

"You mean 'just knows' like she's psychic?"

"Well, let's just say she's extremely intuitive, and I'm sure she'll have plenty of Kabbalistic insights to share with you. Tova is really a special person—very spiritual, very kind and caring, very warm and down to earth."

"She sounds wonderful," I agreed. "But what makes you think she'll be able to help me move beyond my clutter and connect to God?"

"Trust me," Bracha said.

And, coming from my Holy Sister in the Holy Land, that was reason enough for me.

CHAPTER NINE

Starting Over

*"And the end of all our exploring will be to arrive where
we started and know the place for the first time."*
—T. S. Eliot

Early the next morning, I boarded a bus heading to Tova's house
in one of the suburbs of Jerusalem. Bracha had arranged the
whole thing the night before, so all I had to do was show up with
a notebook, a tape recorder, and a thermos of coffee. Tova, Bracha
had warned me apologetically, only drank tea. I was hoping that
would be her sole lapse of good judgment.

I spent most of the forty-minute bus ride—which, the driver
announced several times, would have taken only twenty if the road
had not been under construction for the past two years—looking
out the window and thinking about my expectations. I tried to
imagine what a mystical woman living in a cottage in Jerusalem
would look like.

Bracha had already disabused me of my first misconception: the term *cottage* in Israel simply referred to a small home; it didn't imply thatched roofs, rose-covered trellises, winding walkways, or other fairy tale features. She didn't want me to go off in misguided anticipation of a gingerbread house.

Okay, that was one expectation down. I tried to scan my brain for more; and although I was certain there were none to be found, a number of others soon rose to the surface. The first was that of a healer I had once seen—a tall, ethereal woman with porcelain skin and pale eyes, more angelic than human. This was an easy one to discard, since she looked like she belonged in a Scandinavian ashram rather than on a dusty road in Jerusalem.

The next image that came to mind was that of an archetypal earth mother—better suited perhaps to early kibbutz life—with a ruddy complexion and peasant features, who ground her own grain and could hear ancient secrets revealed in the whispering of the wind through the olive trees and the lemon groves.

I continued to scroll through images of healers and holy women, surprised at how many there actually were in my mental file and how easily I was able to reconfigure them to fit the present situation. I imagined an aged Sephardic woman—in my file, she was actually a Native American, but it was an easy switch to make—draped in an elaborately embroidered robe from her neck to her ankles, her piercing black eyes staring deep into my confused soul.

Then, there was a dark-skinned sabra in a long, flowing dress, headscarf, and biblical sandals; a Bukharan woman in bright Mediterranean colors carrying red strings, crystals, herbs from the Galilee, and vials of sacred water; and the woman from the New Age magazine, still dressed all in white, but now chanting in Hebrew instead of Sanskrit.

I tried, as Bracha had suggested, to move as far beyond these mental pictures as I could. But walking up the path to Tova's house, I realized that no amount of image cleansing could have prepared me for this moment.

As I drew closer, it became obvious that Tova possessed the one quality that had never made it into any of my fantasies—that of an utterly ordinary and unremarkable appearance. Basically, Tova looked just like everyone else—or, at least, like everyone else's grandmother. She was a plump, gray-haired woman sitting in a rocking chair, sipping tea from a little flowered cup with a matching saucer. Unlike the women in my pantheon of spiritual guides and healers, there was absolutely nothing mysterious or exotic about her.

Even her voice had nothing more distinctive to it than a trace of working class inflection left over from her days in Hoboken, New Jersey, where, she later told me, she had been born and lived for most of her life until moving to Israel several decades ago.

"I bet you were expecting someone very different," she said as she took my hand and led me to her kitchen. "But don't be upset at yourself for thinking that way. It's just human nature to try and fit our experiences into familiar places."

I must have looked quite awkward and embarrassed. After all, who wants to have their thoughts read—and graciously forgiven—by the very person they're in the process of misjudging? But Tova quickly smoothed over my discomfort by focusing on lunch, which, for me, was really breakfast—and I suddenly realized that I was starving.

I was well into my second bowl of couscous and chick peas before I could think of anything other than food. And Tova let me concentrate on eating by busying herself at the sink.

"Here," she said, handing me a cup of hot tea as soon as I swallowed my last mouthful of couscous. "Have you ever tried nana before?"

"I don't think so," I said. "What is it?"

"It's special mint tea—I grow it in my garden. I love it with these cookies," she said, handing me a plate of warm, obviously homemade apricot rugelach.

It was a simple meal, but I felt a deeply satisfying fullness come over me after I finished. Tova looked pleased as she piled the dishes into the sink and led me out to the garden to show me her rosebushes.

We were having a delightful time discussing the joys of cooking and organic gardening; but it was already well past noon, and I hadn't written one word in my notebook or turned on my tape recorder. However, I had also not opened my thermos of coffee, which probably said more than anything about how well the day was going.

"It's so lovely spending time together," Tova said, "but you're probably wondering when we're actually going to begin. Don't worry; we already have. Being fully present in the moment is the first step toward change."

I took out my notebook and started to write that down, but Tova gently shook her head.

"If you try to record what we're doing, part of you will feel like an observer. Why don't you put everything aside for now, and let's just concentrate on being with each other. How about going for a little walk? I can always think best when I'm moving."

"I would love to," I said, anxious to see as much of Jerusalem as possible.

As we stepped through the front door, Tova stood still, closed her eyes, and kissed the mezuzah. There is a Biblical commandment to hang a mezuzah on the doorpost of every Jewish home. These parchment scrolls in decorative cases declare the unity of God and are placed at each entranceway as a source of blessing and a reminder to keep God in our consciousness at all times. Tova's gesture seemed to immediately connect her to that awareness, and she was silent for a moment.

"Now," she said, as we turned onto the sidewalk, "you can tell me all about your life and the changes you want to make. Bracha said you're only going to be in Israel for a little while longer, so, with God's help, I hope we'll be able to find some answers quickly."

I decided to begin by telling Tova the recent history of my relationship with clutter, but it wasn't until the moment was upon me that I realized how many different ways there actually were of telling the story.

I could tell it as a tale of things: my personal battle—part love and part hate—with the objects of this world. A saga of lost keys and misplaced manuscripts; of tables and teapots and pottery bowls; of Bewilda and Hippilah; of procrastinated paperwork and unfinished projects and items in need of decision.

Or I could present it as a series of events: My fiftieth birthday; The Project; the dawning of the New Millennium; the tragedy of 9/11; moves and floods; trips to Vermont and Florida; a Twelve Step meeting; my love affair with Jerusalem; my meltdown in Tsfat.

But as I described my life to Tova, it unfolded as a story of people: of Barbie; of the Holy Sisters; of Yankel and my mother; of

Yidis and Yitta and Etta and Laya; of Joanna and Annica and Lisa Marie; of Shaindel and Bracha; and now of Tova as well.

Tova listened, her face intent and compassionate throughout my long description. When I finished, she said nothing for several minutes, but took my hand and held it lightly in hers as we continued walking. Finally, she turned to me and said, "Let's go home for tea."

Back in the kitchen, as she prepared the nana leaves, she said, "Before we get into everything you told me today, I want to give you a crash course in Kabbalah, so that we'll have a framework for it all."

"Is there really such a thing as a crash course in Kabbalah?" I asked her.

"Of course not," she responded, laughing sweetly. "Kabbalah is the deepest wisdom in the world. It takes a lifetime to master— and, even then, it can be done only by the most highly evolved souls. I just want to give you a few drops from the surface. Kindergarten Kabbalah, I call it. Pre 1A. That's the level that most of us are on these days. And, yet, we need all the spiritual guidance we can get to help us make it through these confusing times.

"And I believe that understanding a bit of Kabbalah—and, really, just a bit—will give you a whole different perspective on your issues with clutter and on your relationship with God."

Needless to say, I was sitting on the edge of my seat.

"Okay," Tova said, looking at her watch. "Let's talk Kabbalah for a little while and then have an early dinner. After that, we can talk some more."

But, first, we each took another piece of rugelach from the shrinking pile. "Grounding the spiritual in the physical," Tova declared, raising her cookie into the air, as if she were making a toast on a goblet of fine wine.

"Kabbalah," she began—saying the word as if its very sound brought sweetness to her lips—"literally means that which is received. And this is generally understood to refer to the fact that the wisdom of Kabbalah was received directly from God and then passed down through the ages to special teachers, who received it and passed it on to their chosen students, who received it and continued to pass it along in that manner. "But not only does Kabbalah become ours through the act of receiving, the Kabbalah actually teaches us *how* to receive. And that, my dear Pesi, is what I believe will help you to change the way you relate to the physical world.

"The Kabbalah explains to us how the realms of spirit and substance interact and how spiritual energy—if we do not block its path—moves freely through the higher and lower worlds in order to infuse our everyday lives with God's presence. We experience this through emanations of different Divine attributes, known as *sefirot*.

"According to Kabbalistic teaching, God transformed the universe from an abyss of darkness and chaos into a world that manifests Divine order and beauty. The vessels in our material world, however, could not withstand the full intensity of spiritual illumination. Therefore, the Godly energy contracted and concealed itself.

"Our souls yearn to experience that primordial light in all its fullness. But physical form, which functions in our world as a garment for the soul, can either obscure or reveal the Divine radiance. When we become lost in the physical dimension, the spiritual essence remains trapped within, and our access to it is severely limited. However, when we use physical objects for holy purposes, the Godly sparks are released and become conduits for spirituality.

"Which is why," Tova said, holding one of her apricot ruge-lach, "it's so important to bless these delicious cookies with a full heart and enjoy them with gratitude to God. It's what I try to keep in mind while I'm preparing them."

"And that," I concluded, "is probably why they taste like they're not of this world."

Tova smiled appreciatively.

"How are we doing?" she asked. "Does it make sense so far? Are you able to relate any of it to your life?"

"Sure," I said. "In fact, it all seems very familiar. Darkness and chaos . . . limited access . . . physical objects blocking the way . . . garments that obscure the light. . . . It sounds like a perfect description of my walk-in closet."

Tova and I both burst into laughter at the image of my closet as a Kabbalistic battlefield. But, in truth, that was pretty much the way it felt most of the time.

"I think you may be on to something here," Tova said, still giggling. "There's definitely a cosmic dimension to our closets. Maybe that's why we fill them with all our hidden treasures and most carefully guarded secrets."

"But, kabbalistically speaking," I asked, "what is the harm of all this clutter—in my closet or anyplace else?"

"Well," she explained, "the real danger is that it increases your enmeshment with the material world. And by doing that, it blocks the movement of energy on a spiritual as well as a physical level—to such a degree that your clutter in Brooklyn can affect the flow of Divine light six thousand miles away at my kitchen table in Jerusalem. But the good news is that the opposite is also true. Our own personal transformation alters the universe in such a profound way that eating a meal with holy intent here in Jerusalem can bring blessing to someone in New York or New Zealand or Zimbabwe.

"And, on that note," she concluded, "I'm getting hungry. What do you say we stop for dinner and continue our discussion afterward?"

A few minutes later, we were enjoying a warm spiced lentil soup, whole grain pita bread with feta cheese and avocado, and a salad of arugula, cherry tomatoes, and lemon basil from the garden. We ate mindfully in silence, very aware of each other, the food, and the blessings we were making.

When we finished, I asked Tova to tell me more about the Kabbalah of clutter—and, more specifically, the Kabbalah of *my* clutter.

"Well," Tova said, "as you know, Judaism is not an ascetic religion. It's all about using the physical to connect to the spiritual—and, of course, enjoying the journey as we go along. Self-deprivation denies the role of the physical; but clutter exaggerates it. Neither creates proper balance.

"The Kabbalah describes a universe whose forces are in perfect harmony. That harmony is disrupted when we fill time and space with more than God intended. It's like the words on a page: you need just so much black ink and just so much white space. Black fire on white fire, our sages described a Torah scroll. Without the empty space, there would be no words; and without the words, the empty space would be meaningless."

"And," I reflected, "since I have no empty space in my life, I guess I'm not leaving much of a blank canvas on which to create meaning."

"Or peace," Tova added. "Or joy. Or anything else. But, most of all, you're not leaving any room for the relationship with God that you've been trying so hard to develop. The truth is that you don't actually need space or time to connect to God—you can do that in a fraction of a second wherever you are and no matter how much clutter seems to be in your way. He's always available. But if you want to create a real relationship—that's quite another story. That requires a lot more white fire and a lot less clutter.

"And speaking of relationships, it's not only the Godly one that's affected. When the cosmic flow of energy is blocked, all of our relationships are constricted. And even though you've been blessed with loving friends and family and Holy Sisters, your connections could be so much deeper and more intimate if the channels were fully open."

Over tea and dessert, Tova and I continued talking; and, slowly, I began to see that it was not my clutter per se that was the issue. God didn't really care about the six tables in my garage or the stack of unread newspapers on my living room floor. The real problem was that my overinvolvement with the material world limited my ability to step beyond it. And the irony was that the primary reason for this intense level of interaction was not a desire for physicality, but an inability to cope with the details of my life in a simple and efficient way.

I looked at Tova. She was clearing the table and humming to herself. She had spent half the day preparing food and cleaning up; and the other half, guiding me through a Kabbalistic universe. But the truth is that, for her, it was all one and the same. The nature of her interaction with the physical world—unlike mine—was to participate fully in all its pleasures without ever losing sight of their spiritual source. She blessed those rugelach with the highest consciousness; and once they were blessed, she thoroughly enjoyed eating them, one by one, with the deepest delight.

As the sun was beginning to set, Tova walked me to the bus stop. The notebook was empty, the tape recorder untouched, and my thermos full to the brim with cold coffee.

All in all, it had been an amazing day.

The following morning, I boarded the bus to Tova's house two hours earlier than I had the day before. Other than that, the trip was virtually identical. We got stuck in the same traffic jam; the twenty-minute ride once again took forty; the bus driver (same cranky one) complained about the construction going on; and the passengers onboard grumbled along with him. Late for work in New York, I probably would have grumbled, too; but, today, I was focused on nothing more than my joyful anticipation of another day with Tova.

The walk to her house seemed to go more quickly this morning, probably because I was not carrying anything with me. No notebook, no tape recorder, no thermos. It actually felt quite liberating.

To accompany our morning cup of nana tea, Tova had baked gingerbread squares, which she served warm with homemade whipped cream.

"Tova, you make food that is very easy to bless," I said between mouthfuls. "When did you have time to prepare all this?"

"Oh, I'm an early riser," she told me.

"Yes, and probably a late nighter as well," I added.

"You're right," Tova laughed. "The day is for this world; and the night, for the world beyond. And the truth is, I hate to miss out on either."

After we ate, Tova suggested that we divide the day into three sections, each with its own topic—punctuated, of course, by meals. Clutter after breakfast. Coping after tea. God after lunch.

"I hate to be so regimented," she said, "but, sadly, we're running out of time. Today is Wednesday already. Tomorrow, we can't meet because we need to prepare for Shabbat. On Sunday, my grandchildren are coming to visit—I'll have to show you pictures later. And since you're leaving for New York next week, I'm sure you and your husband will want to spend your last few days here together. So, I think today may be all that we have."

I had already come to that disturbing conclusion myself, but hearing Tova confirm my calculations made it feel all the more final.

Seeing my response, she quickly added, "But this is only the beginning. When you come back to Israel again, we'll continue our work. And, of course, our play. God willing, we'll have many more special times together."

"Okay," I said. "Thank you. I feel better now."

"All right," she smiled. "Then, let's start our morning walk. We have a lot to talk about today."

Before Tova said anything, however, she began to hum a little *niggun* (a melody without words). I recalled that she had done the same thing the day before, so I asked her about it.

"I always sing a niggun before I ask for Divine assistance," she explained. "It helps to open the channels."

"That's good," I said. "We need all the open channels we can get because I want to finally untangle the mystery of how the physical and spiritual pieces in my life fit together."

"Yes," Tova said, "it's very important to understand that. When I was meditating last night, I began to realize just how much your problem with clutter is related to your issues with God."

I stopped right where I was and turned to face her.

"Really, Tova?" I said. "You could see that?"

"Absolutely," she said. "Although probably not in quite the way that you might expect. But let's not get too far ahead of ourselves. God isn't due until after lunch today, and we haven't even had our midmorning tea. So, let's stick with the topic of clutter for now."

Tova hummed her niggun for another minute or two, then stopped walking, cleared her throat, and closed her eyes. When she finally began to speak, her voice had a sharp but gentle clarity to it.

"I believe," she said, "that it is your love of abundance and the illusion of freedom that it creates that is at the heart of your relationship with clutter. You live with a chronic mess because you're convinced that you can do it all and have it all, squeezing more into an hour or a square foot than is physically possible.

"It's a battle of boundaries—and a battle you're bound to lose. The effort to maintain it all is simply too great; and, sooner or later, the system begins to fall apart. And even if it doesn't, the amount of juggling you have to do to keep all those apples in the air destroys any peace of mind you might ever aspire to."

"Still, I don't believe that you seek clutter as a means of distancing yourself from God—although that obviously is one of its effects. Nor do I believe that you seek clutter in order to avoid yourself or anything else. If your mess has become a comfortable place in which to occasionally hide, then you're simply using what's available, which is not at all the same as creating it for that purpose.

"I see the disorder in your life basically as a failed mechanism for coping with a complicated world in which you so desire to experience all that the Creator has given us that you can't seem to find the time or space to connect with the Creator Himself.

"Poetically speaking, my dear Pesi, your garden is simply not large enough to contain all the flowers whose beauty you would like to gaze upon and whose sweet fragrance you long to inhale. And, so, I would like to suggest that you spend less time trying to stock the garden and more time seeking the Gardener. But that, of course, is our topic for this afternoon."

"Now, I'm really sorry I left my notebook home," I said. "That would have made a great quote."

"Well, we can try to reconstruct it over tea," Tova offered, as we walked home—she, peacefully humming a niggun, while I wrestled with this latest insight.

"I love the Twelve Steps," Tova said, as we carried our tea out to the porch. "They're clearly a gift from God."

It was too beautiful a day to stay inside, but the Jerusalem sun was quite intense already, so the well-shaded porch seemed the ideal place to sit.

"The Program has saved my life," Tova continued, settling into one of the rocking chairs. "Many times. But that's another story for another day."

I wanted it to be the story for today, but I didn't press the point. I was just grateful that I wouldn't have to explain Clutterers

Anonymous to her from scratch. I had mentioned it yesterday, but now that we were going to discuss how to cope with clutter, it would obviously figure more prominently in the discussion.

"There's no need to reinvent the wheel," Tova said. "Program is the path to take. Whether your clutter is an addiction in the true sense or just a strong tendency that makes your life unmanageable, the best thing you can do is go to meetings, work with your sponsor, read the literature, and follow the Steps. There's really no better way to deal with the problem on a spiritual level or on a practical one."

Tova sat back in her rocking chair, took a sip of tea, and closed her eyes for a moment. I was never quite sure whether closing her eyes meant that she was tuning into herself, receiving a message from some other dimension, or simply resting. Or perhaps it was a bit of all three.

When she opened her eyes, she looked at me and said, "You know, Pesi, I want to be careful here. We shouldn't romanticize your struggle with clutter to such a degree that we make the whole thing into an epic battle between the forces of order and chaos. I mean, I believe that the issue is primarily spiritual and that there's clearly a psychological piece as well, but we don't want to forget that we're also talking about dirty dishes and unpaid bills.

"I don't want to leave you with the impression that the solutions lie only in the deepest recesses of your mind or somewhere out there in the cosmic realms. Whatever battles are taking place in those areas are obviously being fought in your pocketbook and your closet and your file cabinet as well.

"The fact that you have difficulty focusing and getting organized and working within time limits are issues that need to be addressed in a concrete way. And the fact that you ignore your own boundaries, and consider deadlines little more than suggestions—well, those would probably make good topics for a therapy session. But I really believe that everything will become much easier to cope with once you address the underlying problem."

"And the underlying problem is . . . ?" I asked, leaning forward in my chair.

"Well," Tova said, hesitating for a moment, "I would have to say that the underlying problem, as I see it, is the absence of God in your thoughts."

We were both silent for a moment as I let that sink in. The absence of God? In my thoughts? What was Tova talking about? I was always thinking about God. I may not have done very much about it. I may not have been able to connect in a deep way. But I certainly *thought* about God all the time—probably, in secular eyes, to the point of obsession. So, what could she possibly mean?

"That might seem like a strange comment," she said immediately. "I hope it didn't upset you—it's just what came to me last night when I was meditating about your situation. I thought I would mention it now so that you'd have some time to think about it while I'm getting lunch ready.

"But try not to let it bother you," she said. "I'm sure everything will fall into place once we begin to talk."

I wasn't so sure. Could I be that out of touch with myself that the thing I was certain I thought about the most turned out to be something I rarely thought about at all? This felt even more disturbing than Lisa Marie's observation that my clutter was not merely an unfortunate obstacle to God but a deliberate means of avoiding Him.

Take it easy, I told myself. *You're in the middle of a process here. Try to sit quietly with the discomfort. Just observe it and move on. Breathe. Close your eyes and relax. Now, breathe deeply again.*

But nothing worked. It was more than I could bear to think that the cornerstone of my spiritual life might be a complete illusion. If I couldn't trust my own sense of inner reality, what hope was there for me?

The next thing I knew, Tova was touching my arm. I awoke with a start from a thoroughly unrestful sleep.

"What happened?" I asked her. "I just closed my eyes for a minute."

"You must have been exhausted," she said, looking concerned. "You slept soundly for a good hour."

I followed her into the kitchen, in desperate need of a cup of coffee, and wondering how I could politely decline the meal. But as soon as I saw the lunch she had set out for us, all of my distress began to melt away, and my appetite returned in full force.

On an embroidered linen tablecloth, she had placed a large mesclun salad garnished with grated beets and carrots, cold gazpacho soup with fresh parsley from the garden, warm zucchini muffins, and a mound of shelled pistachio nuts surrounded by wedges of Jaffa oranges. I simply couldn't sustain my angst in the presence of so much love and such magnificent colors.

*B*y the time we finished eating, the sun had moved far enough across the sky to provide a patch of shade in the most beautiful corner of the garden, just beyond the rosebushes. We carried Tova's favorite porcelain teapot and two matching teacups to the spot where the air was richest with fragrance and sat there in silence, inhaling the mingled scent of roses and warm mint, and slowly sipping our tea.

"Pesi, dear," Tova finally said, "did my comment before lunch upset you? I'm really sorry if it did. Perhaps I didn't express myself clearly."

"Maybe I misunderstood," I said.

"Why don't we start the conversation over again," Tova suggested. "And if I say anything that seems wrong or hurtful, please stop me right away so that we can make sure we understand each other."

I nodded in agreement, and Tova began to speak.

"Pesi, I know that you're trying with all your heart to come close to God; but it seems that no matter what you do, you're simply not able to make real contact. It's like you're in a relationship that's barely alive."

"Yes," I said. "You're absolutely right. But I don't know what to do about it. That's why I came to see you—and mainly why I came to Israel. I want to finally understand where I'm going wrong.

"For most of my life, I thought the problem was my clutter—and maybe it is—I'm just not sure anymore. All I know is that whenever I've tried to connect to God—and we're talking about close to thirty years of trying—I can't seem to make it happen, or at least not with any consistency. Most of the time, I feel too distracted by the stimulation of everything around me and inside my head, by the constant drumbeat of things waiting to be responded to. It's like I have some sort of spiritual ADD that comes upon me at these moments.

"Even standing at the Holy Wall—about as far from the details of my life as I could possibly get—I wasn't able to stay focused long enough to feel a real connection, except on that very first night when the experience was so intense that it blew everything else away. Of course, it all came crashing back that night in Tsfat."

"Yes," Tova said, watching me wince at the recollection, "but soon, you'll look back upon that night as a turning point in your life. And I don't mean a turning point downward."

"Do you really think so?" I asked, finding that hard to believe.

"Yes, I do," Tova said. "But before we talk about it, I want to share something with you.

"One of the turning points in my own relationship with God came many years ago when I first began working with the Twelve Steps. I was living in New Jersey at the time and drove to Manhattan one night to have dinner with a friend.

We were supposed to meet on the Upper West Side at six o'clock, and I got there in plenty of time. But I soon discovered that you can't park at most of the meters in that area between 4:00 and 7:00 PM, which made the already difficult parking virtually impossible. This, of course, was in the days before cell phones, so I couldn't easily call my friend; and I certainly wasn't about to park near a phone booth and risk getting a ticket that would probably have cost more than the car was worth. The only other alternative was a parking lot, but I was a small-town librarian in those days and didn't have half a day's salary to spend on such a luxury.

"I wasn't sure just what to do next; but as I sat in heavy traffic at a red light, I took out a list of Twelve Step slogans that someone had recently given me at a meeting and began to read them out loud. All of a sudden, I came upon three simple words that changed my night and the rest of my life forever. They were: Turn it over.

"I had already done everything I could possibly do. Now, it was obviously time to turn it over. But turn it over to Whom? The only God I knew was the Master of the Universe—the One who controls war and peace, sickness and health, life and death. He was a God that I turned to in moments of real crisis or at times of major decision making. Finding a parking place did not quite fit into either of those categories.

"But, then, I remembered that my sponsor—a very wise Israeli woman—had once told me to always keep in mind that the Master of the Universe was also my Higher Power—one and the same God—separated in my mind only because I was not yet able to see their unity. 'Transcendent, yet immanent,' she said in beautiful Hebrew; and then, in not quite as beautiful English, 'up there and down here, all at the same time.'

"And, so, I immediately began to ask my Higher Power up there to help me deal with the parking situation down here. At that moment, I thankfully did not need to be saved from enemy forces or from some terrible illness—but I definitely needed assistance from the world above, since the normal order of things below did not seem to be working in my favor.

"It didn't exactly roll off my tongue, but I managed to express my need and sincerely turn it over. Within five minutes, I was pulling into a parking spot. Now, I'm not saying that this was an act of God in the form of direct cause and effect—although it very well may have been—but the real act of God for me was the miraculous change in my consciousness. From that day on, whenever I've needed anything—no matter how silly or unspiritual it seems—I ask my Higher Power for help. Of course, the answer is not always yes. But even when the response seems to come back stamped 'request denied,' at least I feel that I've been heard."

Tova's story reminded me of so many of my own. I thought of all those times when God had felt too big, too far away, too powerful to call upon for help with my day-to-day issues of limited cosmic significance. But, unlike Tova, I never got past that feeling; and, so, for all these years, I had continued to keep God in his unreachable heaven, while I remained trapped in my layers of clutter below.

Even Bewilda seemed to get it—her weary eyes permanently fixed on heaven. Yet, somehow, it had never occurred to me as I struggled with the day-to-day issues of life to simply turn to God and ask for help with the details.

"Tova, what are some of the little things that you ask your Higher Power for help with?"

"Oh, that the food I'm making should turn out well, that the shoes I'm buying should feel comfortable when I get them home, that all my roses should bloom and have a beautiful fragrance—things like that."

"Wow," I said.

"Wow?" Tova asked. "Why wow?"

"Because it's so obvious," I responded, "but somehow I never thought of it. It's simply not something I do. I just don't talk to God that way. Which, of course, probably explains why I have no real relationship with Him. My conversations with God—if you want to call them that—are too lofty and far removed from me and my everyday life to create any sort of genuine connection. I try to meet God where I think *He* is—somewhere out there in the great beyond—instead of speaking from where *I* am, right here in the midst of my own earthly mess. And the result is that we don't really meet at all."

"Except for that night in Tsfat," Tova reminded me again.

"I wish I could forget that night already," I said, cringing once more at the memory. "Why do you think it's so important?"

"Because I believe it was one of the few times in your life that you spoke to God from an honest and vulnerable place. Now, for some people, raging at God is not a particularly enlightened act because it doesn't lead anywhere. It's more a venting of frustration than anything else. But, in your case, I think it was a major turning point in your relationship.

"It's kind of like that first fight you have when you're a new-lywed. It's usually not one of the highlights that makes it into the scrapbook; but, when you look back, it's often the beginning of a deeper and more mature phase of your marriage. Hopefully, over time, we learn to work things out before an explosion occurs. However, for many of us, that first quarrel is actually something to be grateful for."

"So, in the end," I asked, "how do you think what happened in Tsfat will change my relationship with God?"

"Well," Tova explained, taking a long sip of tea, "I think it opened a new pathway for you. Hopefully, in the future, it won't take an event of that emotional magnitude to get you to talk to your Higher Power from your heart. But, sometimes, clearing a passage requires a stick or two of dynamite to get things moving.

"What strikes me about that night is that you weren't simply angry at God because everything was going wrong. You were really hurt because He seemed to be continually erecting roadblocks in front of you as you were trying harder and harder to reach Him. There you were, walking around the Holy Land, where God's presence is supposed to be accessible to all, and it seemed that one door after another—and then the washing machine lid—were being slammed in your face. It must have felt like the ultimate rejection."

"Yes," I said, reliving the awful feeling once again, "that's just what it felt like. I wanted to wash my laundry and be done with it, so that my mind would have one less bit of clutter in it, and I could finally connect with my Higher Power in a more focused way. But, suddenly, it seemed that my Higher Power wasn't particularly interested in connecting with *me*. Not there in the ancient city of Kabbalah or in the Old City of Jerusalem or anyplace else."

As I spoke, the memory became excruciatingly vivid. Not just as a memory of something that occurred at a moment in time, but as an archetypal image that had somehow woven itself into my soul. It felt as if I had always been chasing after a God who apparently had more important things on His mind. Or, maybe, as Tova said, He was simply waiting for me to show up and be real. Which, sadly, took an emotional meltdown to bring about.

"Should we rest for a while?" Tova asked, watching me fidget in obvious discomfort.

"No, no," I said. "If it's okay with you, I'd rather keep going. I really need to understand how to change all of this. I don't want my relationship with my Higher Power to be so shallow that it takes a middle-of-the-night breakdown to give it any depth."

"Okay," Tova said, "then, let's move on to the next level."

This time, I closed my eyes; and, without thinking, I did something I had never done before. I asked God to help me hear what Tova was about to say—without becoming defensive or resistant or too upset to really listen.

Tova must have sensed what was going on because when I opened my eyes, she smiled at me and lightly brushed her fingers across mine.

"Well," she began, "when I said before lunch that God was often missing from your thoughts, what I meant was that you were not thinking of Him at the times of greatest potential. Those are the moments when your life feels the most unmanageable, and you could grow so much closer to Him by reaching out and asking for help. Instead, those seem to be precisely the times when you turn away and try to handle the situation on your own."

I could feel Tova circling the truth, heading toward an insight that I felt desperate to understand, but was not entirely sure I was ready to hear.

"The moments I'm talking about," Tova continued, "occur whenever you lose a battle with your clutter. The losses are so much larger than they seem. It's not just about broken washing machines or lost keys or misplaced paychecks. For you, each defeat is a major setback in your war with the physical world. And each loss feels like a deeply personal failure. But because the battlefield seems to be a secular one, you don't bother to call upon God to send in spiritual reinforcements. And that, I'm afraid, is a major flaw in your thinking."

Tova waited a minute to see how I would react, but sensing that I was okay and braced for more, she went on.

"And not only do you ignore your Higher Power at those moments, but you seem to remain convinced that He is unreachable. In your eyes, it appears that your clutter is preventing you from finding the secret passageway that leads to Him—as if He were the Wizard of Oz or a reclusive guru hiding in a cave somewhere. Suddenly, it seems that the only path to God is through some spiritually transforming experience—an afternoon spent peacefully meditating in an open field or a few hours of quiet contemplation by the ocean or a three-day silent retreat—none of which is likely to occur, especially not while you're cleaning up from your latest flood or racing to meet your next deadline.

"Your mess then becomes an impenetrable barrier, since it now stands in the way of your entire spiritual journey—which seems to grow longer and more complicated by the minute. The truth, however, is that all you really need to do at any moment is utter the most basic one-word prayer. If you would simply stop where you are and cry 'Help' from the bottom of your heart, you could move heaven and earth and connect with your Higher Power in the deepest and most personal way. Most of the time, it's just that simple. And all the transcendent levels you aspire to can follow later."

Could that really be true? For the first time, I began to wonder if I was making my relationship with God as complicated and impossible to navigate as everything else in my life. Was my vision of the perfect mountaintop encounter keeping me from the very real but imperfect possibilities down below? And how about my fantasy of a life of perfect order and simplicity? Was that getting in the way of a normal life of less-than-perfect order and simplicity? Maybe my Higher Power wanted me to lower the bar a few notches—or maybe, as Tova suggested, He just wanted to hear from me from time to time as I tripped over it.

"Tova," I asked, "do you think that my reluctance to ask God for help is the reason I'm plagued with floods and endless moves and household disasters of all sorts?"

"Well, we can never really be sure why God does anything," Tova said, "but it certainly makes sense that when you don't respond to His first wake-up call, He's likely to follow with a second and, if necessary, a third and a fourth."

"I think I've had enough wake-up calls for one lifetime," I said. "But now that I'm finally awake, what do I do next?"

We both closed our eyes and sat in silence for a few minutes, as if Tova were searching for just the right words and I was trying to clear a space in which to receive them.

When she finally began to speak, her eyes were still closed, and her voice sounded as if it were traveling a long distance to get here.

"The first step," Tova said slowly, "is to see your clutter as the gift that it is. Whatever brings us to the awareness that our lives are not totally under our control is something to be grateful for. However, the purpose of the gift is not to enlighten you through pain, but to provide you with a special opportunity. In that moment of feeling powerless, you can either choose to hold on to the reins more tightly or let go and ask your Higher Power for help."

She opened her eyes and looked directly into mine.

"And if you choose to turn it all over to God, you'll see that He's not hiding on the other side of your clutter. He's right there— in the moment, in the pile of laundry, in the very mess that you think is blocking your way. The only obstacle you face is your own resistance to seeking His help.

"To express it in Kabbalistic terms," Tova explained, "releasing the flow of Divine blessing from the Higher Worlds often requires an arousal from below.

"Or, to put it in simple English, in order to receive a gift, we sometimes have to ask."

Saying goodbye to Tova was more difficult than I would ever have expected. In our two days together, she had become a friend, a therapist, a spiritual guide, and a bit of a fairy godmother. She had invited me to share her home, her garden, and the healing love of her homemade food; and she had generously given me the gift of her wisdom, which had changed the entire course of my spiritual journey.

There were other difficult goodbyes to say that week as well. Sadly, I bid farewell to Bracha and her Jerusalem Jewels and to Raezelle, Reizl Malka, Elana, and Leah; to the land of Israel, whose milk and honey my ancestors had never stopped longing for; to the Old City of Jerusalem, which would always remain my first love: to its winding streets and hidden gardens and to all of the gates it had opened for me; and, finally—with the deepest sadness of all—to the Holy Wall, where I spent our last night with my cheek pressed against its warm stones and my tears melting into its ancient crevices.

As I walked down Misgav Ledach Street for the last time, I called the Holy Sisters, as I had promised them I would, leaving middle-of-the-night voice mails for each. I thanked them for always being there for me and told them that if my plane should plummet into the ocean, I wanted them to know that I loved them and would try to make contact from the other side. Yidis was actually awake when I called and picked up the phone to tell me that she thought my message was ridiculous but that she couldn't wait for me to come home. I agreed on both counts.

The last few hours were a whirlwind of frantic packing, final goodbyes, and airport challenges. (How was I to know—with my limited flying experience—that it was against international law to bring a bag of cherry tomatoes from Tova's garden back to Brooklyn with me?) As Yankel ran around trying to resolve that issue as well as the one of our overweight luggage, I stood on the check-in line, hoping to capture a few final reflections in my journal.

I was returning to what would almost certainly be a study in chaos—a house under construction, a kitchen with no appliances, a duffle bag overflowing with my latest accumulation of dirty laundry, a stack of unpaid bills I had completely forgotten about, and the general mess that—under the best of circumstances—I always left behind. But I was also returning to the people who loved and supported me and who would do everything they could to make my landing a gentle one.

I wished I were coming home utterly transformed—or at least partially rehabilitated—but, in truth, I felt just as disorganized and overwhelmed as ever. I had lost my beeping watch somewhere on the trip and hadn't bothered to consult my calendar in over a month. When I looked down, I realized that my socks didn't match, and the hem on my skirt was coming undone. And, needless to say, I had no idea where I had last seen my keys. I certainly did not appear to be a woman returning from the Holy Land with deeper consciousness and a new grip on reality.

And yet, no doubt, I was.

My ability to function in the physical world might not have undergone much of a change, but my desire to include God in the process certainly had. I was no longer struggling with the details of life alone while pursuing a deity who dwelled in the distant heavens. My Higher Power was still the all-knowing, omnipotent Master of the Universe, but He had become my personal God of parking places, washing machines, and flying phobias as well.

Nothing was too big for Him—but neither was anything too small. While He was busy making certain that the sun rose every morning and set each night, He could still help me choose the perfect shade of yellow for my kitchen and find the painter's phone number that I had scribbled on the back of a misplaced color chart. And once I returned to Brooklyn and resumed my quest for order and simplicity, I planned to ask Him for help—one day at a time— every step of the way.

When I looked up from my journal, I saw Yankel walking in my direction. He must have had to pay the excess baggage fee again because he wore the resigned expression of one who has done battle with bureaucrats and suffered inevitable defeat.

"The next time we fly," he said—as if he were talking to someone who had the slightest inclination to ever get on a plane again—"we're not going to pack like our grandparents coming on a boat from Europe."

I looked over at our towering pile of belongings, which had grown considerably higher since our arrival, thanks to the addition of new books, Jerusalem pottery, original artwork from Tsfat, bath salts from the Dead Sea, and a large assortment of gifts and souvenirs. It was quite a sight to behold.

"Yankel," I assured him, "after this trip, I can honestly say that I want nothing more than to want nothing more. And for a clutterer, I would say that's real progress. I only hope I'll remember how I feel now once we return home."

"Don't worry," he said, starting to breathe heavily as he pulled my one-wheeled suitcase and dragged my torn duffle bag, "In case you forget, I'll be sure to remind you."

Epilogue

This book has been written pretty much as my life has been lived—with one hand hard at work on the task and the other trying to fend off all the distractions and minor disasters that have come my way during the process.

Some things, it seems, never change. But, then, others thankfully do. And one of the things that *has* changed is that I've come to see the interruptions to my journey as part of the journey itself, sent not by an uncaring Deity that randomly hurls lightning bolts and leaking pipes at befuddled mortals, but by a God who delivers to us the experiences—pleasant and not so pleasant—that can bring us closer to Him.

Originally, I set out to write a book about my relationship with clutter. That soon evolved into an exploration of my search for a deeper spiritual connection. However, in the end, the book has turned out to be as much about my friendship with the special women in my life who have helped me try to put all the pieces together.

Coping with clutter still remains a constant challenge. Despite my many insights and breakthroughs, the war has hardly been won. And as soon as I gain a bit of control over one area of dysfunction, another one seems to step right up and take its place. Missing keys now share the stage with forgotten passwords and lost ATM cards; unsorted items in old cardboard boxes have been replaced by unsorted items in shiny new plastic containers; and the papers in need of response stacked upon my desk have been eclipsed by the neglected emails waiting on my screen. Times change, it seems, and so does my clutter. But no matter what form the piles take, I can rest assured that—like Patt's extra pound—sooner or later, they will pop out somewhere. And, so, I have chosen not to judge my progress solely by their diminishment.

As Yidis once pointed out, the difference between a human being and a chicken is that we can see our attempt to cross the road as a worthwhile experience, even if we never get to the other side. That's because, unlike chickens, we recognize that there's more to success than reaching a destination. And, in writing this book, I've come to realize that the goal in my battle against clutter is not merely to step beyond the piles and the procrastination and make it across to whatever awaits me, but to open myself fully to all that I encounter along the way.

For most of my life, the wall of shame and chronic busyness to which my clutter gave rise kept the innermost parts of myself well concealed from others and beyond my own reach as well. It took every bit of the embarrassment and upheaval I've described in these pages to wear me down to the point that I finally allowed the Holy Sisters into my private sanctuary to witness the chaotic universe that I inhabit.

Thanks to their ongoing support, I remain optimistic that—despite all evidence to the contrary—I will someday find my way to a simpler and more orderly life. In the meantime, however, I'm no longer claiming success based upon the amount of old newspapers I discard or the number of overflowing drawers I reorganize, but by how often I remember to stop and ask God for help and how willing I am to openly share the difficult moments on the journey with my Holy Sisters. And that, I believe, is the true measure of growth for me—and, hopefully, the first step toward real freedom.

Acknowledgments

This is one of the few areas of my life in which a bit of excess still feels welcome. The more people there are to thank, the happier it makes me. And since, as Gertrude Stein wisely pointed out, "Silent gratitude isn't very much use to anyone," I'm thankful for the opportunity to give voice to my appreciation.

First and foremost, I would like to thank my dear friend Yitta Halberstam, who used every technique at her disposal to encourage me to write this book. For years, she alternately applied praise, peer pressure, and gentle doses of guilt to get me started. That finally accomplished, she introduced me to her agent and guided me through my book proposal, cheering me on every step of the way. Without her support, this book—and so much else in my life—would probably never have come to be.

I'm also more grateful than I could ever express to Yidis (Judith) Leventhal, who, from the very beginning, has stood by my side, reminding me always to look inward and go deeper. Like the angels in the Talmud whispering to each blade of grass, she continually urged me to "grow, grow." To whatever extent I have, I believe it's largely because of her faith in me and her own unwavering commitment to truth.

Special thanks are due as well to the following close friends and Holy Sisters, who have been the pillars of The Project from start to finish: Laya Bracha Adrezin, always available in the middle of the night with a sympathetic ear, a few lines of her latest song, and just the right words; Etta Ansel, on the morning shift—the best combination friend-therapist-coffeemaker I could ever imagine having on my team; Atara Grenadir, whose artist's eye and uncluttered view of things helped bring clarity to my own vision; and Yehudis Zahava Michelson, who kept me going day-to-day with her wise, compassionate insights and Divinely inspired muffins.

Also, thank you to Lili Budman, my very first Holy Sister and literary muse. Thank you to Heather Burns for appearing at the perfect moment and adding so much to my life and to the writing of this book. Thank you to Chaya Leah Kaess for making certain that I was lovingly nourished on all levels as I toiled over the manuscript. Thank you to Ruchama King Feuerman, whose life-changing workshop on creative writing set this whole adventure in motion. And thank you to Carrie Drum for managing the details of my life with loving devotion when I couldn't.

To all the other Holy Sisters everywhere who helped me wrestle with my clutter and write about it in these pages, I'm deeply grateful. Thank you especially to Lian Sae Bloom, Marjorie Ordene Brown, Annica Davis, Geula Dickerman, Bracha Din, Elana Friedman, Enid Gil, Frumma Gottlieb, Golda Hoffman, Reizl Malka Hupert, Sharon Jacobs, Myriam Kalchstein, Leah Kops, Judy (Chaya) Kruger, Raezelle Lazar, Janet Maulbeck, Orah

Moshe, Mindy Ribner, Jill Kaplan Shimansky, Theresa Suraci, Rochel Winston, and Fran Yesner.

Of course, my efforts might all have been in vain if not for the encouragement and hard work of my outstanding agent, Jane Dystel. Always accessible and supportive in every way, she and Myriam Goderich have skillfully guided me through the often mystifying world of publishing and made the experience a truly delightful one.

In addition, I owe much appreciation to the excellent staff at Perseus Books. Thank you especially to Krista Lyons—my wonderful editor—for the beautiful job she did in transforming my manuscript into a real live book and for her infinite patience in dealing with the many delays that arose, as every distraction imaginable seemed to gravitate my way during the writing process. Thank you, too, to Brooke Warner for all her help—above and beyond the call of duty—in getting me across the finish line; to Lisa Lee, the Mac Goddess of Seal Press, for walking me through one technological challenge after another; to Elizabeth Mathews for her fine and sensitive copyediting; and to Krissa Lagos, Eva Zimmerman, and everyone else at Perseus for being such a pleasure to work with.

I would also like to express my gratitude to several very special rabbis and their special wives for providing the inspiration and wisdom that eventually led to this book: Rabbi Tzvi and Chaya Shaindel Mandel of Brooklyn, Rabbi Meir and Dr. Ruchama Fund, also of Brooklyn, Rabbi Yaacov and Bayle Haber of Jerusalem, and Rabbi Shlomo Carlebach, presently residing in The World Beyond. Their friendship and guidance over these past decades have shaped my life and my spiritual journey. I thank them for being there for me—now and always—in so many ways.

In more recent times, my path has led me to a few wonderful rabbis and rebbitzens here in South Florida. Thank you to Rabbi Sammy and Irma Intrator for being, as Reb Shlomo would say, the sweetest of the sweet, the deepest of the deep. Thank you to Rabbi Yisroel and Gutel Edelman for their exceptional warmth and kindness. And thank you to Rabbi Yidel and Pessa Kayla Stein for bringing so much joy and possibility to my life.

Along with my Holy Sisters, there are a number of Holy Brothers also deserving of thanks. In a class by himself is our extremely thoughtful and generous friend and neighbor, Yaakov Dovid (Gerry) Hoffman who, since we moved to Florida, has gone to great lengths to keep us well fed, well stocked, and—against his better judgment—well caffeinated in the face of hurricanes, floods, power outages, and looming deadlines.

I would also like to thank my good friend and colleague, Peretz (Paul) Camhi for the many hours he has devoted to helping me create order at school and at home. No matter what the nature of the mess, his wise advice to me has always been, "Edit, edit, edit." Great advice, Peretz—I'm still working on it.

Thank you to all the other Holy Brothers who have played such an important role in my journey. Thank you to my real brother, Larry Jacobs, for always being there when I need him, and to my nephew Aaron Jacobs for inspiring me with his own great writing. Thank you to John Sollami, who—despite his aversion to all things cluttered—has remained my lifelong friend. Thank you to Dr. B. J. Adrezin for being permanently on call and ready to help—even three time zones away. Thank you to Bobby Minkoff for continuing to remind me that within the chaos of life lies a poem waiting to be created. And thanks to Dan Smith, Matthew Goldstein, Jeff

Chester, and Bobby Plonchak for helping to dig me out of my mess time and time again.

A special thank you to my dearly missed father, Albert Jacobs, who—among his many extraordinary acts of love—always showed up in the middle of the night to rescue me when I lost my keys or locked them in my car. Thanks, Dad—I hope you're finally getting some rest.

And, most of all, I would like to thank my mother and my husband—both substantial accumulators themselves—for encouraging me to share the story of my clutter with the world, even though it included a few rather revealing snapshots of their own collection as well. Thanks, Mom; thanks, Yankel—I could never have done this without you.

Author Bio

Pesi Dinnerstein (a.k.a. Paulette Plonchak) recently retired as a full-time faculty member of the City University of New York, where she taught language skills for close to thirty years. In addition to contributing to several textbooks and an anthology of short stories, she has also written selections for the bestselling series *Small Miracles*.

Pesi has been an aspiring author and self-acknowledged clutterer for many years and has spent the better part of her life attempting to get organized and out from under. Despite heroic efforts, she has not yet succeeded; but she is still trying and hopes that her journey will inspire others to keep trying as well.

Selected Titles From Seal Press

For more than thirty years, Seal Press has published groundbreaking books. By women. For women.

Pretty Neat: The Buttoned-Up Way to Get Organized and Let Go of Perfection, by Alicia Rockmore and Sarah Welch. $14.95, 978-1-58005-309-9. Funny, irreverent, entertaining, and helpful, *Pretty Neat* offers readers unorthodox, surprisingly simple methods to reduce clutter-induced stress, and insists that perfection is impossible—and unnecessary—in this messy, unpredictable world called real life.

DIRT: The Quirks, Habits, and Passions of Keeping House, edited by Mindy Lewis. $15.95, 978-1-58005-261-0. From grime, to clutter, to spit-clean—writers share their amusing relationships with dirt.

Free Fall: A Late-in-Life Love Affair, by Rae Padilla Francoeur. $16.95, 978-1-58005-304-4. In this erotic memoir, Rae Padilla Francoeur recounts the joys, benefits, and challenges of embarking upon a surprising love affair late in life, and inspires women over 50 to discover their deepest sexual self.

Marrying George Clooney: Confessions from a Midlife Crisis, by Amy Ferris. $16.95, 978-1-58005-297-9. In this candid look at menopause, Amy Ferris chronicles every one of her funny, sad, hysterical, down and dirty, and raw to the bones insomnia-fueled stories.

Second Wind: One Woman's Midlife Quest to Run Seven Marathons on Seven Continents, by Cami Ostman. $16.95, 978-1-58005-307-5. The story of an unlikely athlete and an unlikely heroine: Cami Ostman, a woman edging toward midlife who decides to take on the challenge to run seven marathons on seven continents—and finds herself in the process.

The Quarter-Acre Farm: How I Kept the Patio, Lost the Lawn, and Fed My Family for a Year, by Spring Warren. $16.95, 978-1-58005-340-2. Spring Warren's warm, witty, beautifully-illustrated account of deciding—despite all resistance—to get her hands dirty, create a garden in her suburban yard, and grow 75 percent of all the food her family consumed for one year.

Find Seal Press Online
www.SealPress.com
www.Facebook.com/SealPress
Twitter: @SealPress